Ba'al Perazim

The Breakthrough

Jetta Dya Jones

ISBN-13: 978-1986323031

ISBN-10: 198632303X

Cover Design:
Life Chronicles Publishing
http://www.mylifechronicles.org
Editor: Jetta Dya Jones
Copyright © 2018

All rights reserved. No part of this book may be reproduced in any form or by any electronic or mechanical means, including information storage and retrieval systems, with or without permission from the publisher or author, except in the case of a reviewer, who may quote brief passages embodied in critical articles or in a review.

Dedication

EuWin, Indiefemme, Ethaan, CCSF, Skip, Jimmie, Kurt, Herbert, Ronita, Connie, Sheff, Leo, Margaret, Warren, Lola, Walt, Keith, and Paul.

April 3, 1997

To my new friend,

I have carried you in my heart since the day I received your letter. I can't describe the impact it has made. You see, I am like a loaf of Wonder Bread, packaged, enriched by years of opportunity, but ultimately devoid of substance. My experiences and upbringing in an upper middle class white world have given me much and yet I am always feeling the need to seek out those with different life journeys. I am floored how the world presents opportunities.

When your letter arrived without warning or solicitation, I knew it had come for a reason. I am still unsure what that reason is but I do know that you are giving me an education in life! I have thought daily about you and shared your letter with an African American woman with whom I work. We are both looking forward to the day your book is published. It <u>must</u> be published for the tale told is one of substance and truth. It <u>must</u> be told so that white women like myself will open our eyes to the reality of our world.

I admire you so much. Your mission to provide opportunity for your children has never faltered despite roadblocks and detours. They have had the greatest of role models – you should be so proud. You have committed yourself to them and I know they will be better people because of your dedication. While I sit in this lovely area with a wonderful husband and two healthy, incredibly wonderful children (10,

14), I am distressed to think of your struggle. I know that God has a plan but fairness does not always jive with the picture. Anyway, you have come into my life via a letter that has made me look at the world differently. Something will come of it, I know.

My friend Michelle tells me that she never enters a store or restaurant without thinking, "Do I belong here? Or, is this ok?" It would never occur to me to question. And so our different experiences growing up in America have shaped our lives. Perhaps the greatest result of your letter has been open dialogue with friends. I talk about you frequently – you must get your story out so that others can share your history. It needs to be told.

I have been teaching 4th grade at an independent school in Carmel for a few years. See what I mean? Your letter has sat by my bed. I wanted to write something profound to you. Something to help. I think I've been afraid in a way to answer. You have given me much and I am touched that you thought of me in spite of the little contact we've had. Yes, I always have been interested in your projects and will continue to be. I see you up there with Toni Morrison – keep fighting for your voice. You have much to teach us.

Love,

Cindy

So, David went to Baal Perazim, and David defeated them there; and he said, "The Lord has broken through my enemies before me, like a breakthrough of water." Therefore, he called the name of that place Baal Perazim. 2 Samuel 5:20

Acknowledgements

My beloved friend, education guru, and mentor, Dr. Margaret "Maggie" Hill; the SBCUSD; and to my former students and the wonderful youth who frequented W21 . . . those who taught me far more about life than I could have ever shared with them.

"The committee" including the husky and all those who helped to save him.

The writings and inspiration of Bishop T.D. Jakes, Pastor Joel Osteen, former pastors Martin Ban and Scott Penrod, Beth Moore, Ann Voskamp, Iyanla Vanzant, Oprah Winfrey, Nelson Mandela, Steve Biko, former First Lady, Michelle Obama, Maya Angelou, Marion Wright Edelman, and Malala Yousafzai.

Leilani Latin Duke (former Executive Director for the J. Paul Getty Education in the Arts – Discipline Based Art Education Program) who, in the late 90s, helped to save my life.

The phenomenal work of Singer Rankin, founder and executive director of **World Women Work.**

Those who encouraged me; never judged me; and seemed to understand and care: Jenasis, Jo, Betsy, Minnie, Freddie, Eric, the Wilkes, the Gillettes, the Lujan/Montanos, the McCurines, the Higgins, the Barbers, the Storys, Louise,

Ellie, Rudy, Alexzand, the old red van, and the cowboy from San Lorenzo.

Leigh and Emily whose powerful e-mail inspired me to complete this book.

Sharon Blake, CEO **(Life Chronicles Publishing)** for never giving up on this project or the author, and being the only other individual who understood how the following content came together 'against all odds'.

Contents

Dedication

Acknowledgement

                                                  Page

Prologue

1 – The Devil In The Alley 1

2 – Embraced By Grace 17

3 – YOU Didn't Have To Do What YOU Did But YOU Did - And I 'Thank You' 29

4 – A Shepherd's Heart 51

5 – Grandma Jemma's Prayers 77

6 – A Lizard In The Woods 93

7 - Seasoned Warrior 111

8 – Coming Through The Valley Of Weeping 133

9 – Letting It "Be" 159

10 – Ya' Know, Father, I'm Good 179

11- Flowers Of Blessedness 199

Aftermath 227

Prologue

The most important days in your life are the day you were born and the day you found out why. Mark Twain

One of my favorite theologians, Bishop T.D. Jakes, describes a basic truth I would have to embrace on some of my toughest days . . . the results being really painful sometimes, yet necessary life lessons. Our responses to these kinds of hard-hitting times requires much contemplative action comprised of a calm demeanor so we can think sharply; pray with confidence that the battle is HIS; and sustain faith that tomorrow the sun will shine, or the rains will come to replenish the earth and us making both stronger and prepared to bloom.

My tattered, dingy pink "Woman Thou Art Loosed! *Bible*" has been my saving *grace* and constant companion. *When you commit to bring forth all that God has for you,* the anointed preacher man warns believers in one of his Biblical essays related to scripture, *you may have to 'push' against everything anybody ever did to you or said about you. You may have to battle years of suppression, oppression, and depression. You may have to push with all your might to release the treasure God has put within you, but He wants to bring it to birth. He put the treasure there. He'll help you bring the treasure out. But it is up to you to push. In fact, it may not happen if you don't.* I've been pushing for a mighty long time. Still have a little 'ump in my comings and goings' . . . pushin' and a pullin' myself up Langston Hughes' crystal stair. (poem – "Mother to Son"). *Satan* was spitting fire. *Its* last assault was pretty brutal and left permanent scars. But "Ba'al Perazim: The Breakthrough" was about to go press.

Brethren, I do not count myself to have apprehended; but one thing I do, forgetting those things which are behind and reaching forward to those things which are ahead. I press toward the goal for the prize of the upward call of God in Christ Jesus. **Phil. 3:13-14**

The sentiments chronicled by the Bishop in his multitude of powerful essays definitely summed up where I'd been most of my life journey and where I was currently as a 'winter woman'. Push! And then *push* some more . . . again and again if necessary! Unbelievable! "How strong do You expect me to be," I'd have the audacity to ask the Lord sometimes when my back was up against a wall?

With so many blessings to count, I continued to take the plunge . . . to risk taking a risk. I felt I had no other options and was truthfully quite proud of how I had survived the best I knew how while enduring *satan's* ambushes. I too thought it was pretty cool to be 71 and writing books; still visualizing my children's line of clothing and unique baby blankets I have had for 40 years; and still wanting to establish a foundation.

The Word . . . and the Bishop's interpretation for some of the most inspiring Biblical stories I grew to love . . . could be really instructive if only I would stay quiet, listen to my heart, truly connect through reverent prayer, trust in the Divine, and then activate this wisdom through my thoughts and actions. One day I did earnestly start paying closer attention to directives from the Heights and thus this book began to take shape out of a place I had never been.

I had been editing my children's books written over the past 30 years and began working from an outline for a romantic script for the Hallmark channel I had planned to submit. It became quite obvious the Lord had a Bigger design . . . messages HE wanted to relay through the chapters of this book. I have been totally shocked and amazed throughout this entire literary process as to how this all happened ... how I knew better to ever think about quitting until it was done. The creation and finality of the project saved my life. It had taken one last blow to bring clarity. I could look at the manuscript pages in front of me and now understand why. I thankfully had a publisher who understood, as well.

There was a pressing need for candor, truth, a morality dose, commonsense wisdom to guide us, a message of hope, and a call for a faith-action revolution among the spiritual warrior ranks. Children are struggling to garner believability for a rewarding and prosperous future and a happy life when their friends and classmates lie riddled with bullets right beside them as they huddle in closets and under desks on classroom floors.

Many churches have few answers especially when mothers and fathers cry uncontrollably and angrily declaring 'a moment of prayer' is no longer the answer – it's not working – it's not enough - when their child cannot go to school and feel safe while also enjoying a normal childhood and a rewarding academic experience . . . when there is little help coming from those tax exempt dollars supposedly to be used to help those in need, but when called upon are asked if they are members or if they tithe. Many American citizens like me are growing weary of the tumultuous political, economic, amoral, and blatantly divisive racial climate of our country and I intend to use the days of my 'winter season' through my writing and my speaking to do something about it . . . to make a difference.

It's difficult to explain to anyone how chapter titles, quotes, scripture associations, and content began to appear again from another place. I began keeping a notebook in my bed and wrote down notes in the dark. Information strangely showed up in books and articles for research and then came together in the pages I began to write. The first message was clear: if we connect through heart felt prayer and we hear this Voice telling us 'reserve power' is within us... and when that same Voice encourages us to build a David-like faith in order to hold our grip, navigate the darkness, and find the light, we might want to listen, remain cognizant, and then follow through.

As I have tried to explain to close childhood friends and beloved new friends too, I had never heard of 'baal perazim' (2 Samuel 5:20)...the title of the book meaning 'breakthrough' in Hebrew. And I would shamefully admit I never read or studied the Bible with any consistency nor had I been on any quest to learn from the Scriptures. Some stories seemed a little too far-fetched in my estimation at the time. The tale of a young shepherd boy killing a giant with one of five smooth stones specifically selected by God from all the rocks in HIS entire universe . . . released from the young man's sling shot, hitting just at the right spot to lower the enemy . . . a gifted writer and musician; strong enough to wrestle a bear in the wilderness . . . then later would be a king appointed by God, despite having to wait for almost two decades to reach his throne while he served another king . . . all seemed quite implausible. That was until the dots started connecting and day by day living with a more meaningful purpose seemed to make more sense.

I began to understand and feel the power behind the virtues of *faith, love, and gratitude.* I no longer asked questions regarding matters of Divine knowledge and reasoning unexplainable through human logic. I thought about the main character of my all-time favorite novel whose name was also David, and later down this rocky road I was traveling, the shepherd boy became my chosen Biblical hero. His beautiful Psalms enhanced my closely followed script for living. David also loved to dance, and I had long found praise dancing deeply moving and a sustainer of spirit and hope.

When I first saw the globally acclaimed Alvin Ailey Dance Troupe perform their famous piece "Revelations" years ago, I can still recall feeling the presence of this invisible force blossoming inside my soul. There was so much gratitude for having the privilege of being mesmerized by such magnificently bold, creative geniuses as Ailey and Jamison . . . to have the blessing just to be alive to witness this entrancing, celebratory exhibition. Generations of fine young dancers, coached by new generations of gifted and passionate talents in the business of imagination and artistic body art movement still thrill audiences worldwide with sermons of song and dance following the musical offerings of a variety of genres including blues, jazz, gospel, Broadway theme songs, and familiar spirituals.

As a writer and a timeworn witnessing soul wanting to spend my "winter season" sharing what I knew to be true of Divine knowledge . . . to touch even more lives in a positive and welcomed manner with inspiring exposes . . . I began delivering Biblical narratives and choreographing accompanying praise dance presentations that have pleasantly surprised worshipers in quite a few churches around the country.

For generations of African Americans, *revelations* have long been our story . . . a mixture of joy and grief; of struggle and triumph; of love and hate. They continue to be with the hatred and wickedness becoming more intense and mystifying . . . so sadly destructive. *Revelations* is a component of my story and it was David's too. We had a lot in common. We were both writers; pretty good with words and phrases, I must say. We loved to dance and give God all the praise and honor we could muster. We had to wait for years before we received our freedom and could fulfill our destiny. We were both flawed and had committed obvious sin, but we also experienced and attested to the Lord's grace, goodness, mercy, and forgiveness. We stood up against giants with confidence and God's promise, and often endured painful circumstances and outcomes. We remained steadfast, resilient, and determined while being confronted by *satan's* affronts and piercings.

The shepherd and the 'winter woman' eventually understood the power of God's unconditional *love* and the necessity of our *faith* becoming our strength and protection. When this last season came upon me so suddenly, I realized it was time . . . time to surrender; time to seek serenity; time to 'let it be and let go'; and time to trust the Master to know how my life script would conclude. The content of the following pages would be positioned in the light so that others could see the **good** life still had to offer . . . even during such disheartening and perilous epochs in the country we were once so proud to call our home.

So many memories, the good and the bad, flow towards me like rushing ocean waves. The force of nature (life) knocks me over and I am lost and disturbed. It had been a wicked start to my "Hey World, here I am" first moments. This eventful occurrence happened on the basement floor of the only hospital where 'colored' babies could be delivered by one of the few 'colored' doctors in a small Midwestern town. The year was 1947. This beautiful woman's (my mother) heart suddenly stopped momentarily for fear of the cold, silver forceps about to be used in my delivery. The actual size magnified instantly in her mind as she would describe to me so many times throughout my teens when I was old enough to understand the danger we both faced.

My mother would lug the memories of that harsh throbbing of my earth's entrance while simultaneously being elated with the sounds of my cries to her grave along with the anguish and sad loss of the four other babies never having a chance to live. It wasn't until recently that I would acknowledge to my silent partner how grateful I was for being the only one of my parents' five creations to have survived . . . a 71-year gift. Perhaps selfishly, I always thought it would have been nice to have had a sibling. My life might have been different; happier; or maybe not.

I can't imagine the anguish and broken hearts of both my parents who dealt with their personal grief in their own separate ways. Upon leaving the army base on the day of my never-to-be brother's birth and passing, my father was handing out cigars with a blue ribbon tied around the middle in a bow only to return to the hospital hours later to find his wife near death and a son . . . yes, the baby boy he'd always wanted . . . having taken his last breath three hours after birth. Daddy drank and smoked a pack of cigarettes a day for many years after that first tragedy with others to follow. But what was so admirable was that he always provided for his family and completed his job responsibilities as best he knew how. He forever honored his beloved wife, his oldest sister, his mother, and especially God.

Both always worshipped and constantly prayed no matter how tempestuous the storms outside of the space where they found God. Mama loved to cook and found solace in trying new recipes and proudly preparing huge holiday meals. The delicious cuisine was where she buried her anguish and found temporary relief. It was really a joyous and special occasion when my favorite uncle came to town. He loved Mama's cooking and meant the world to both of us. It broke our hearts when he left this world so young. I don't think Mama and I were ever the same.

The prayers of my mother willing my existence all those years ago on that frigid March morning ushered in my human space on planet earth. Now as a 'winter woman' I often feel so ashamed and empty at my sometimes lack of wise, rational choices and hurtful decisions of my past. I was resentfully lonely and at times had simply stopped caring about anything with the exception of my dogs. Arrogant. Unappreciative. There seemed to always be this need to describe my pain to anyone willing to listen. Those conversations eventually destroyed so many potentially great relationships. The baggage was far too heavy for anyone else to help carry.

And then there were many times I thought God was never listening when I prayed because every time I asked HIM why my hair wouldn't grow; why I couldn't get into the ocean and surf like I'd always dreamed of doing; and why Daddy wouldn't let me buy a ticket to Fairyland Park on the one day a year 'colored people' could attend; HE never answered and neither would Daddy. In addition, I foolishly surmised because Jesus looked like "them", "they" would be His favorites and get all the 'good stuff' life had to offer in the land of milk and honey while black people continued to sharecrop on a plantation called America.

I had long lived life simply going through the motions; not feeling but getting by . . . surviving by *grace*. In the meantime, I lost the spring and autumn seasons of my life without noticing time had just disappeared. It was a complex and painful roller coaster ride at a frightening rate of speed and before I knew it, I was a 'seasoned warrior' in my final season and life as I had always experienced, in laughter and in sorrow, was about over. The era of aging had barreled into the place where I stood. As one of my favorite sports reporters, the late Craig Sager would always say . . . *time is the life you live*. Time had stolen precious days of my life I honestly didn't remember living. I take total responsibility for allowing this wasted energy to escape while caught up in continued darkness . . . an abyss where **grace** would not allow *satan* to take me out and where faith and gratitude kept me being 'me' with a few alterations.

If only there had been a way Mama could have predicted or given me fair warning that my destined, God-scripted journey was going to be so lop-sided and would bring forth more tears and heartache than life should before she fought to bring me into this world. But then it wasn't like she could have touched a magic button and suddenly been in control of anything anyway. If that were the case, I would have had four brothers. A large and supportive familial clan enjoying annual reunions and holidays together was just not in the cards.

But no matter the circumstances or our chronological years, there would always be a chance **good** and **caring** people would find themselves in a place where they could welcome the sunrise after being lost in the darkness of night for so long and that included me. The void of logical reasoning pertaining to ancestral matters could not be easily explained to my own offspring and that reality hurt deeply. It was important we acknowledged that being grateful for blessings such as the privilege of life and health was our main task contrary to fretting and worrying about things we couldn't explain, change, or within our control.

There was a story told by Grandma Jemma of this handsome gentleman doctor with limited knowledge in advanced gynecological medical methodology (especially for women with a negative blood type and at high risk) hovering over his patient in preparation for yanking me from my mother's body with a quick, burning tug. My loud cries in the wee hours of the morning of my earth's entry gave this grateful mother and paternal grandmother hope that perhaps this 9 lb. 12 oz. mortal might live to see another day and maybe another one after that. Heartbeats. Precious, precision breathing in and out.

It was for-certain serendipity that these two wonderful people would find each other when they did. They were . . . their family members were . . . their friends were . . . such fine-looking, hard-working, and genuinely noble people (for the most part) who loved God, each other, their neighbors, and having a good time too. They wore gorgeous gowns and tuxedos to cabaret parties and would sometimes save their coins for summer excursions and cross-country trips. Both had suffered such heartbreaking, emotionless childhoods (there WERE occasional family celebrations); were impressively self-taught with only elementary academic opportunities; and had escaped so many life-threatening racial and physical occurrences. My mother was such a stunning young army bride who was assumed to be any ethnicity other than African American . . . who just so happened to have been married to a black soldier. Imagine that! The year was 1941.

The couple was just starting their lives together while my father was stationed in the Deep South. What a true blessing so many dark days of their lives would be joyously balanced with 60 plus years of a devotional friendship bond and 'real' love even the best Hollywood screen writers couldn't describe. Unfortunately, to complicate this very small family unit with such a fragile and unexplainable dynamic was this sad and lonely little person I had become . . . never satisfied with Divine favor I seldom recognized and just wanting to occupy a space where lil' colored girls growing up in my formative years could only dream.

I had this insane notion I could design my own life the way I wanted it to be . . . out of the chains of finite opportunities afforded 'chocolate baby boomers' and the expense and physical pain of making my black hair presentable and acceptable for young girls like me. This hair thing was pretty important in my day. The white people we came in contact with had referred to our time consuming and costly tresses' inconvenience as a "curse". I considered it to be an unwarranted injustice. From very early on, I refused to crawl into a box labeled 'for colored girls only' with my kind of hair. I was left trying to figure out what I was doing in this world . . . come up with some feasible explanation I could hold on to as to what God had in mind instead of my running and running and running here and there in search of something or someone I probably could never find . . . that was never meant to be . . . and was never intended to stay if they did come.

As young children, we all remember with intense delight hearing the (never-tiring-at-the-time) Disney fairy-tales of the beautiful blonde-haired, blue-eyed princesses who were always rescued by a gorgeous prince with emerald green eyes and soft, glowing black-as-coal-hair. There was always this woeful understanding that this perfect person in the fantasies I dreamed about all the time could never be in love with someone who looked like me; someone who could never be royalty... whose position sitting on a bejeweled, velveteen throne in some foreign country bringing servants and squires to their knees would never happen in my lifetime (at least not to my knowledge at the time). On May 19th, 2018, a beautiful bi-racial, dark haired, brilliant actress and humanitarian walked down the aisle of St. George's Chapel in Windsor Castle escorted by her future father-in-law... the future King of England . . . where she first acknowledged and smiled at her teary and proud mother and then met her handsome red-haired Prince at the golden altar and exchanged marriage vows while millions watched and celebrated the magic of the love story . . . a reprieve from the ugliness in the world today. Thank you, Lord. What the Dutchess of Sussex did for young black girls on that day could never be measured or denied.

Because of this conundrum found in my fairy tale books, I continued asking even more questions. I found some of the answers while researching my prodigious ancestry in graduate school . . . the true facts about African kings and queens with regal statute, military brilliance, innovative minds who designed and built great edifices with crude tools; and celebrated great feats in institutions of 'real' learning . . . where students studied advanced math and science; published classical literary and musical masterpieces handed down through the ages; but sadly where the ruling class took credit and profited from their arduous work ethic and ingenuous inventions. They were the legends whose descendants endured such barbaric cruelty but continued giving God all the praise and honor while singing gospel songs around a big camp fire during rare slave quarter gatherings.

We eagerly followed the fluctuating affluences of the good boy or girl ever protected in the hour of crisis from evil machinations of the scheming witch always clad in black. Because my favorite uncle and the rest of my mother's family looked like the white Jesus I looked at every day and having a father who was 'black like me', I was constantly exploring whether this mixture of the same color of red blood made something terribly abnormal about me . . . if I was an 'in-between' race. "If I'm as bad as other people say I am, then why did God even bother to make me?" I would ask when I got old enough to express my disdain with the illogic of it all and no explanation offered.

For a while, I thought I was pretty cool as a child model at six although never tall enough or white enough as a teen and young adult to make it professionally. I had started 'strutting my stuff' at the local 'colored' YWCAs and social clubs like the ones Mama and Daddy were members for 50 plus years. They were never allowed to socialize with whites in mainstream America, so they formed their own social and humanitarian outlets. I suppose I had what most folks called in those days . . . 'the look', but my 'look' was the wrong color. Later, I would ask why the YWCA (Young Women's <u>Christian</u> Association) wasn't called (Young Women's Colored Association) since we had to go our separate ways all the time. I had been a fashionista and designer from a very early age . . . just a few decades before my time.

Unfortunately, for some of my blunders from pre-teens to adulthood, my parents paid dearly for my contempt. At 71, I have just begun to forgive myself for the pain I caused them. And for some strange reason, I believe they heard me say "I'm sorry" during one of their 'committee meetings' all the way up in heaven. Fighting for my dreams and possibilities with relentless vigor and willful determination, I would begin my search for my own 'five smooth stones' to slay the goliaths blocking my success and 'oh' happy days.

As a 'chocolate baby boomer', I witnessed disappearing white neighbors totally confused. Those living close by were frantically running and running fast. It was doubtful many ever understood why they had to get away from 'people of color' or where they were running to. Standing fearlessly on the front line demanding justice and equality as a teen activist, I grew up asking if this white Jesus treated 'them' (white folks) the same way the old white man next door had treated me and why there were all-white churches and all-black churches if there was just one God?

Imagine someone so viciously hateful he would call the police on a four-year-old 'charcoal child' because her tricycle had touched the edge of his driveway! Mr. Hess had been a holdout while most of the other white neighbors seemed to disappear overnight. 71 years later, I have lived to tell the story of a 'seasoned warrior' survivor having had a mediocre "measure of success" and spurts of joy, love, complexities, perplexities, sadness, painful shock, and awe-inspiring moments. Childhood friends of 65 years often provided wonderful, fun-filled memories through old black and white photos and surprisingly a lot of holiday and birthday celebration memorabilia . . . those rare occasions in my life filled with laughter and happy, peaceful contentment.

As difficult as it has been to wait out "in the meantime" until the *breakthrough* came, I grew adamant now that I understood (as much as possible) how to hold tightly and wait for God's next move. HE hadn't failed me yet, and if my prayers had gone unanswered and I became weary, HE would always step right in to inform me HE had a bigger plan. I would hold the Lord to HIS promises, surrender, and be glad. If my heart was right and I was obedient, I believed success and 'good times' would visit me soon. As Muhammed Ali would always say . . . *if your mind can conceive it, and you can believe it, then you can achieve it.* Repeating over and over again . . . **I CAN DO THIS!**

Having honestly lived so many different kinds of existences, it has been difficult to admit how I jumped off the tracks over and over again . . . how I once walked on the waters of academic success and gifted creatively . . . a life filled with so much pride in achievements and passions of both children and mother . . . to where I found myself in my final season. At one time, I was this great 'Mom' who received the Father's Day card too for going beyond the call of duty trying to fill the role of two parents . . . a successful educator/role model who generously and unselfishly touched the lives of many young people and their families in quite a few cities over the span of a 40-year academic career . . . always having heart-filled, virtuous intentions to do the right thing for the right reason for others; and having once enjoyed waves of romantic bliss, sometimes so unbelievably deep and powerfully sustaining but only for short periods. Those in-between, great memories continued to give me hope. When I became so hurt and simply feeling cheated, HE always managed to give me a clear sign as to why I had to come this way.

I never understood how potential 'significant others' for life went away so quickly taking commitment, responsibility, and apparently little regret with them. As one of my favorite authors, Chinua Achebe once wrote . . . it seemed like 'things were constantly falling apart'. Aloneness, isolation, and living in environments where only the 'super strong' survived created circumstances capable of permanently silencing me. What amazed my small circle of caring friends was how my vision for 'breakthrough' success and joy never blurred; never faltered. My desire was to do something great, so I could breathe in gratification, experience the life I had long desired for my children and for me, and more importantly glorify the Father so that others would know the truth and learn how to do the same.

Moving upward, there I was, side by side with the phoenix as a demonstration of how to rise from and above the ashes with the resolve never to return to the pit of hopelessness and gloom again. I refused to give into *Satan's* sophisticated disguises as I appeared to be one of *its* prime targets. With almost every breath, I was thanking God in advance for HIS Promise to rebuke the *darkness* if asked and for giving me favor in granting an opportunity for redemption and restoration. As actor Pierce Brosnan, one of the many fine actors who played the role of the famous character, James Bond, attested in one of his popular Bond movies . . . *there's no reason to be alive if you aren't living.* I wanted to live.

Congratulations to me!! I had made it. God had answered my exhausted mother's prayers that snowy winter day, but invisible demon predictors and predators lurked in the shadowy potholes of my future . . . those intermediary diversions every mile or so down my personal highway. There were quite a few exit ramps suggesting alternative routes I suppose I could have and maybe should have taken. I chose to take 'the road less traveled' for 'lil' colored girls' growing up in the decades I had been given. Maybe it was this idea of compensating for having gone through so much misery early in life. In addition to my body being covered with this ugly and painful rash most of my childhood (with no cure for years), my teen and early adult years took me through near fatal episodes of hives . . . the dangerous and severe kind that made my eyes swell and close shut; my lips double in size and in aching discomfort; and the closing of air passages in my throat on several occasions when life and death were just minutes apart.

Every time I would get excited about an important event, get angry about an unwarranted, often vicious occurrence (especially racially tainted or an injustice perpetrated against my children), or showing up for a presentation I had to make, I would be so embarrassed because my face would immediately start to puff from stress and nervousness. Even in the steamy hot and humid Midwest summer months, long sleeves, long pants, and high collared blouses were my mode of fashion in order to cover the festering splotches. I was bullied even then by my own peers who thought I had a contagious disease which only added to my aloneness . . . and by the remaining remnants of 'white flight' residents who freely labeled and constantly referred to me as the 'lil' nigga baby'. They never bothered to ever ask me my name.

While attending a predominantly white elementary school, my youngest offspring went through a similar experience as I did 30 years later while standing out in the aisle of a school bus . . . one of two black children in each class. After getting the denim jacket begged for and was so proud wearing, two 3rd grade white boys decided to show off their superficial toughness by shoving my 1st grader to the hard rubber floor landing face down. The word 'nigga' spewed from one of the boys' lips. Disgusting spit landed on the back of the jacket my broken hearted little one never wore again. The bus driver claimed he saw and heard nothing 'out of the ordinary' in his rear-view mirror when questioned by school authorities.

Running home in tears as did I, my child begged me to explain what a 'nigga' meant. Again, my face began to immediately swell and distort. I could not speak. Ambulance ride. Oxygen. Benadryl. Saving my life. The red-neck boys would be forced to write letters of apology meaning nothing to any of the participants involved. No words or gestures would ever soften the blow of that kind of pain 'children of color' endured then and now. Haunting nightmares of such raw offenses seldom go away. We would go to church the following weekend but nothing the minister had to say would ever be believable again. No young child deserved to feel that kind of hurt and helplessness. Despite my anger and confusion, God never let go.

While wrestling with the goliath of inadequacy and operating on an empty barrel of stamina, I tried putting everything I had into my teaching because I felt I owed my students all that I could possibly give them. It never seemed to be enough or enough of me. Several months later after one child's introduction to the real world for a 'charcoal child' living anywhere in the world, a group of Skinheads arrived on my oldest child's high school campus in the same school district. One of the most prominent and so appreciated civil rights activists in the city and a representative from the Department of Justice in D.C. made their presence known to the local media and hate groups showing up in the suburban schools and residential areas across the river. While all of this had been happening, I was administering a standardized test to my students.

Despite the tragic memory jolts of my survivor beginnings, there were strange yet vivid surges of pleasantness and rare delightful times. In the first decade of my childhood years, my life slowly opened as cupped hands used as a vessel assessable to the gifts of God . . . boons I would be unaware of until the beginning of my 'winter season'. I never understood at the time just what was happening regarding the complexities of a universal cultural shift in a changing society relentlessly resisted by white power brokers and associated with my brown skin. Our newly formed 'colored' communities 'isolated' us from many racist disrespects, dangers, and injustices and provided us with security; quality academics where white favoritism and twice as many suspensions were not an issue; and a sense of pride and expectancy in who we were and who we could become were demanded. We were judged on character and hard work and motivated to strive for excellence in everything we pursued.

When it came to my continuing to try and figure out just where Grandma Jemma's God stood when it came to people who looked like me and the lack of favor we seemed to endure, I think of the stories my mother would tell me about Robbie Newsome, my very first 'real friend'. According to Mama's recollections of my early childhood years, by the time I was calling out "mornin' Robbie" to our favorite neighbor, he was on his third or fourth cup of black-black Jamaican bean coffee.

I would later become convinced in my innocent young mind that this God everyone talked so fondly of was actually my friend, Robbie . . . this black man who was as black as the coffee he drank . . . a striking dark skin tone totally the opposite of his bright, pearly white perfect teeth. Robbie always donned Afro-long, bushy silver hair and a big tangled beard he would twirl between his fingers. He would sit for hours at a time reading thick books about his native Jamaica and the African slave trade.

The day Robbie disappeared from his old rocking chair and his empty coffee cup had sat on that dilapidated bannister for months, I was told my dear friend had gone to heaven and if

I looked hard enough, I'd find him smiling down on me from the clouds. For years, I found myself looking up at the sky searching for him, especially after it had rained, thinking maybe he might miraculously appear. When a rainbow broke through the parting clouds, I became even more intrigued. But the mythical gold supposedly found at the end of the prism of colors or Robbie never materialized.

Sixty-five years later, I still feel as though I'm getting messages from my friend possibly as a member of "the committee" . . . those loved ones who continued keeping a watchful eye on my children and me from high above. Sometimes I envision a few members of the celestial commission asking the Lord for a favor or two in order to save us from *satan's* wrath. Where did he go . . . that black-black man from the coffers of my childhood memories . . . my friend whose love was pure enough for me to remember all this many years . . . one who like Mr. Teaberry, the really nice white mailman in our quickly evolving 'white flight' neighborhood, made me feel so good about being "me".

Deeply battle scarred from my journey especially losing almost everything and close loved ones I held dear, I hoped the highway I was now on would lead me to my final destination . . . perhaps a place I could find peace and finally call home. Right before heading west, a dear friend asked me if I really knew where I was going, what I was going to, and if I had any kind of plan mapped out. I did not. I was far too broken and afraid. Six years ago, there it was . . . this stark omen staring me right in the face – eye to eye. No question of the obvious. And six years later, those sad heart songs never changed their tune.

As I drove my treasured Jeep around the bend heading toward the Cajon Pass in route to L.A., traffic seemed to slow down to a snail's pace. Suddenly, there was immediate concern. My car was loaded down with a 30-year collection of African American art along with everything else I couldn't fit into small storage bin 800 miles away. I had given away most of my possessions, something I had done far too often. Alas, I knew I would eventually lose my prize vehicle as soon as I reached the address where I would reside longer than I anticipated. There would be no way to keep up the costly payments without employment. Although AARP made gallant strides in encouraging seniors to "Disrupt Aging", the reality of age, gender, and racial discrimination in the work place still existed. With my lack of knowledge and experience in the quickly evolving technological marketplace, the likelihood of my finding meaningful employment was rather remote.

I also knew I was pretty tired and had lost my passion and hope after my work on the pueblos was politically terminated. Painfully I had to sacrifice but necessary awareness of a personal reality became imperative. At 71 I had written a book . . . one that was soon to be published. Few would understand that the story and the messages were instructed and created by a silent partner.

The tough circumstances, environment, and processes were surprisingly mystical and often bordering debilitation, but the results became a tribute to infinite grace and forgiveness of self and others. "The committee" is now in charge of public relations. If the publication is to be successful, it will be. Perhaps the content of the pages will somehow make a difference in the lives of deserving, genuinely 'good' people, especially those charged to mold the lives of our beautiful children and those desperately needing an angel of mercy. I had been so blessed with old age and I was setting out to make the best of it.

Mine had not been a normal ride compared to what most human beings expected the typical steps of living to be, but I gladly acknowledged the fact that my march through this dark and light spectrum could have taken place in a shantytown or fleeing the ravages of war. It took me quite some time to be able to say . . . *Ya' Know, Father, I'm **good**! I really am! I'll gladly and with much gratitude accept Your blessings.* As one of my favorite female entertainers, Jennifer Hudson declared after going through one of the most painful periods in her young life (the murders of her mother, brother, and nephew) . . . *"God told me - I've got this!"*

Chapter One

The Devil In The Alley

... and that they may come to their senses and escape the snare of the devil, *having been taken captive by him to do his will.* 2 Timothy 2:26

The sun rose at our backs and cast different shapes of shadows on the lines of cars forming what resembled a chain-linked fence stretching and winding for miles and miles. A brush fire had jumped the highway by the Cajon pass heading into L.A. Both sides of the highly traveled freeway had been shut down. Some drivers, like me, entrusted their unlocked cars to total strangers after several hours had gone by and in case the CHP started moving vehicles.

Long rows of drivers and passengers waiting for the two or three restrooms available seemed so far away. Having left Phoenix around midnight, still quite numb from the devastating losses (especially the husky) and fear of the uncertainty of what lie ahead, it had all pretty much pushed me right to the very edge. Here in a web of even more curious doubt, snarling traffic had been halted by uncontrollable flames. *Satan* tiptoed on the scorching embers giving me a clue of a possible future of doom.

One could hardly watch the disaster unfold without wondering just how much more pain a place like L.A. could bear. In a city scorned because it had no seasons, some residents jested they did have four different natural vicissitudes . . . riots, earthquakes, fire, and mudslides. The city of angels and dreams was out of breath; its spirits deflated, and now quite fragile. The Northridge earthquake, the one I had missed while facilitating a weekend symposium in Laurel, Mississippi on Martin Luther King Jr.'s national holiday, was hardly the worst quake in CA's history, but it turned out to be one of the most expensive natural disasters in U.S. history at the time.

While the rest of the country was iced over and snowed in, we all watched the reconfiguration of California's coastal nightmare play out on the air waves. This natural and bureaucratic disaster tested the city's resilience and threatened hopes for any kind of economic recovery. It also jolted some of its scared population into packing up and leaving for more solid ground. Although Dr. King was no longer an earthly being, he was still saving lives. His spirit continues to motivate those of us yearning to be inspired and to gain useable knowledge focused on one's interests and passions in order to pass positivity and hope on to the next generation.

And now here I was going back to the land of 'this thing' I knew could happen at any time of the day or night again. But what I didn't anticipate were "the mean streets" where I would have to live and walk until the *breakthrough* came. Don't get me wrong. I would always be grateful for a roof over my head. With raw activism rooted in my blood and numerous devastating personal experiences tucked tightly under my belt, I was befuddled and angered by the bold impudence of callous and brazen individuals (many former and current gang members) who carried out selfish and inconsiderate dangerous escapades in an alley they considered their own private backyard. The *devil* has always been like that, you know. The mean and fiery assault forces come after 'warriors in God's army' with a determined and unyielding lashing. It all began the very first day I laid my head down and attempted to sleep through the emotionlessness and anguish of yet another life transition.

These were cold, heartless people like I had never known before and I had lived a lot of places – 19 to be precise. They were the kind of parents who taught their children such awful lessons about how <u>not</u> to be compassionate, respectful, and caring for others, especially mothers and grandmothers. After some had struck fear in many residents by setting off bomb-like explosives or aiming bottle rockets at dried-out palm trees close to perishing from the five-year California drought, 'something got a hold of me.'

If no one else would stand up to these merciless individuals, I certainly wasn't going to sit back and let them rob me of my much-needed rest, sanity, and peace of mind. It was 5:15 A.M. and they were not entitled to honk their horn 15 times until someone hollered out they would shoot their tires! When they got angry because someone challenged them, they would push a car alarm button from inside their apartment. 25 – 30 times and no one called authorities. "How do you get used to this and let it go on year after year?" I would ask neighbors. The safety and well-being of my children, neighborhood children, and for the most part, wonderful neighbors having been residents for a long time had to be addressed. Tolerance without consequences of such dangerous and asinine behavior was ludicrous.

This was a game for the occupants of one specific apartment in one particular building on the block where I resided. They were smart enough to know they might be forced to move eventually but no one could stop them from visiting. It would be then they would return throwing dynamite like bombs at one or two in the morning; run as fast as they could inside an apartment; celebrate for just a few minutes; and then jump in their cars and speed away. Unless the explosive was caught on their person they knew they had never been nor could they ever be stopped or caught. No more striking terror. I had come to the same conclusion about the devil. *It* would not rob me of my soul or pierce my heart any longer. There was such an antidote called 'God-power'.

I couldn't believe what I was watching and hearing . . . the celebration and the gloating in another victory of avoiding a police helicopter. Their young offspring who reveled with them were some of the very same children taught by frustrated teachers in the neighborhood elementary school . . . children who should have been in bed on a school night; were supposed to care about and respect what their teachers had to say; and to love themselves and be concerned about their future. While frightening sounds and dangers of fire loomed on a day when some celebrated a nation's history they were proud of and those of us paying homage to the brave individuals who protected our freedoms, toxic poisons of carbon monoxide, sulfur, and particulate matter filled the earth's atmosphere surrounding our living space and especially our children's lungs.

Some older residents came close to suffering strokes and heart attacks from the sudden intrusion of extremely loud explosives with the strength of dynamite being rolled up to their door, thrown at them, and quite a few thrown at moving vehicles. It just wasn't fair for these really nice folks that already struggled to pay pricey and escalating rents to have to endure consistent, terrifying, and extremely hazardous living conditions. Instead of having the luxury of relaxing and celebrating, holidays and weekends became times to be dreaded and feared as they acted out these same horror shows year after year and year round. It was disappointing in one sense and understood in another that resident had become so desensitized and afraid they would say or do nothing. No complaining. *Just stay to myself so I can be safe. Don't let folks get too close. It's what was to be expected.* Nonsense . . . part of the nation's insanity! I was not afraid and informed both the 'devil in the alley' and *its* crew and a few city officials of that very fact. They could be on the attack for *satan* but I was going to crusade for the decency of human rights that these people would not take anymore.

Facebook postings described the days and nights of fright and terror from the bombings and the 'fire in the sky' as the likes of the beaches at Normandy or the reverberations of the kind of explosives miners used in search of gold. It was happening all across the country. People were scared and angry all wondering just what could be done to stop the madness penetrating their lives and of those they loved and wanted desperately to protect. To add insult to injury, the main *devil* would then rev up the pipes on his motorcycle setting off all the car alarms up and down the block right at dawn the following day.

Helicopters would hover again and again but could never catch the 'mean ones'. Since the city refused to stop selling so-called legal fireworks on every street corner where illegal ones were said to be sold on the down low from the same vendor, it appeared city officials, through their own inactions, were condoning this ruthless and dangerous behavior. There were no legal weapons the neighborhoods could use to combat the atrocities every year and seldom were there any consequences. The *devil* had *its* maneuverings down to a science. Trick. Torment. Terrorize.

What was happening was a good example of what results when the have-nots . . . the underserved . . . possible deportees... the disenfranchised with few skills and no employment opportunities create a culture of not caring about anyone but themselves and their own. It was again all about the opened containers of half-eaten food and the can of soda sitting on the bench inside a bus carousel with a trash can an arm's length distance away on both sides. 10 or 15 miles down the freeway, as rapper Eminem sadly described in a 2002 movie "8 Mile" . . . tall skyscrapers; enriching cultural exposure (especially in the arts); fine dining; elite shopping venues; state-of-the-art academic institutions; safe play and exercise sites; and the availability of nutritional food outlets were in most cases foreign to those who looked up and over or passed by and wondered what it would be like to visit 'their' world.

What was it about this picture that appeared askew? A multi-million-dollar business complex and billion multi-billion-dollar sports complex surrounded by neighborhoods plagued with gangs and explosives. The city and its police department continued to do everything they could within the law to curtail the violence perpetrated against innocent citizens by the *devil in the alley* and his crew, and I remained confident some effort would be made to rid of the domestic terrorists eventually. Hopefully, I would be afforded the opportunity to move on. The wind beneath my wings had dissipated.

Saint Michael, the Archangel, defend us in battle. Be our protection against the wickedness and snares of the devil. May God rebuke him, we humbly pray. And do thou, prince of the Heavenly host, by the power of God, thrust into hell satan and all the evil spirits who wander through the world of (seeking) the ruin of souls. Amen

(Pope Leo XIII, 1884) after a vision he had of Our Lord conversing with *satan*

"He" looked up from his thumb presumably in the middle of punching in a text on his IPhone. I could look into his eyes and pretty much guarantee "he" assumed it had been me . . . the old-wicked-black-witch who had decided . . . ENOUGH! *You WILL NOT punk me, my children, or my good neighbors anymore! By any means necessary, I will stop you!* NO MORE!! Since most of us couldn't afford to move right away and we rather liked our neighbors, it was time to step away from apathy and take up the cause for what was right and just. We owed this fight to our precious children.

It was the day I had gotten word my dear friend and attorney had left this world at the age of 64. His heart had suddenly stopped beating. We had just talked about ways to raise money for a book tour and a possible investor for my famous children's blankets. He was really proud, as was my late literary agent who transitioned at 64 as well, in that I had never given up. When I left the Southwest, I promised Mrs. Marshall I would not. Like my children, I was committed to keeping my eyes on the prize to the very end.

Shock. Sadness. Anger. *The devil in the alley* refused to stop. As a matter of fact, his antics got worse and far more perilous. "He" just kept pumping the music so loud that it was heard from one corner of the block to the other. NOT TODAY! It just wasn't going to happen TODAY . . . not a minute longer. I didn't care about the repercussions. After knocking on the opened door for several minutes, there he was... gold chains, tattoos covering his entire upper body, and shirtless . . . standing on the other side of the screen.

"I'm asking you nicely, Young Man. Would you please turn the music down? People work at night and a lot of them have two jobs. Have a little respect. Would you be just as rude and inconsiderate to your mother or grandmother," I asked him without hesitation? "He" responded by announcing he wasn't going to turn down a damn thing. And I boldly responded by saying, "When I tell you not TODAY, take me at my word. I am quite serious!"

For a while, the music got even louder. While contemplating my next move, surprising silence came upon the block. Really strange but gratitude was quietly exuded. Several weeks later I learned my brazen and fearless confrontation had taken place with a hierarchy kingpin of a famous Hispanic gang. I was scared and shaking like a leaf after the danger had long been over. The incident reminded me of my battles with *satan*. At first, *it* won't budge! And then the Lord steps right in and peace hovers over the place where I stand.

A decade or so prior, a police gang task force had convened to addresses mainly in this particular block. It had been absolutely stupid and treacherous then, too. From day to day . . . night after night . . . no one knew where a body would be found. Many times, residents were unable to distinguish between gunshots and firecrackers or when there would be an occasion to awake to the smell of gasoline having been poured over a car in an apartment building driveway. A resident's ex-suitor had threatened to light a match and throw it toward the vehicle nearby. Fire and fury. That was *satan's* way.

An apartment complex running an illicit business of ill repute continued to operate a few blocks away. Blue and red bandana wearing drivers and passengers in low riders had begun to claim their respective turfs once again. They would stop and ask old ladies walking their dogs early in the morning where the best place was in the area to have breakfast. I was quite sure they already knew. Perhaps it was the 'shake-in-my-boots' reaction they were hoping for but didn't get. Instead I drew them a map on a napkin. Blue and red incomprehensible lettering had appeared spray painted on the sidewalks surrounding the elementary school. The taggers knew their message would be far more difficult to remove from cement.

Fortunately, a few 'good folks' at the county animal control helped rid some of the neighboring blocks of numerous vicious pit bulls, some known for jumping fences and chasing innocent walkers on the hoods of parked cars. They rightfully feared they would be mauled and face a horrible, untimely demise. This entire scenario reminded me of what 'hell' . . . *satan*'s playground and factory . . . must be like.

Down these mean streets a man must go who is not himself mean, who is neither tarnished nor afraid. He is the hero; he is everything. He must be a complete man and a common man and yet an unusual man. He must be, to use a rather weathered phrase, a man of honor—by instinct, by inevitability, without thought of it, and certainly without saying it. He must be the best man in his world and a good enough man for any world. Raymond Chandler

Several years ago, we would shockingly hear the sounds of gunshots go pop! pop! pop! out of the blue. A 16 year-old black male had been murdered just up the street from where we lived. Classes were going on inside the elementary school near the corner where the bus stop carousel was located and where the shots had rung out. This was the last place the young man sat before it was all over . . . before he would take his last breath.

The police informed concerned and frightened neighbors it had been an unfortunate and isolated incident . . . that no matter where the young man had traveled in the city, those who were after him . . . who were determined to get him for whatever reason . . . would have eventually gotten the job done no matter how long it took. Was this not just like *satan*'s markings when 'warriors' run out of heart ammunition in order to fight back? There was nothing authorities could do to stop the inevitable.

Like atrocities happening to our youth in the urban streets of Chicago and other major cities, what explanation could anyone have for this degree of anger, hatred, and self-loathing some had for themselves and each other; that some officers of the law had for those in which they were charged to serve and protect? *Satan* continued *its* crusade to destroy our will to prevail over evil. My promise to myself would be to never cower before any oppressor and their threats . . . that my lineage included standing tall before giants; making my own decisions (good and bad); continuing to believe in my creations; and facing the world boldly and unabashed declaring . . . *this I have done against all odds.*

I was left asking why the children had to hear the deadly commotion just outside their classroom windows and how they were expected to just bounce back and be interested in why George Washington crossed the Delaware River . . . why some on the playground would be unintentionally forced to witness the horror of a young boy having slumped over in his own blood on the heavy plastic enclosure?

Were our youth not entitled to a more positive academic and nurturing neighborhood culture where they were being taught to be kind, confident, polite, and courteous . . . having respect for self and others and looking people in the eye to say, 'good morning' and sincerely meaning the sentiments? Should they not be offered rigorous and relevant curriculum organized and presented by highly qualified professionals willing to work hard to make a difference in the lives of our youth and their families? The young man who lost his life that day had been somebody's brother, nephew, grandson, and friend and within hours of learning his fate, a mother and father's entire existence would be changed forever. So would some of the children who witnessed this shocking barbarity.

Journal Entry (June 21st, 2016) - *The electric company had given the residents in my neighborhood fair warning that power would be cut off in a 10-block area from 8 p.m. until 6 a.m. the following morning. They were updating the technology in the circuits, whatever that meant. From the minute the darkness was upon us and the only lights seen were from the workers' protective metal hats, reflections from flashlights, and candles inside residences, the "devil in the alley" and his crew (both male and female) went wild throwing M80s and cherry bombs at the workers on the poles. All we could hear were men screaming back for these crazy maniacs to stop, but they refused. No one could see them coming and going. It was so frightening hearing the workers' holler and to feel our hearts pound for fear of fire. I couldn't imagine how scared the men had to be. It was even too dangerous for the police - with their red and blue lights flashing - to enter the 'war zone'. What could these people possibly be thinking? Someone could get killed. Why are they doing this? "What did that loud sound of a blast do for you? Why did it make your children laugh and cry to hear more," I wanted to ask them?*

The battle against the *devil* and "him" would be strategic, consistent, and daring. I had always been battling on the front line for one cause or another. *Enough. No more hurting people. PEACE!!* This was the message left by the youngest victim of the Boston Marathon bombing tragedy in 2013. The words had been printed on a bright green poster and held proudly in the midst of the crowd right before his and others' senseless murders. I would never forget Martin Richard and that beautiful smile on a day when the laughter and joy we all shared while watching this exciting, historical race with thousands of runners from all over the world shockingly died in a pitiful sorrow. Enough of the danger just outside my window. NO MORE! I had really enjoyed talking to my neighbors, especially when we got into conversations about flowers, dogs, and sports. As long as I was still living on the block, I certainly wanted to continue that pleasure.

Was it too far-fetched for me to assume we were capable of having the kind of community where residents could walk our streets like people did in Beverly Hills and on Rodeo Drive, safe and secure and taking great pride in their manicured lawns and gardens, and in the success of their offspring in some of the finest schools and athletic outlets in the state. We all deserved that kind of freedom whether our bank accounts had the same number of zeroes or not. Neighborhood children were entitled to play freely without fear of a dangerous firecracker blowing up in their faces or witnessing a possible drug overdose of a young man falling off the wall just up the street.

Too many young people of all colors and all walks of life are growing up today unable to handle life in hard places . . . without hope, without adequate attention, and without steady internal compasses to navigate the morally polluted seas they must face on the journey to adulthood. Marion Wright Edelman – *The Measure of Success*

I stared into "his" face unfazed . . . and "he" stared right back. That's how *satan* acts . . . audacious and intimidating when confronting *its* targets. I was like the renowned 60s civil rights activist, Fannie Lou Hamer declaring . . . "I am sick and tired of being sick and tired!" "His" egotistical, foolish actions were taking up too much of what little valuable time I had left but I couldn't turn my back on people losing their dogs when dusk came upon the block due to the loud booms coming out of nowhere and stopping our hearts momentarily. I also couldn't imagine how the late Viet Nam war veteran who had lived in our building for 20 years felt every time a dynamite sounding blast went off right by his windows, as well. I would guess the loud detonations took the kindhearted gentleman back to the hell he lived and survived on the battlefield and jungles decades ago... in an environment where the enemies and allies all looked alike. Like the neighborhood, no one knew who to trust or what to expect next.

It was the same with *satan*. When evil descends upon us, sometimes we might not have the intuitiveness and strength to fight back. *It* wakes us making *its* presence known. Depression. Fear. Uncertainty. Aloneness. Hopelessness. I remember hearing Canadian Prime Minister Justin Trudeau when he declared in a speech . . . *You cannot let yourself be defined by the hopes that you will fulfill the darkest wishes of your opponents.* That was the key . . . not that *the devil* won't win, but that I would have gained enough stamina from having to fight so many satanic battles that I would be far more prepared when the next round of attacks were about to land.

Several years ago, childhood friends lost all their possessions when a bottle rocket landed on the roof of their townhome. *Please, God, don't let the same thing happen to us. Rebuke satan! Make 'him' and the fire go away!* I was huddled in the corner of a small hallway in a fetal position praying we would all make it through another night of terror. Dogs bark and whimper . . . some howling loudly and frantically running under beds, tables, and chairs seeking refuge. To those who have ruled these mean streets for a decade or more, I say again . . . *No More. I'm done!!!* The basketball bounces under my window. I holler out unafraid. "He" looks up and moves a foot or so away and continues to bounce the ball . . . faster and louder. "He" is DEFIANT! I am too! It's 6 A.M. 20 minutes later the blaring sound of a saxophone now comes from "his" apartment window. This is HELL!!

But He turned and said to Peter, "Get behind Me, Satan! You are an offense to Me, for you are not mindful of the things of God, but the things of men." **Matt. 16:23**

I see "him" standing on the nearest corner with a few members of "his" crew. They stare rudely, not budging from the middle of the sidewalk. I pick up the Basenji and walk around them. I speak silently to myself. *You will not bother me, satan! I've learned to fight in the lion's den!* I look back over my shoulder after I put the Basenji back on the ground. Someone had informed the police who had graciously stepped up their patrol of the neighborhood and they informed the *devil* that we didn't hang clothes outside and down the front and side railings of apartment buildings for sun drying . . . that we were fortunately not a third world country.

Someone had also called the Animal Control informing them that breeding pit bulls in a residential back yard without a license and located across the street from an elementary school was dangerous, against the law, reckless, and inhumane . . . that allowing them to run loose without a leash was an accident waiting to happen? How did you get to this point in your life where you have no conscious or meaningful purpose? What is it about hurting others that gives you such great satisfaction?

Loud booming sounds are heard close by and far away. *Satan* manages to penetrate the hearts and souls of **'good'** people the same way . . . close by and then sometimes at a distance. Sirens resound unnervingly in the early morning hours and the booming never stops. Where do they get the funds to pay for their rampages? It's Christmas Eve. People are exiting church services and children rush to bed in anticipation of Santa Claus. Let them have their magic! Don't you have children? Talkin' 'bout those mean streets. Clearly *satan's* way. We never know what's coming or when *it* will strike especially if we're getting ready to grasp God's favor. But we are confident God does know; that the wind will blow where it wishes; and that we are all born of the Spirit. I prayed the explosions causing me to jump and my ears to pop in pain to cease . . . for the fire in the sky to smolder and turn to ash.

In 2008 in Seattle, Washington, spiritual guru, the Dalai Lama; South African Archbishop Desmond Tutu; and a number of other religious leaders gathered to talk about how adult caretakers could teach compassion to younger generations, so the world would be a more peaceful, less violent place. Ten years later, it seems any recommendations coming from that meeting have gone by the wayside by certain divisive segments of society and especially leadership at the top. Perhaps another meeting with a similar agenda is in order for so-called grown-ups and then the children.

There "he" was... just standing there looking back at me. It's quiet on this particular night; quite a rare occasion. There are times when *satan* is quiet too. And then in an instant, right when we've caught our breath and think *it* is gone . . . when we can stand without swaying, *it* wakes up and starts chasing us through the traffic of our minds until we're all tuckered out again and tired of fighting. *It* is like *its* cohort in the alley . . . hell-bent on melting faith in *its* fire and breaking hearts with a sledge hammer. *It* tosses bombs of discontent when we least expect to experience the explosions, stealing our security and peace. We need God and prayer in our lives more than ever now. *I can't give up . . . I can't give in . . . please help me, Lord. Satan is back again!* I would open the envelope of my soul and abide by the directions contained inside.

There were shocking lessons learned by the enemy as the battles of good and evil played out. They discovered there were people who would boldly stand up to them . . . who would refuse to live in fear and be terrorized when they walked the streets. Sometimes the ones orchestrating the affront against their continuous wrath would be the very ones *the devil in the alley* might or might not ever expect. No one would ever know for sure.

My children and I would continue to pursue our literary and entrepreneurial endeavors, hoping to soon be able to escape the perils of evil on these 'mean streets' . . . the remorseless demons that persisted and found ways to have their own way. That's how the *devil* operates, as well. The strength required and the cries to God to rebuke the enemy's wrath would have to intensify. "He" would not stop nor would he be made to move or be told he could never come back to the neighborhood. "They've been trying to get me out of here for three years. I'm not going nowhere," I heard him tell a neighbor. There was no truth explained as to why residents wanted him to find another city, but there was also the realization that he was probably correct. I would be gone before he would. It's what they called the rudiments of "The System."

Where You have already opened the door, let me come in; where it is shut, open at my knocking. Let me always remember You, love You, meditate upon You, and pray to You, until You restore me to Your perfect pattern. Augustine of Hippo – 354-430 A.D.

Chapter Two

Embraced By Grace

Oaks, massive with the memory of Lynch
Pervasions, bend to grip my knees and rustle
A moan for our burned visions.
The trees may weep. I must stiffen my back.
Quieten my face and teach a lesson in Grace.
. . . from "Now Sheba Sings the Song"

Maya Angelou

Only when I learned to forgive myself and others and to "let go" . . . "let it be" . . . was I to understand the true essence of God's **grace.** At first, I believed 'Grace' to be a popular girl's name because I knew a pretty girl named Grace when I was in elementary school. As I grew older and having survived two close-to-death experiences and several of my children, I have come to comprehend and embrace this concept of **grace** for the incredible power it possesses.

Grace, as theologian and mystic Thomas Merton once wrote **is not a strange, magic substance which is subtly filtered into our souls to act as a kind of spiritual penicillin. Grace is unity, oneness within ourselves, and oneness with God.** It is this reality of 'oneness' that gives us strength and the courage to move forward. I am frequently perplexed as to why my journey, although in no way compared to the passages of my beloved parents or ancestors (to whom my children and I refer to as 'the committee'), had to be so hard and lonely. But the fact remained that through it all, I had obviously been carried and still live because of HIS **grace**.

I was reminded of this simple truth one day by my former pastor, a brilliant man of God leading a powerful, faith-action congregation unlike any color-blind group of people and place of worship I had ever been part of on my long, quite disconcerting spiritual passage. Of his many blessings were his beautiful family and his very wise interpretation of Biblical scripture. He made it relevant and useful by providing a map escort through the maze of struggle and heartbreak in troubled times. "People like you and so many others who still don't totally understand the Divine offering of **'grace'** shouldn't complicate matters," he told me in a counseling session one day. "You're still being carried by **'grace'**. You always have been. You've just never known it as that. Recognizing this power of **grace** and *faith* now for what it is? Now that's certainly moving in the right direction."

Life was very dark and scary at the time, more so than usual. My losses were far more than I could absorb and happening all at once, especially the sudden death of my beloved friend and literary agent and the murder of a young man who was 'like a son'; the forced retirement from my very rewarding academic position (especially halting revolutionary project-based student/adult learning labs on a few Southwestern pueblos and rural school districts); the loss of most of my personal possessions; and more than anything else, the painful separation of my beloved canine companion of 10 years. The gorgeous blonde, blue-eyed husky had been saved by a community of wonderful animal lovers. These kinds and loving human beings contributed funds ($2,500) to help pay for a surgery that ultimately saved his life. It was a wonderful example of true *grace* and so much gratitude.

Theologian John Wesley once wrote of **grace** saying *. . . it does not depend on his endeavors. It does not depend on his good temper, or good desires, or good purposes and intentions; for all these flow from the free* **Grace** *of God; they are the streams only, not the fountain. They are the fruits of free* **Grace**, *not the root. They are not the cause but the effect of it.*

In order for me to understand my life trek as a woman and mother of color living in a really sad (state-of-affairs-and-heart) America, now homeless and staying afloat on a well-earned Social Security check, temporary unemployment, and the goodness of 'genuine' Christian folks, I had come to the altar where faith and *grace* merged and resided. There was no safer place to be. Mentally and emotionally battered and lost, I honestly didn't know where to turn, what I was praying for, or how I would start to rebuild at this late stage in my life. I knew if I could get stronger, move pass the devastation of a really bad broken heart, and stay positive about the possibilities, **I COULD DO THIS** . . . come through the murky waters of despair . . . the valley of weeping . . . in my quest of finding and sharing the light.

I had met **Grace** when I opened the door one morning to feed the stray black cat that roamed the estate property where I had been staying. It had snowed overnight and now the querulous creature was searching for food as were the bunnies and squirrels. Standing in my long, cantaloupe orange terry cloth robe and bright multi-colored rubber boots, I swept away the freshly fallen white crystals from the bird feeder and poured a hefty helping of wild bird seed I was sure would attract a variety of my fine feathered friends.

Holding a steaming cup of coffee with both hands after completing my task at hand, I *thanked Him for His Grace* since being given a temporary living arrangement on this Hollywood-like property of total strangers at the start of winter. I would be given time to stand still and allow God to speak to my heart as HE had done day after day. I just never took the time to listen close enough on previous occasions when I thought I might be hearing a distant whisper from an unknown source.

Constantly, I fought to steer my thoughts away from this idea of victimization and to rationalize circumstances and the actions of heartless people I had just walked away from after losing my education administrator's position as totally beyond my control. I could have stayed and fought this corrupt, racist bureaucracy I had tried to succeed in for 6 years, but I knew I would always be 'their' target like I was *satan's*; always watching my back or over my shoulder; always believing I wasn't good enough. They would get me out sooner or later. **Grace** sat on my wall of pain and shame and waited for me to *trust*. What I later learned to be true was that **grace** would illuminate my life and turn dreams to opportunities and joy in the blink of an eye. That's how quickly the darkness could be extinguished by the light. *Grace* accepts us whole without regards of physical beauty or ugliness; wholesale; regardless of mistakes or shortcomings; with no possibilities of rejection.

I was accepting of the truth life was about choices and I realized rather late, I must admit, that I had made some good ones and quite a few bad ones, too. I personally charged myself with the responsibility of the consequences I had and would suffer as a result. Perhaps in the final accounting, I would have done more positive than harm. Again, as the phenomenal Maya Angelou frequently reminded us . . . *then you forgive yourself and say, 'Well, if I'd known better, I'd have done better.'* There were so many life lessons my parents couldn't teach me because they had never been taught themselves . . . so therefore I couldn't impart important knowledge to my own offspring. The Cycle of struggle and despondency continued.

Just like it was yesterday, I can see Grandma Jemma sitting on her front porch, leaned forward in the new wicker chair she had gotten for Mother's Day. She loved her new chair. Said it made her feel like a queen. "You ARE a descendant of African kings and queens," I informed her. I saw her familiar smirk and knew she wasn't much of a believer in what I had just told her . . . facts I knew were definitely true. A medium-sized silver kettle was secured between the inside of her knees and the calves of her legs as she broke and rinsed freshly picked green beans. Her plentiful garden, planted just a few feet from the old streetcar tracks, supplied the family and many of the neighbors with vegetables and watermelons for months.

Never looking up, I remember her saying to me as a teen, *"Ain't nothin' in life gonna just come to ya'! Gotta work for what you want and go after it with everything ya' got. I never had that chance. Lil' bit late for me, but not for you. Don't waste yo' time, Chile. Remember, David made good use of his time. You're one of my grandbabies that's gonna' do some good things someday. Your Mama and Daddy gonna see to that! Us colored folks just don't see lots of dreams come true these days but there's a few folks like me still thinkin' stuff ya' really want to do can happen! But some things are just what they are and it ain't nothin' we can do about those! That's good enough for now. What we got is God's **grace** for the takin'. Ya' can get it all day long and 'specially when ya' sleep and you wake up the next mornin'. That **grace's** been paid for long time ago.* I was one of 45 (maybe a few more unknowns) grandchildren and generations of great grands, so our conversations were few.

The ones we did have provided life-long lessons I would never forget.

Amazing Grace*, how sweet the sound!* No matter one's spiritual journey choice, the new heights are indeed accessible. All that is required is to honestly love God; appreciate ourselves and other beings given life; and abide by often challenging Divine rules as outlined in the Scriptures. This kind of ***grace*** has the power to save us but will often require God's troopers fighting tough battles with the *devil*. By now *it* is quite miffed with our David-like 'conquering faith' giving us strength and the proper armor to withstand *its* fire surges. We can rely on ***grace***. . . that heavenly gift of unconditional love. Its value is infinite.

Believing God is for me and HIS desire is that I have success, love, and happiness in my life, I find a bit of grit keeping me from giving up. The God in Grandma Jemma's conversations and my personal declarations in discussions with HIM are about the same. Are there times when I feel nothing . . . emotionless . . . because *satan* has beaten me so mercilessly I can hardly move? You betcha!! But I won't fall into the 'doubter ranks'. I inhale air (as fresh as possible). My heart beats like it should as blood runs through my buried veins and opened arteries of my heart. Walking three or four times a day with the Basenji, and before with the husky for 10 years, certainly helped support good health. I pump my fist discretely looking up to the sky, and whisper, 'thank you' and to You I offer praise and honor. *And He says to me, "My **grace** is sufficient for you, for My strength is made perfect in weakness."*

I call upon the Lord to shower HIS ***grace*** upon my children and me . . . and all those who believe in justice and miracles. I believe God wants us to be everything we could possibly be as we become more and more of our own true self. What if instead of discounting the current moment . . .

the uncontrollable . . . the simply 'given' . . . that we would count our abundant miracles as obvious **grace**? What if we focus and depend upon the God who controls it all?

When we look back on our life's journey will we view an earth term of thanksgiving for the gifts God sent quickly, barely in time, or not at all, or will our registry read of complaints, anger, envy, and disbelief in the goodness of the Most High? Whether we merely asked, sought, or knocked incessantly, we would eventually learn that every occurrence; every tribulation; and every joy happened for a reason we just might not ever understand. It's all about God's timing and HIS offering of eternal and loving **grace** in all forms, measures, and matter.

Isn't the only thing that really counts to God in the end is that we're a good person? Wouldn't that give us the chance needed for redemption and finding true joy?" Maybe. This all sounds great, and being and doing good are obviously central to what it means to be a decent human being, but can we look at the other side . . . the subtle belief system just below the surface of this conventional way of seeing God? That question often flows from an acceptance that God operates according to a good and bad tally sheet, and if we do the good . . . the upright . . . or the 'religious' thing, then we will earn all the 'brownie' points' we need for God to be pleased. Bah! That's not the kind of gospel the Scriptures describe or that Grandma Jemma taught.

Genuine gospel is **grace** and this kind of grace is a special present. We receive this gift from a caring Source. We don't have to do anything to earn it or try and make it happen. Wake up and it's right there resting on our pillows! This kind of *gospel of grace* is revolutionary, provocative, and counterintuitive in moments of our greatest despair, pain, sin, weakness, loss, dilemmas, sojourning, and whenever we fall short. God meets us right there . . . right in the place where we are and HE announces *I am on your side. I've been there all along.* When we remain stuck in the same old points program, we waste time trying to earn what is already ours. Just know there is revolutionary news at the heart Jesus's message that God is for us . . . that God is love. This kind of gospel of **grace** isn't about us always hitting the target so that we can have God's favor. This gospel is all about us finding God exactly in the moment of our greatest brokenness. HE is indeed a 'breakthrough' God!

In so many instances, we read about Jesus going to the edges . . . reaching out to the poor and hungry; the disenfranchised; the marginalized; the lost and the losers; and those betrayed, abandoned, unloved, and in trouble. In His insistence to show that His Father was on the side of all followers, Jesus challenged the conventional wisdom of His day that God was only on the side of a select few. In His standing with the poor, He confronted the system that created those kinds of conditions. In His declarations that God can't fit in any one temple, He provoked and angered those who controlled and profited from that very edifice.

It was the amazing, awe-inspiring athletic and soul feat of the then 64-year-old swimmer, Diana Nyad that encouraged me to strive for new heights even in the 'winter season' of my life. She convinced me we should "dare greatly" all the way to the very end. After four failed attempts to swim the 110-mile trek from Cuba to the beaches of Florida, Nyad achieved what many believed would be an impossible exploit for any human to accomplish, especially a woman of her years.

Like this very brave lady, I wanted to be introduced to my authentic self, creating a life I could truly admire . . . one focused and driven to achieve what I could with what little time I had left and with the gifts I had been given. More importantly, I wanted to be remembered not by the things I did wrong or right, but by the woman I eventually became . . . one still believing in love, finding my way, and landing in a place where I could STAND proudly. Where did Nyad find the strength . . . the belief she would not be satisfied until she had succeeded in her quest? With every stroke in cold and dangerous waters, *faith* splashed to the left and *grace* was carrying her on the right.

The **grace** and love of God whence cometh our strength and salvation are free for all and free in all to whom it is given. It's often dire distress that drives us into deep devotion as we reach for our **grace** potion. It's when all else fails but HIS love never does. This is why we are a people that can take the pain that is given, give thanks for it, and transform it into a joy that fills all emptiness. This has indeed been true in the writing and the completion of this book with my co-author in the sky.

This task has indeed been a challenge especially under some pretty crippling circumstances. It became necessary that I counterbalance and overcome the natural law on the brink of knocking me out. Gathering all he spiritual oomph possible, I continued to tell myself . . . **I CAN DO THIS!** Like a factory or any city using electricity (the grid), the switch had to stay on so the power can always be available. Our sustaining power comes in the form of a 'for certain' stance against the *evil* guises of the <u>*devil*</u>; the habit of faith under <u>all</u> circumstances; recognition of and appreciation for true **grace**; and an unwavering will to achieve and find joy.

There was no shame. I had humbled myself before the Lord, living by the old adage that had sustained my parents and their parents and generations before them. "The will of God will never take us where the **grace** of God will not protect us." Those brave and unconditionally loving human beings, often bewildered by the voids and injustices of their lives, simplified it for us all with their personal convictions and by finding a little laughter in their sorrows. We are all capable of doing the same. God's **grace** was for them and continues to be for us as well, indeed satisfactory for now. Striving to always do better, be better, and enjoy life more abundantly would forever be our charge.

I am momentarily content and smile at *grace* as the icy rain pounds steadily on the thick glass window panes of the guest house. Leaves plop down with a thud . . . drenched and now clinging to the cold, soaked ground. It's the peaceful, reverent hours of the morning when wild animals in the woods budge from their resting places in search of food . . . when God speaks through the breezes conducting the wind chimes in a pleasant melody for my meditative spirit. HE mystically whistles HIS presence in between the branches of the dense acreage of captivating foliage and budding blossoms.

Giving God thanks and constantly acknowledging HIS daily allotment of *grace* has made me an overcomer in places and during chapters of my life trail where and when I was convinced there was no escape . . . a total dead end. Like Paul and Silas within the prison walls, I found it was when grief and *grace* kindled in the same flame of gratitude that my heart gained strength and the will to conquer my demons. Like David, I dance and pay homage to the Source from where I find pure **grace** and heart stamina in order to endure. Standing against the punishing storms . . . the rocky and bruising circumstances of my life . . . I have learned to fly on God's wings of **Grace**; grasp the wonders and beauty of the world; and usher in *wholeness*. HE began to show me HIS kindness in so many different ways . . . gifts of love and blessings having been in front of me all along, even when there appeared to be no reason to give thanks.

For the Lord God is a sun and shield; the Lord will give *grace* and glory; no good thing will He withhold from those who walk uprightly. **Psalm 84:11**

- Suffering does deliver *grace* if one manages to survive evil's onslaught. Our eyes must be wide opened. HE asks, "In me, is anything ever really lost?" Be confident that all is *grace*, God is always **good**, and those who know, and love God also know they are loved too and never alone.

- God makes all *grace* real because HE transfigures all that is pure, good, and lovely. I marvel at God's simple gifts of the sun, the clouds, the trees, the flowers, the birds, and the morning dew.

- *Grace* helps us hold our heads high and no matter the steep hurdles, we can continue to sustain a happy heart. The knowledge of true *grace* will help us celebrate what an unbelievable life we have had so far . . . the accomplishments; the blessings; and yes, even the hardships because they have made us stronger.

- The real mystery of the powerful force of *grace* is that it always shocks and pulsates our being. With a passionate love of God, it always stuns, it's always just what we need, and it always arrives right on time.

- It's only when our love for God ignites a pure blaze of glory and we become totally devoted to the truth when we finally realize peace. While we may not always be happy, and heartbreak might take our breath and faith away momentarily, God still asks us to give thanks in all things because HE knows the feeling of joy begins in the action of appreciation. It's when HE offers us HIS *amazing grace.*

- One of the great truths of the Bible is that when we are helpless, God is not. "Of this, I am sure," the unknown author wrote. "There is a God and it is not me. And if this God I know doesn't answer prayers in the time and manner we've asked, it's because HE can see what we cannot." The Scriptures tell us of this truth, of God's promises, and of HIS unexpected blessings for the people of Biblical times and believers of today. When we run into the arms of **Grace** provided by the One who bore it all, into the embrace of HE who is more than enough, we are safe, and we are free.

There is indeed *grace* for every season. And because there is, we may walk unafraid as we are wrapped in the kind of *love* knowing no end and no equal. I come to deliver a message from my silent partner . . . my co-author who one day just up and announced that HE wanted me to write this book . . . that the opposition would be punitive and only a few would understand. I was to always stay in direct communication with the Infinite Source and prepare myself for unforeseen goodness and peace of mind. My numbness and distress would diminish, and my life would have new meaning, a more purposeful direction, and a voice to be heard along with the children's cries. I hoped to see myself accomplishing impossible dreams.

But may the God of all *grace*, who called us to His eternal glory by Christ Jesus, after you have suffered a while, perfect, establish, strengthen, and settle *you.* **I Peter 5:10**

Chapter Three
Ya-didn't-have-to-do-what-you-did-but-you-did
And I Thank You

If the only prayer you said in your life was "thank you" that would suffice. Meister Eckhart

    Human failure beginning (Adam and Eve) was, has always been, and might continue to be that we aren't satisfied with God and what HE has given. We hunger for something more, something other than what we have. I have always wanted "good" hair as we used to call "white" hair in my day. I was ashamed of my half coarse/half of my father's Native cold black hair wavy locks that never grew for a long time. I would ask in innocence if colored folks did something really bad to upset the Lord when this hair curse came upon us. I certainly had a lot of nerve dictating to the Master and Designer of it all how HIS people and the universe should be operating.

    Processes such as steaming hot pressing combs and curling irons, and chemicals to straighten the hair so it would be presentable and acceptable in the white world hurt sometimes; it was expensive and time consuming; and denied us of the freedom to walk in the rain and be splashed at an amusement park and to enjoy the conveniences and fun things others took for granted. Society told people of color we were not their definition of 'true beauty' but we fought to defy that negative stereotypes and ugly myths. I learned 50 years ago that I had to make the best of what I had been given, look at myself in the mirror, and say in heartfelt silence . . . "you're still living; you're healthy and feel pretty good; you look good today – a good color; and you're going to be all right." Hallelujah! It's a brand-new day!

For so long, I wanted to jog down the street with my non-fake pony tail swinging or drink champagne in a steamy hot tub with someone special and not have to worry about my thick head of nappy hair reverting to an uncontrollable and messy looking texture, rising like baking powder. Some referred to our having a separate section of black hair care products in most grocery and drug stores used just for our grade of hair as a disgrace . . . an embarrassment . . . and especially in all white settings where others would not have a clue, nor would they care about this albatross-like plight we endured daily. I always kept a scarf and a hat on my person just in case of emergency. Often times I would clip a couple of Mama's clothes pins on the ends of my thin braids. In my young logic, I surmised the pins would help stretch the length of my non-growing hair and encourage the scalp follicles to loosen up and magically produce long, flowing golden locks. Wow! What a wild imagination! It hurt so badly when it never happened.

This hair stuff we'd been given at birth was known to fry and crackled in putrid smelling Dixie Peach hair grease when the steaming hot pressing comb touched it. The irons had set in the fire on a stove burner for quite some time. There were occasions when the person holding this smoking hot instrument would accidently, though unintentionally, let it slip from their hand leaving a burn on my scalp, forehead, or ear lobe. Those occurrences were quite painful.

Several decades later, big name beauty product companies began developing permanent straightening chemicals with lye that often burned, and then safer black hair care products emerged on the market for those preferring more flowing and versatile hairstyles rather than stunning natural style varieties not yet feasible at the time. How sad that if we ever took a dip in chlorine swimming water a few days after paying $100 for a perm, we could possibly come up the pool steps after a relaxing, good-for-the-heart workout, with green hair. The chemicals on the hair and the chlorine in the pool would have clashed. I used to be so proud that black people had their own hair care section in the drug and grocery stores until I understood why.

Later in life, I was baffled at the fact that a lot of Asian Americans found themselves owning beauty supply outlets geared towards black hair care and expensive hair extensions and wigs. I asked an owner one day, "Tell me, what do you know about my hair; which shampoo, or hair oil would be best? You go home and stand in the shower after an hour or so in a sauna. What I know now that I didn't know then was that there were so many grateful ways to make the best out of what we have been Divinely given.

I was always mesmerized by the ocean waves, but never learned to swim because of my hair. Having that safety net that might have been necessary to save my life and that of my children was just not feasible. A swimming cap over my big head gave me headaches and never held the water out. Still none of these female realities seemed to matter to Daddy especially when black children were only allowed to go to the major swimming outlets on one or two selected days of the year anyway. He wasn't about to entertain the possibility of my joining a few friends who didn't care. They just wanted to swim in the big pool.

What was even more pitiful was right after the 'colored days', the public works authorities would come and disinfect the entire facility starting with draining the pool. It was insinuated 'colored kids' could have some kind of contagious disease. I always dreamed of surfing and even designed surf boards for my storybook characters to ride on when they hit the water. Recalling how hard I cried, that 'hair' pain seemed to never go away. A towel had accidently slipped from my head and the steam from a long hot shower destroyed my upsweep hairdo for my senior prom. I promised myself if I ever became a mother, and my offspring might be girls, they would not suffer as I had. Today, at 71, I remain so *grateful* to still have hair, no matter the texture.

Mama would rationalize that black hair gave a lot of talented and deserving 'colored' folks a constant source of income, especially when corporate America was not rolling out the welcome mat for people brown like me, especially women . . . that we should be grateful for the jobs and qualified beauticians to make us look and feel better about ourselves. With the exception of a few blessed and brilliant "chocolate baby boomers" fortunate to have conquered new frontier career opportunities . . . for most of us, 'charcoal children's' choices were quite limited. My quest to become a photojournalist in 1965 was pretty much unheard of and most university journalism schools would not enroll a woman of color.

Grandma Jemma would always say our thick, coarse hair was what made little 'colored' kids special but I knew then it was a lie proven with the pain of the detangling and straightening process. But Jemma's sentiments were coated in enough love to seal our innocent hearts from an unwarranted kind of hurt. I knew again when the little white girl standing in front of Mama and me in a grocery store line stared at me with such nasty condescension and then turned quickly with her silky, blonde hair flying right in my face. I never forgot that humiliation . . . a feeling I really didn't understand at such a young age but never forgot. Mama told me I got really mad, but I wouldn't cry . . . thus, the beginning of my defiance. I was too young to understand where the hurt was coming from, but I fought throughout my life, often times to no avail, never to feel that pain again.

As I went about my stewing and protesting about the injustices of such blatant prejudices and bondage (mind, body, and spirit), Jemma would always remind me that no matter how unfair or how unfortunate circumstances might be or appear to be, one should want to give 'thanks' anyhow for all we did have, plain and simple! "You still breathin', ain't cha' Honey Chile? The way I see it, everything else should be a 'thank ya' cakewalk'! Get up! Dress up! Show up!" That commonsense directive came through loud and clear and most of the time I stuck to the 'Jemma order' throughout this journey.

People of color have long struggled with the bias and unfairness in it all, believing sometimes as Job's wife and friends tried to make him think . . . that all his 'bad luck' and loss was somehow connected to a crime he might have knowingly or unknowingly committed. I wasn't perfect . . . never claimed I did everything right, especially when it came to single motherhood. But one truth I would announce without hesitation. That wasn't how God operated. Since HE created us, HE would surely accept us and love us, with our flaws and nappy hair too. I was enough for now just as HE wanted me to be. I sat high on the ash heap next to Job refusing to slide off until the Lord said to me, *"Come, my child, and I will give you rest."*

I heard my beloved friend and late literary agent who had just up and left this world one day without any notice speak to me in a dream. We were having lunch at Harry's right before I was about to leave the Southwest, sadly closing another life chapter. She could read straight through my façade of hurt. I had lost everything and was feeling quite sorry for myself. I had no idea at the time that my dear friend was dying. "You can't give up, J.D. I know that's rather cliché, but it's true. It's going to happen. Believe as I do in you." What a classy and beautiful woman she was! I was so *grateful* the day I met this lady in pink alligator cowboy books and fancy skinny jeans . . . so classy and confident in her presence and delivery when she handed me her business card with just her name and an e-mail address. She reminded me of one of my all-time, favorite actresses, Kathleen Turner.

Believe as I do in you. I meditate often on that dream . . . the last conversation my dear friend and I would share. I had to get my projects to market to help support my children's dreams as well as my own. They had done all they could on their own when few who could help would help or believe. There were other young people depending on me to believe in them as well . . . a constant natural act of kindness and caring that could make a difference in someone or an animal's life. I stop to write a gratitude list today. No complaining. No worrying. No defeatist mind games. Taking good care of "ME" . . . my mind, my heart, and my body. My hours would be filled with good thoughts and actions and always in gratitude for the privilege. I rub a premium Argan oil through my hair.

It has been my admiration and the inspiration of powerful women like Oprah Winfrey; Iyanla Vanzant; and the late Maya Angelou . . . of Kathleen Cleaver; Assata Shakur; Angela Davis; and Ruby Bridges . . . of JoAnn Jenkins (CEO of AARP); Marian Wright Edelman (founder and executive director of the Children's Defense Fund); Cher, Chaka, and Tina; our one-of-a-kind, so appreciated, and will-always-be-reveled former First Lady Michelle Obama and the former Second Lady, Dr. Jill Biden; my mentor, author, and education guru, Dr. Margaret B. Hill (Highland, CA); my beloved mother and Grandma Jemma . . . coupled with a David-like faith and repeating 'thank you,

Lord' that has kept me from being scorched in the devil's smoldering fires of perdition .

What powerful role models these beautiful women were and some continuing to be, providing genuine encouragement and giving me hope through some of my darkest and most trying days! All know and knew firsthand about *'gratitude'* . . . the power in simply saying . . . *thank you, God; I'm good! These blessings are just fine for now* . . . as they kept on improving, finding more joy, thriving and achieving, and paying-it-forward.

It has been said that life has treated me harshly and sometimes I have complained in my heart because many pleasures of human experience have been withheld from me . . . if much has been denied me, much, very much, has been given me.

Hellen Keller

(The Miracle Worker)

Beautiful roses of every color imaginable grow most of the year in the warm California sun. I pass right by the fragrant buds at one of the corners in the neighborhood where I walk the Basenji. There is sometimes an added bonus . . . the greeting of that pleasant smile from the genuinely spirited and gracious Mamacita, the wonderful lady who tends her flower and vegetable garden at dawn or at dusk. She takes great pride in their sudden blossoming and pleasant natural aromas and often shares some of the blooms with me as I head back home. Although she speaks little English, this very kind soul gives me hope in the goodness and graciousness of humankind. She is just that kind of lady and I am truly grateful. In November, she was fanning herself with her big, broad rim, straw hat complaining in a comical manner of protest . . . "'Spose' to be cool – not so hot, Mama (as she always called me). Roses 'all mixed up'," she grimaced. "They bloom . . . they don't bloom! It gets cold . . . it hot!" She shook her head, put her hands up to her plump jaw cheeks, turned, and waved good-bye.

Whiffs of breakfast bacon and pancakes linger beside the lovely fragrance of the roses. Mamacita's smile is infectious. She makes me smile too because she exudes such genuine joy even when she pushes her grocery cart filled with recyclables the neighbors have saved for her. Often times she just isn't well at all but never wants to make a fuss.

There were just some things in life we could not change or control especially when it came to Mother Nature and the callousness or affability of people's hearts. In all the muck of the world, I strive to find and keep the roses in my life and reckon if things get rough, they'll either get worse or better. I pray for the latter without the prickly thorns. "I know, God. YOU're walking right beside me, keeping me safe. I can feel YOUR presence. What a *revelation*!

"Talk about being **grateful**," a pastor friend declared in a great message that stuck with me over the years. "Any time, on any day, take a stroll down the corridors of a local hospital, especially the children's ward, or go visit a nursing home. Then step outside and look up to the sky. Will HE then hear your moans and grumbling, the pastor challenged, or will HE see you smile, spread your arms like an eagle in a worshipful gesture of praise and honor, and proclaim in gratitude, *to Thine be the glory?"* Take time and stop to really smell the roses, my friends!" he encouraged his parishioners.

My pastor/friend continued by reminding his faith-action congregation.... "Want a way to not wake up numb and afraid of the 'bad things' you might have to encounter in your day? Imagine not being able to wake up at all! It's a privilege when you think about the heart wrenching carnage and survivor aftermath in mass shootings all around the world and natural disasters we simply cannot control. Think on these things, my friend . . . the blessings of your days when all human body functions are working properly and void of disease and danger. Study the complexities of the physiology of living beings. Then you'll understand without a doubt and have no confusion what this gift of being who you are really means."

If one were to try to duplicate the functions of the liver, it is doubtful that a fully computerized, four-story laboratory could accomplish the myriad of chemical and enzymatic processes with anywhere near the precision of the four-pound liver. And if one would study the central nervous system, one would discover that in the brain there are over 14 billion units (cells) . . . all multiply and all interconnect. These cell units process all the incoming data from our senses of vision, hearing, touch, smell, and taste, and send messages to the appropriate body organs and limbs, and with perhaps millions of interactions occurring every minute.

The one-pound organ that resides within the human skull makes the internet system appear like a simple tinker toy by comparison. And at the base of the brain there is a gland no larger than a thumbnail which constantly analyzes the chemical composition of the blood, especially the various hormones and mineral levels, and regulates it with an uncanny precision by sending messages to the appropriate glands and organs. This refers only to the brain itself. We know very little about the actual function of the human mind although intimately associated with the brain. It's not accessible to examination via a microscope or MRI machine.
(Sun Books, Santa Fe)

And so the message is quite clear. Cherish your health. *Give thanks.* Keep yourself in condition to do life as well as it can be done. If it's still good, do everything you can within your financial limitations to preserve it by eating nutritionally, exercising, and following through with preventive care. If you're hurting in places and you feel out of balance, search for resources and utilize their availability wisely. I want my mind and body to stay strong and to share all these life lessons with those who believe so called 'old age' means the end. It's a transition and a 'what is' we can still enjoy where we are. We have the experience gained through previous seasons to make the best of the time remaining in our lives. But I also know people need to have the freedom and independence to learn and decide on their own and that definitely included my own children.

Gratitude is the most fruitful way of deepening our consciousness informing us we are indeed a Divine choice. HE chooses that HIS children fully live and HIS children choose the discipline of always giving *thanks*. That's how life works properly no matter what *satan* slings our way. Waiting for such a time when God aligns the stars, we have penetrated the whole mystery of life by giving thanks for everything including the majestic power of the galaxies and the simplicity of breath leaving our lungs.

Journal Entry (August 21, 2017) *Excited spectators, especially scientists, had come from as far as Scotland, Australia, and Germany to see the total solar eclipse traveling from the Northwest to the Southeast . . . one of the most amazing scientific, God performances in modern day history. I couldn't believe one of the largest school districts in the country did not prepare in advance to afford their students the sight of such a spectacular galactic miracle. Caring, innovative educators could have developed lessons for a semester just based on this one event . . . the merging of earth, sun, and moon. In St. Joseph, Missouri, and I'm* *sure in a few other locations as well, it ended up being cloudy and raining steadily on the day of the impending spectacular event. Dejected onlookers headed for their cars having given up on seeing the phenomenon unfold through their protective glasses. And then suddenly . . . within minutes . . . the clouds began to part and move from side to side. The sky breaks open right at the moment of the* **total** *eclipse*. That's how God works. Right when we're just about to give up and think all is lost . . . about to throw in the towel . . . there Our God comes to the rescue galloping down a white sands beach on HIS beautiful stallion named **Grace** and carrying with him a collection of *blessings* and *wisdom nuggets* safely tucked away in HIS saddlebags.

Start your day in *gratitude* feeding what you want to grow in your life. It's an emotion that generally opens the pores of compassion and love, especially when we find ourselves giving praise and thanks in times of darkness and despair. It is one of the most profound testimonies of faith when we are willing to surrender . . . "to let go" and trust the process.

I am a divine instrument of universal power! I am a divine reflection of universal love! I am perfection at its best! I am whole and complete! I am unlimited and abundant! I am divinely capable! I am a beauty to behold! I am joy in motion! I am the greatest miracle in the world! I am the light of the world! I am all that I am, and life is graced by my presence. For this, I am so **grateful.** *And so it is!!* **Affirmation by Iyanla Vanzant**

I had learned all too well that no one receives the **grace** of God unless they are truly grateful for who God is and what HE has already done in their lives. As difficult as life lessons might be, especially for a person of color, the beauty in *faith* and *gratitude* is honoring the graciousness of a living God no matter what. In the midst of bitter actualities and a lack of understanding as to why disappointments, betrayals, uncertainties, and hurt appear to occupy our very existence more than we'd like, giving thanks is still a must. Count blessings for all things, big and little. Discover life yielding much more than what might appear to be possible. We'll never understand HIS ways, but few questions would remain pertaining to the pureness of HIS love when we have occasions to laugh and feel joy.

I thank you God for this most amazing day: for the leaping greenly spirits of trees and a blue true dream of sky; and for everything which is natural which is infinite which is yes. e e cummings

Once I heard a story about a man who had a young eagle that he put in the hen yard with a clog on one of its feet so that it couldn't fly, and there it grew up. At last, when the man was going to move away from that part of the country, he decided to set his eagle free. He took off the clog, but the eagle went hopping about just the same. So very early one morning he took the eagle and set him upon the wall just as the sun was rising.

The eagle opened his eyes and looked for the first time at the burnt orange reflections peaking gradually from behind the mountain ranges. Then, lifting himself up, he stretched his mighty wings and with one screech launched into the upper air. He belonged up there all the while and had simply been living in the wrong place. When we find no meaning in life because we're not in the right place... mind, body, and spirit . . . when we can find no reason to hold on because we are blinded of our blessings and find no reason to be thankful, then we have not had the chance to follow the Master's map across the rising sun just like the eagle.

Another lesson I had learned was that feeling and expressing gratitude for the good in my life didn't give me permission to passively accept the tough aspects of my daily journey and the pieces just not fitting. *Gratitude* lays out the tightrope of trust. I can walk the thin, wonky wire from one destination to another and know even if I fall, I will have another chance to try again if my injury is not too serious. I longed to have the opportunity to spin my lack into gold and my fear of uncertainty and limited time into hope and reality.

An attitude of gratitude in the midst of all things allows us to make all things new. It allows us to make something better out of both the best and the worst that comes our way. This mindset puts us in the right relationship with God, the creative power of our lives. How do we manage to allow God to be seen through the cracks in our hearts and souls during our most difficult days and the times we feel so alone? How can we find happiness and meaning when we're constantly angry and resentful and unappreciative and the world appears to be so mean and insane?

I had found over the years that the best instructional text teaching humankind how to embrace appreciation instead of bitterness was in the Psalms . . . David's songs of praise and thanksgiving sung during times of bewilderment, pain, sorrow, and trouble as well as triumphs. Even after God appointed David king, HE sent the young shepherd boy back to the pastures to herd his sheep until he was prepared . . . until it was the appointed time for him to assume his duty. Through it all, the Psalmist's faith never wavered. Being so grateful and captivated by God's goodness having been chosen to one day be King, David still danced in praise and wrote some of his most powerful love letters to the Lord. He was confident his heavenly Father was ever-present, running the universe, and creating ultimate **good**.

The road to blessedness, peace, and happiness is paved before us as long as we recognize the key . . . that of *gratefulness* for the blessings already received. The grateful mind is always an open mind . . . amenable to the new, the higher, the better, and therefore invariably coming into possession of more and more of those things. And in order to be grateful in the best and most perfect manner, appreciation and kindness are required. Both virtues enlarge our inner consciousness and promote the expansion and authentic expression of love.

The beholden, dedicated mind has a natural tendency to look upon the better side of things, eliminating sadness, fault finding, and criticism. This tendency becomes complete only when an optimistic attitude is added. To be optimistic, however, does not mean to think that black is white and that everything everywhere is all right. The true attitude of mind is to be content with things as they are now and at the same time reach out constantly for greater things . . . for circumstances to improve . . . to emanate an ambiance of superiority to all that is imperfect.

- Gratitude, being filled with **grace**, is giving thanks every time, we can rev up our senses and know we have been blessed to see, smell, and listen to the wonders.
- Gratitude is an expression within our lives and with others blossoming into the realization that we are whole and complete within ourselves. One of Oprah Winfrey's many mantras . . . *seek to be whole – not perfect.*
- Gratitude and appreciation taken all the way to the Source of life comes when we surrender to its hidden intelligence.

- Gratitude fills our hearts with gladness and allows us to see the truth, empowering us to make the right decisions and take appropriate actions. With a grateful heart, we can see the best in every situation and in everyone we meet.

- Gratitude is an attitude of mind and heart. It starts from within and flows through every part of our body and soul. It leaves no area of our being untouched. It encompasses all that we are and ask for . . . the highest and best we can envision and aspire to be.

- Gratitude is a state of being rather than doing. It is unending love for the Creator and all of life's creations.

- Gratitude is important because it's not just a cold, mental acceptance of something. It is warm like the sunshine that makes the flowers grow. It unfreezes negative conditions, making it possible for desired good to manifest. Prove the power of gratitude, and we will be practicing what some refer to as the highest form of prayer.

- Gratitude is not only the memories of our heart; gratitude is a memory of God's heart and to thank the 'unseen' is to remember God.

- When we live with grateful hearts, fear cannot enter, guilt is dissolved, and there is only peace, love, forgiveness, and understanding. That's what life is all about. Successful manifestation of this contentment depends upon affirming that our needs have already been met, believing this is true, and being *grateful* for our supply.

➤ Gratitude leads to two delightful results in our lives. First, it creates a deep sense of joy. It is said that if we pursue happiness as our goal, it will elude us. But if we practice *gratitude*, living in a consciousness of contentment, being thankful for what we have (even if it's meager), we will realize a personal experience of abundance and prosperity. The energy of gratitude in our lives draws more and more of the things we desire, almost like magic.

➤ Counting our blessings is one of the surest ways to lift one's spirits. It always shifts the energy to something positive and desirable. Love is the power that heals our lives, and love is the power that will ultimately heal this country. Gratitude comes from love. It is the natural expression of a caring and grateful heart.

➤ Gratitude, like faith, helps us understand that suffering is not the whole picture. Circumstances can change overnight; hurts can gradually subside; and promises can become realities. Once we begin to pay closer attention to the beauty around us and exhibit thankfulness for the normalcy of our days, our soul will be warm and contented and peace of mind will overflow.

➤ Gratitude gives us altitude above all earthbound concerns and worries. With unconditional appreciation, we are assured of eternal growth and abundance.

➤ Gratitude projects positive vibrations into the atmosphere and our benevolent Universe responds kindly. The fact we exist and are experiencing the gifts of life and love is a tremendous privilege in an age of effortless conveniences giving us far more freedom than our ancestors. Each new day always brings about new possibilities. Each new day is another opportunity for us to begin again . . . perhaps the last chance for a second chance. We remain consciously **grateful** for every person, place, and thing that helps us learn to love.

- Gratitude is one of the greatest secrets of a fulfilled life. It is full cooperation with God. This revelation might change the way we view ourselves. In the healing arts, gratitude is basic to the emotional bonding of the parent/teacher/student interaction.

- Gratitude is indeed like a gearshift that can move our mental mechanism from chaos to peacefulness; from numbness to inner peace; and from fear to love. When we find ourselves stuck about all the things that seem wrong, we might want to remember to say a prayer of gratitude for all the things that are right.

- Life is not meant to be isolated and for one's self, but is meant to be shared in the context of love and peace. Gratitude comes by virtue of doing for others, or what some would call Honda-like *random acts of kindness* . . . whether for a total stranger or someone we've known all our lives.

- Gratitude enriches and deepens the colorful fabric of our lives by allowing us to see more. It is impossible to feel worry, anger, depression, or any negative emotion of any kind in the presence of thankfulness.

- Gratitude is a way out of difficulty, pain, and broken heartedness. In the face of adversity and distress, practicing gratitude requires us to give up our own ideas about what we think is happening to us.

➢ Gratitude is a miraculous force like a magical magnet generating and then attracting so much more than we have already received. The more grateful we are for everything in life, the more reasons we find to be appreciative. Focusing gratitude on anything makes it grow. Gratitude takes almost no time to convey but can have a tremendous impact on our achievements and joy.

➢ Expressing gratitude for the miracles in our world is one of the best ways to make each moment of our lives special. The positive effect of thanksgiving gives us strength and hope to cling to. As is often said . . . *life isn't about surviving the storm. It's about learning how to dance in the rain.*

➢ Gratitude is sometimes about slowing down our pace, opening up our senses to the world around us, and feeling the impact such awareness has on our thoughts and actions. We cannot be grateful and unhappy at the same time. It's emotionally impossible to do both.

➢ Those of us who understand the importance of gratitude can encourage others to recognize their own special moments.

Be thankful for blessings already yours . . . one being that the soul knows no such thing as time. All the good we can ever experience is ours now and the more we believe it, the more we rejoice in it. If you are reading this, you're breathing, above ground, and on your third bite of Vanilla

Bean cheese cake. Some of the happiest people around are those who have comparatively few accoutrements and some with severe physical impairments... Jeison Aristizabal (2016 CNN Hero of the Year), Travis Mills (veteran), and Amy Purdy (Paralympic) to name a few. Often times these individuals might require constant medical attention, iron-will strength, and dense courage to sustain their urgent need for balance of joy, physical pain, and perhaps a little sorrow from time to time. But their lives stand for something. They have reached out and helped so many others in spite of handicaps and hiccups having the potential of blocking their visions and destroying their dreams. They have inspired. They bring clarity to the true meaning of living.

    Every year I watch *CNN Heroes*, I ask myself, what is it we can't do if these passionate, giving human beings could achieve so many great feats with such daunting odds against them. Their gratitude list grows longer and longer and their accomplishments more and more remarkable. These champions of life teach us the more melodious our song of thanksgiving is sung for what we have, the sooner we realize it in actual everyday experience. Happy, contented people radiate victory wherever they go, maintaining an attitude of confidence in daily tasks and a game plan for the tomorrows. Choose happiness perhaps by making someone else happy. The person who bestows happiness always gets much more of it in return.

    Seek out constructive distractions. Think about what always gives you pleasure and do it. Be grateful that you can! Don't wait for the activity to come to you. Buy the tickets, call your friend, have a glass of wine or a cup of coffee, even if it's by yourself. Get on a bike, pick up a tennis racquet, or take a train ride north up the California coastline. And in your heart, silently scream .... *Thank you, thank you, Lord!* Do one thing at a time, at least for one or two hours a day. Multitasking can sometimes make us feel tense. Focusing on one activity is calming and allows us to enjoy the experience fully. Spend more time with friends and loved ones. Choosing to change, even with small steps, is itself a mood-enhancer allowing us to see unmistakably just how blessed we really are.

The art of blessing comes through our willingness to 'let go' and surrender to the angel of the present who carries beauty and hope in her wings. The key is to realize *something* is operating under the surface and we must trust the One who has designed it. To give thanks and praise to the conductor of the universal orchestra in times of darkness, anguish, physical and emotional pain, and uncertainty in the tomorrows of our lives is the toughest test, but when successfully and consistently accomplished, is the most profound testament to a *faith* that pleases God tremendously. It has been proven that by doing so, we will attract more good as a result. The art of deep seeing makes **gratitude** possible. And it is the art of gratitude that ushers in joy and prosperity in abundance.

Hall of Famer John Wooden (legendary UCLA basketball coach) knew all too well about the saving *grace* of being thankful. As a high school and college basketball coach, he practiced a "thank you" rule believing that if one didn't show their appreciation to others, they'd have no way of knowing their contributions were recognized. Coach Wooden believed that without recognition, people would start to pull back both from performing and from cooperating with others. *Thank you expresses extreme gratitude, humility, and understanding.*

I often wonder what would happen to the wickedness of humanity in modern times if we would all practice what Jewish people refer to as *brachot* . . . blessings or prayers of thanksgiving throughout the day. These are praises of gratitude giving honor to God for creating a world of infinite amazement and possibilities - though today somewhat fractured and frightening in its current state. For example, there is a blessing upon seeing a star, a full moon, or a rainbow. There is a blessing for the gifts of food, wine, and water. There is even a blessing upon going to the bathroom for internal organs that function healthy and normal.

When we celebrate and uplift the spiritual energy of our ancestors – 'the Committee' - we say "thank you" for paving the way and loving us beyond measure. When we take the time to recount the blessings God has poured out in our lives already, we sing praises as did Mary. We accept that **gratitude** is an essential part of being ever present. When we delve deep into the present, **gratitude** arises spontaneously. A simple occurrence of joy and thank you for me was watching my husky gallop up and down the snowy hills with other dogs at the dog park . . . just as the sun peaked over the mountain ranges at dawn. A smile embraces my heart as I remember the sleigh rides in Brooklyn Park six decades ago when our childhood innocence and laughter was so intense it made us cry so many happy tears.

If *gratitude* is the highest form of thought a human being can have, I would always make it my first thought the minute I came out of the mystery of the darkness of sound and healthy sleep, and like Augustine, my ultimate goal, without exception, would be finding joy in the painful horridness of things and sharing this awareness and elation with others.

We live in a culture that programs us to expect instant gratification and to devalue processes that involve large amounts of time and close attention. It's easy for us to read a few books, go to several workshops, and then expect immediate enlightenment. Some call it a mentality of 'microwave spirituality'. But in order to learn how to connect to the Divine . . . how to love . . . how to forgive . . . how to find lessons in the chaos and confusion hovering over our existence, we must embrace life's experiences, both the sublime and the dreadful. We learn often the hard lesson that it's truly a challenge to become grateful for our pain as well as our joy.

The majority of those who have earned the accolades have been great thinkers throughout their lives. They were awestruck by the plethora of fascinating phenomena of the universe that made them feel a welcomed serenity. They were so **grateful** for it all. So am I. It is believed that if we are brave enough to seek what appears to be impossible, it is a place where fear meets faith and in our sometime victories, we can see the face of God. When we live with **grateful** hearts, fear cannot enter, guilt is dissolved, and there is only love and contentment. As long as giving 'thanks' is possible and acted upon, joy will most certainly follow. As I practice forgiving myself and others, I feel the swell of **gratitude** moving within me, humbling me each moment in proof of God's love and generosity.

Dark clouds lighten their load of much needed moisture for the once parched earth and now rise above the mountain peaks. I stand in the crisp, cold temperatures of the morning, and as always, in awe and in thanksgiving. My heart and spirit has long been broken and I am lonely . . . my future uncertain, but I would find a piece of pleasantness watching the chipmunks appear and disappear into the holes they have dug through the cold wetness of the forest grounds. At first I thought I was seeing things until I zoomed in on a larger animal with my camera lens. Who would have thought it? A bear cub roaming the woods not far from town in search of its mother, I would surmise. "For your *grace*, Lord, I am truly **grateful**.

Chapter Four

A Shepherd's Heart

All I have seen teaches me to trust the Creator for all I have not seen. Ralph Waldo Emerson

All throughout the Scriptures, *faith* is emphasized as a tremendous power. It was by *faith* that Moses led the children of Israel out of Egypt, safely across the waters of the Red Sea, and through the wilderness. It was by *faith* Elijah, Isaiah, Daniel, and all the other great Biblical prophets performed their miracles. The whole spirit of the Bible encourages long life through sane and healthy living and by building day by day on one's *faith*. It points to the duty of living a useful and noble life . . . of making as much of ourselves as possible.

God's plan focuses on the conscious union with the Father's life as the one and all-inclusive thing. We are never to forget we are One, for only in realizing this unity can we hope to know the power of true *faith*. How can I love God but by loving HIM in the universal all – in rock and plant; in bird and beast; and in all humankind? Until we have found HIM in these things, we search for HIM elsewhere in vain.

Faith was the remarkable characteristic of Christ Himself. He always shared the necessity of consistent belief. *According to thy faith, be it unto thee.* As the great healer and restorer, Jesus often referred to it as "the measure of what we receive in life." Whenever He healed, He laid the entire emphasis upon the *faith* of the healer and the one being healed. *Thy faith hath made thee whole . . . believe only and he shall be made whole.* He often reproved His disciples for their lack of faith which prevented them from healing, and when He addressed them, he said, *O faithless and perverse generation, how long shall I be with you and suffer you?* God sees our failures and HE knows we need answers . . . that we need help. Through *faith*, we can calm our own heart waves and be encouraged all will be well in time.

Now when He got into a boat His disciples followed Him. And suddenly, a great tempest arose on the sea, so that the boat was covered with the waves. But He was asleep. Then His disciples came to Him and awoke Him, saying "Lord, save us! We are perishing!" But He said to them, "Why are you fearful, O you of little *faith*?" Then He arose and rebuked the winds and the sea, and there was a great calm. So, the men marveled, saying, "Who can this be that even the winds and the sea obey Him?" **Matt 8:23-27**

Jesus knew the power of this ultimate degree of *faith* and taught only what He had found to be true. When He began to feed the hungry multitude in the desert off five small loaves of bread and two fish, He demonstrated *undying faith*. He was confident the Infinite supply would never fail but would increase in His hands. He reverently blessed the bread, broke it, and gave pieces to His disciples. The disciples fed the people, some once non-believers, until every human need was satisfied.

This was the authentic truth Jesus knew without question and spoke of as revealed in the Word. Generations and generations later, I would come into this world and experience similar miracles. My survival as a newborn was a testament in itself. Even more and finally, I now live by my *faith* and desire to testify to its truth. When life was at its ugliest stage, and that was quite often, I would sing in tune to gospel sensation Kirk Franklin . . . *yes, I can . . . yes I can . . . yes I can, can, can! all because I got faith!* And then I wrote a book and edited it on my own over and over until I got it right. My faith assures me 'the best is yet to come."

Christ came into this world with a peculiar aptitude for understanding the intricacies of the Spirit of the Lord. He taught believers that the Father's love within them could be absolutely trusted to guide, protect, and provide when we believed it possible. *Faith.* We could live simply, care deeply, communicate with kindness and sincerity, love generously, and then the best advice I could offer my children and other believers was to 'leave the rest to God'. What many often lack is a big picture view of things . . . a vision. We forget we can't know what God has working for us in the future. It's important to tell ourselves over and over that things can turn on a dime and often do. See the possibilities before and not after the fact. Remember, God doesn't ask us to understand. HE asks us to obey. That's where true *faith* comes in. I have complete *faith* in the Lord and pray HE is not finished with me yet.

Sadly, I had gone from Baptist to United Methodist to African Methodist Episcopal to Catholic to Church of God in Christ and finally to Presbyterian in search of answers; a solution to my conundrum of loving God with all my heart but angry about a lifetime of racial injustices experienced by my children, many of my students, and me. Some sense of it came together during my battles in the 'valley of weeping' when I knew I could no longer carry the load alone. Thank you ccsf, and thank you Grandma Jemma, that wonderful, funny, very wise lady who taught me so much about prayer and believing in myself.

With few opportunities or exposure to the world on the other side of the tracks and with very little societal compassion and respect afforded a woman of color in the beginning decades of the 19th century and continuing into modern times (it's gradually changing, thank you Lord), Jemma still found joy in God's small miracles like the opening of her tulips and star gazers; a new puppy; and a big piece of lemon meringue pie. Her *faith* was so inspiring. When God set out to find those with David-like obedience . . . believers with a 'shepherd's heart' . . . HE found Jemma Alexander, her cold bottle of Pabst Blue Ribbon beer and all.

Scholar theologians remind followers that it is often our lack of *faith* that keeps God from delivering HIS promises. Still we ask . . . how do we have **faith** in God's love when it sometimes feels like the world and everything else in it is in such a vicious, scary mess? No one's there to depend upon anymore and those who were there are now running away or were never truly for us in the first place. When there are no siblings and maybe one or two extended family bonds after the ones close to me had left this world so soon, the road became mentally and circumstantially life-threatening as I constantly fought a vicious *satanic* war with the devil.

It became necessary to reinforce my *faith* by returning to Jemma's teachings . . . plain old common-sense inspiration. She introduced me to heroes and heroines of our ancestral heritage and other famous warriors who made history by stepping forward with their staunch *convictions* bearing witness to God's love and mercy. These brave men and women believed they would find true peace and joy on the other side of their struggles. We (and they) just had to have the discipline and the will to 'hold on'. We owed it to their memory and all the sacrifices they made . . . for the generations who paved the way for 'chocolate baby boomers' to move just a little higher up the success ladder.

Today we owe our children the same kind of love, truth, protection, freedoms, and dedication because truth be told, we are in a crisis and our children are crying out. Listen. One-night rainy night, I was awakened by a group prayer coming from "the committee". I could hear familiar voices of my past asking the Lord to intervene in our troubled times... *Give them this day their daily bread.* I heard the husky bark back as well. He heard me tell EuWin and him just how much I loved and missed them.

Jemma loved telling stories about Biblical characters from her 'good book', especially when she knew we might be hurting for one reason or another and needed to be encouraged and strengthened in our *faith*. "Job told God HE wasn't being fair . . . that no man should suffer as he had. And then God gave Job back everything he had lost, and even more." Of course, her skeptical grandchild . . . that would be me . . . believed Job probably missed what he first had more than he liked the new stuff. "David hadn't done right by God, and he hurt too just like you do now!" she assured me. "But then everything turned out just fine, yes it did, now! God saved David from a giant and made him a king." Jemma always made people laugh by the way she explained things even when she was trying to make a point.

The beginnings of my infinite anguish as I discovered my 'charcoal child' status began with an early experience while waiting to use a nasty, roadside park restroom until a white child and her mother came out. We couldn't be in the same place at the same time. Go figure! Frequently, I would have released nature in my clothes by the time the two exited, strangely walking as far away as they could from where Mama and I were standing. It was obvious the pair had taken their time purposely. Mama would quickly clean me up, first wiping my tears and then hers and never commenting on this particular incident among so many similar ones until I was much older. She knew she just wasn't equipped to offer me any kind of explanation that would ease the hurt and confusion. What had I done to them, I remember thinking? They didn't know anything about me or where I was from. And again, they never asked me my name.

I realized then I would not think, grow up, or live my life the way the majority of white people felt a little 'colored' girl should. My great grandfather who fled Kentucky in the late 1800s after he slapped a white man for spitting in his face had paid the price for me to be free . . . free to pursue the dreams coming from my gift of creativity and imagination; from my red View master showing me other worlds; and from the books and articles in magazines (especially *Ebony* and *Jet*) confirming what was possible for those who believed and looked like me. I later learned this was what was known as *faith* and I would pass this *faith* on to my children and students. I would always tell them they were capable of making life happen the way they wanted . . . it just might not transpire overnight or without a struggle and perhaps heartbreak.

Members of my estranged, extended family interpreted this brazen mindset of 'coloring outside the lines' as my thinking I was better than others . . . uppity!! That was never the case. I had this gorgeous, brilliant uncle who had traveled the world and told me fascinating stories about beautiful landscapes he had seen and the wonderful people he had met in all the different cities where he had worked as an electrical engineer. Like my mother (especially in her younger days), my uncle passed for white and enjoyed all the perks available in the white world. He had introduced me to the Southwest and I fell in love.

Yes, I suppose I wanted more than maybe what I should have ever imagined possible at the time for a 'charcoal child', but I started very early deciding I would settle for nothing less. I taught my children to dream just as big. The difficulty was trying to fulfill their lengthy plan-to-achieve-list on a teacher's meager salary . . . a 'champagne mind and a beer pocketbook' as Jemma would always quip, and with no other support with the exception of my beloved parents. They had long depleted their golden years' savings at our expense never losing *faith* in God's promises and their *faith* in the future of my children and me. I never blamed them for not agreeing with many of my choices and decisions. There were times I didn't even agree with me. I rationalized numerous plights as what was 'supposed to be' without my having the freedom to make those decisions. I kept on pursuing my dreams with dogged aggression knowing I had a 50/50 chance of success or failure in order to gain the life I had always wanted for my children, for me, and for other children who have called upon their caretakers to take a stand and help save their lives and this country.

Circumstances definitely weren't perfect nor were they always happy or easy. But my bumpy road would never cloud my vision. There would be no personal satisfaction or awe with being on a Hollywood tour bus looking at movie stars' mansions. I would always announce I wanted my own super cool place to live and own. Even then, it didn't matter how long it took to get there or if I'd ever get there. I just knew I would never stop trying nor would I be trapped by the illusion or the devil's snide mocking that an uncaring, capricious fate would determine my destiny. Racism, poverty, and emotional hardship would not be excuses for failure. Loving God and striving for excellence would occupy my efforts.

What I did know was Job and David had undeniable *faith* and pure love for God without question. "People who don't understand God's timing can become spiritually spastic, trying to make the right things happen at the wrong time," maintains Bishop T.D. Jakes in one of his many powerful messages. "They don't get HIS rhythm and most folks can tell they are out of step. They birth things prematurely, threatening the actuality of their God-given dreams. Can God trust you with rejection . . . accepting you won't always get what you want from HIM?" the Bishop asks. "Be reminded, people won't always respond to you the way you'd like either. Can you be trusted to remain faithful? Can God say "no" and trust that you will still dance, still pray, and still praise HIM?" At this point in my life . . . not before . . . HE now most certainly could.

God trusted the young mother Mary. Obviously, HE trusted her **faith** giving her an incredible responsibility at such a young age. She remained devoted and obedient even when her son . . . the son of God . . . went to the Cross. When the Lord has extraordinary work needing to be done . . . when HE has a special calling that requires a "certain someone," how does HE choose? I had to believe HE chose me to write this book with HIM. There is no other feasible explanation upon its completion. What was it about Mary that persuaded God to choose her?

The Father knew HE could trust her even though her heart would be pierced again and again. She didn't understand at the time that through her Son's death God was reconciling the world to HIMSELF. She had no idea that in three days, Jesus would be resurrected to a new life. She just stood there at Calvary watching painfully yet trusting and praising a God she couldn't comprehend but loved with all her heart. Can HE trust you through this kind of disappointment?" the Bishop's concluding question asks.

Picture the omniscient eyes of the unfathomable El Roi – the God who sees – spanning the universe in panoramic view, every galaxy in HIS gaze. Imagine now the gradual tightening of HIS lens as if a movie camera were attached to the point of a rocket bound for planet Earth. Not a man-made rocket, but a celestial rocket – a Divine messenger - of the living kind. Gabriel has been summoned once again to the throne of God. This time heaven's lens focuses northward to a town called Nazareth.

I dare guess where Mary was when Gabriel appeared to her. She must have been stunned when he spoke . . . "Greetings, you who are highly favored! The Lord is with you." How could this young girl of thirteen or fourteen years (as has been assumed) comprehend that she was 'highly favored' by the Lord God HIMSELF? "You will be with child and give birth to a son. Not just any son, but "the Son of the Most High."

I now invite you to imagine what Mary's first moments might have been like as a mother. Her young body lay sapped of strength, her eyes heavily closed, but her mind refusing to give way to rest. She hears the labored breathing of Joseph sleeping a few feet from her. Only months before he was no more than a stranger to her. She knew only what she had been told about him and what she could read in his occasional shy glances. Those that knew Joseph said he was a good man. Over the last days before the birth of Jesus, Mary found out he was far more than just a 'good man'. No man, no matter how kind, would have done what Joseph had done for her.

Finally, picture Bethlehem a day or so after Jesus' birth. A calf, only a few days old, awakens hungry and unable to find its mother. The stir awakens Jesus who also squirms and whimpers. Scarcely before Mary can move her tender frame toward the manger when Jesus begins to wail! She scoops Him up in her arms, her long, dark brown hair draping His face. She quietly slips out the gate.

Gingerly sitting down, Mary leans her back against an outside wall of the stable, propping the baby on her small lap. She takes a strip of muslin from her dress and ties back her hair. For the first time she sees the King of Kings in the light. She stares lovingly into His tiny face. Just down the path, the sun begins to peak over the roof of an inn full of unknowing souls who had made Him no room. They would never know they were within a few steps away from our Savior who had come to save sinners and believers like them . . . and today, like you and me. Luke 1:26-33 – (resource) ***Jesus* by Beth Moore**

What great *faith!* Mary moved from a dangerous predicament of being pregnant and unmarried . . . to the unfortunate conditions of where the Lord was born . . . to the separation from His parents when He traveled to the temple and challenged the vindictive power priests . . . to looking up at her child, our Lord, on the Cross all bringing her much angst, confusion, and sadness. Yet, as the Lord's mother walked away from Calvary she carried in her heart an awareness and an acceptance of the true will of the Father. She never walked away from God. I couldn't either . . . not ever, no matter what I didn't understand, or think was so unjust.

"Have you experienced the piercings that Mary did?" Bishop Jakes would ask. "Are you someone who has survived hell and high water and still says, 'I love you, God? Not my will, but YOUR will be done?' Are you able to praise HIM not only through the good times but when everything is going haywire, too?" Mary would believe "all things would work for good" and she must and would abide and believe even when her heart was broken into pieces and her soul pounded like drum beats in the wilderness. As Mary's son grew into a young man, He also exemplified a powerful *faith* and belief of expectancy on so many occasions.

The supremacy of some of the greatest benefactors of the race came largely from the inspiration of *faith* in their mission... their belief that they were born to deliver a certain message while simultaneously making an important contribution to humanity. They could attest to the fact that this virtue of *faith* was the greatest power in civilization. It has been and will always be the foundation of courage, initiative, and enthusiasm. It has built railroads; has revealed the secrets of nature to science, medicine, and technology; has led the way to all our inventions and discoveries; and has brought success out of the most inhospitable environments and exigent conditions, especially when so many, including me, had come so close to giving up.

There is no magic like ***faith***. It elevates, refines, and multiplies the capability of every other faculty. George Washington, in a letter written when he was but twelve years old, predicted.. "I shall marry a beautiful woman; I shall be one of the wealthiest men in the land; I shall lead the army of my colony; and I shall rule the nation which I helped to create." General Grant, in his *memoir,* wrote that as a boy at West Point he saw General Scott seated on his horse reviewing the cadets. Suddenly, something within him said, "Ulysses, some day you will ride in his place and be General of the Army."

Hopefully, Harriet Tubman's photo will soon be on the front of the U.S. $20 bill. It would be a shame if that never happens. How ironic 150 years prior Tubman would need $20 to get her family out of the south via the Underground Railroad. Rumor had it they were in grave danger of being captured. Surprisingly, townspeople came forward to help when an abolitionist Tubman trusted had refused. Decades later, this brave conductor of a 'freed people' escape passage would need $20 dollars a month to keep her home in Auburn, New York, opened for those who continued to need shelter and food. While doing so, she was penniless and supported herself through private donations, raising pigs in her back yard, and selling produce from her garden. A staunch *faith* and fearless spirit helped Harriet make 19 trips to the South over a 10-year span and rescue (it is estimated) 300 slaves.

Much of Napoleon's power and early success came from a tremendous **faith** in his mission; the belief that he was a man of destiny; he had been born under a lucky star; and he was ordained to conquer. When warned by his generals not to expose himself to the enemy, he was said to reply that the bullet or cannon had not been cast which could kill Napoleon. This invincible belief in his future added immensely to his natural powers.

It was her conviction that she was chosen by God to free France from its enemies that made Joan of Arc, the simple, unenlightened peasant girl of Dom Remy, the savior of her country. Her unwavering *faith* in a Divine mission gave her a kind of quiet dignity; a miraculous force of character; and an ingenious military strategist encouraging all the commanders of the French army to obey her as private soldiers obey their superior officers. **Faith** in her potential and in her calling transformed the peasant maiden into one of the greatest military leaders of her time.

In Elbert Hubbard's (100-year-old book), *A Message to Garcia* he wrote, "When war broke out between Spain and the U.S., it was deemed critical that the President communicate with the Spanish leader, Garcia. He needed to secure his cooperation quickly. No mail or telegraph missive could reach him. A fellow by the name of Rowan was sent for and given a letter to be delivered to Garcia who supposedly had been fasting somewhere up in the mountains. Why Rowan? Why could he be trusted? Why did this 'someone' of a distinguished nature have so much *faith* in Rowan? Rowan took the letter and asked no questions. He just did the job because that was what had been requested of him. He was a man of his word and his word was his bond. That 'someone' had *faith* Rowan was a dependable soul.

The idea of the telephone was flashed into the mind of Professor Alexander Bell by the drawing of a string through a hole in the bottom of a tin can and by means of which he found the voice could be transmitted. The concept took such complete possession of the inventor that it robbed him of sleep and for a time made him poor. But nothing could take away his vision or prevent him from struggling to work it out of the imaginative stage into the actual. It was Bell's *faith* in himself and the process that allowed the improbable to become real.

Rahab was a prostitute living in Jericho. Because she put her *faith* in God and confessed it to the Jewish spies, the Lord used her to help the children of Israel win a mighty victory. She could have easily felt too guilty and condemned to step forward. But while she couldn't do anything about her past, she could and did do something about her present moments in order to help the infiltrators. Joshua's soldiers must have believed him to be crazy when he explained the *plan* he had been given by God to carry out. While Joshua was talking, God was working with his soldiers' hearts preparing them for what HE was about to do. Joshua also believed victory was at hand as he told the general he was going to win before the war began. He had total confidence in God so he acted upon Divine instructions. (Joshua 6)

It wasn't going to be easy having Joshua-David-Mary-Rahab like *faith* . . . that which requires submitting to the total will of God. Though time was limited now, I would endeavor to live a new and more *faithful,* victorious kind of life. For this, I prayed.

Faith Mantras

- ✓ Let no one shake your *faith* in yourself or in the possibilities and future of humankind. That's what brings you into the closest connection with God. It is your mainstay.

- ✓ Don't step back in fear. Step forward in *faith*.

- ✓ Be convinced there is no spot where God is not.

- ✓ Faith isn't believing God can. It's knowing God will.

- ✓ God isn't alarmed when we hit rock bottom. HE made the rock.

- ✓ Our *faith* puts us in touch with Infinite Power and opens the way to unbounded possibilities and limitless resources.

- ✓ No one can rise higher than their *faith*. No one can do a greater thing than they believe they can.

- ✓ Binding yourself to a God-centered code of obedience is a necessary cost of living in *faith*. Unless we stand for something, we will fall for anything.

David knew in order to live a life of great accomplishments, God's followers would carry with them the "risk of belief." There would be skeptics who would be diehards in their opinions. Some would venture to believe God could not be all that generous and gracious when the world was in such a scary, sad state of affairs and so many people were hurting and hopeless. Just as the Lord empowered David, HE will direct and strengthen the tools HE has given us, and we will find joy early in the morning hours, just before dawn.

The young boy did not waste his youth. He was active; got strong and fearless; and worked productively and diligently. He learned how to labor outdoors; how to focus on music and poetry; how to follow God's law; how to love people; and how to become a man after God's own heart. Because of how this young man spent his time, God was able to take David – whom few thoughts would amount to anything – and turned him into a King. (Flurry – 2012)

Though not clearly comprehending many ways of the Father, David eventually possessed a "mystical-type spiritual power" that brought him to a place in the wilderness where he was confident enough to proclaim, "Thou art near, O God. Let Goliath do his worst; he shall know there is a God in Israel." Like David, I had to secure myself in this omnipotence that would provide protection from the beatings of the wicked one. I, too, was in the wilderness physically and in my mind and heart. Like Mary, I would have to find the courage to say to the universe in the midst of my heartbreak and tears and with all my love and praise, declaring again and again and again . . .

Trust in the Lord with all your heart and lean not on your own understanding. In all your ways acknowledge Him, and He shall direct your paths. **Prov. 3: 5-6**

"Just like David, the Wise Men, and Mary, God chooses people who will give HIM the glory and show others how *real faith* works," declared the esteem Bishop Charles E. Blake (West Angeles Church of God in Christ – L.A.) in a powerful Christmas message years ago. I had kept my notes folded in my Bible all this time. "God chooses ordinary people to do extraordinary things! That's how HE does things." The master Biblical scholar and prominently honored theologian went on to inform dedicated followers listening intently that Jesus was not limited by a system . . . that He went 'outside the box' to choose His disciples. "If He chose shepherds and fishermen, no one is disqualified."

Often times when we do the right thing and the wrong thing happens, the challenge becomes halting the discouragement and making our mess our message. The dilemma is how to stand tall in the precious hours 'in between' . . . the days of walking lifeless; the years calloused and simply going through the hollow motions but fulfilling one's personal and professional responsibilities; self-protecting by self-distracting; and often times self-medicating leading to self-destruction.

The body never wakes. It has lost all its capacity to fully feel. In the meantime,... the moments between now and *'the breakthrough'* . . . how do we hold on to our **faith**? Even when our plans don't happen, how do we still enjoy our lives? I come upon the beautiful coral roses hanging over the chain link fence where I turn left on the familiar block in my walk with the Basenji. The winter rains have caused them to multiply and bloom twice in size. *I'm good, Father. I really am. Bring on the rains of hope so I may bloom in faith quadruple in size.*

Through the prayer Christ prayed just before His death on Calvary, the people were given undisputable truth of the commitment to His **faith** and a glimpse into the *grace* of the Father. Jesus' flawless character, the confidence in which He spoke and prayed, and His simple lifestyle demonstrated what HIS Father was like. As recorded in John 17, Christ spoke . . . "I have made Your name known to them." It is our *faith* in the "living bread" that takes us to new heights and brings us within the Oneness of God. Were not all His teachings and all His words directed to the end that He might show men and women how full and complete life could be?

Those who do not see the Designer behind the design everywhere . . . who cannot comprehend the might of Intelligence in back of every created thing . . . cannot have that inspirational *faith* which buoys up the great achievers and civilization builders. Our supreme aim should be to get the best from life, the best in the highest sense life has to give, and this we cannot do without ultimate trust in the Infinite.

Without confidence in the Architect of the great universal plan, we cannot have much assurance in ourselves. The whole of the individual has to be centered in God – lost to all objects of the physical world, and absolutely apart from the sense. Spiritual warriors have the same privilege and responsibility Jesus did to reveal the Father to others. Paul reminds us that God "always leads us in HIS triumph in Christ and manifests through us the sweet aroma of the knowledge of HIM in every place."

Humankind begins to deteriorate; to go toward failure not when we lose all of our material possessions, not when we fail in an undertaking, but when we lose *faith* in ourselves, in our ability to overcome, restore, and ultimately make our dreams come true. We are and will probably always be confronted with things that threaten to destroy faithfulness and contentment. But *trust* tells us we can proceed safely even when our mental faculties see no light or encouragement ahead.

Abraham and David lived in different eras and fulfilled different positions, yet they shared one commonality relating heavily to the concept of *faith* being credited as righteousness. Both had sinned so grievously that faith was demanded for them to believe they were still who God said they were: a father of multitudes and a king whose kingdom would have no end. True restoration demands dedication and hard work. 'Walk on by Faith' requires virtue with no doubts and the epitome of trust in the Unseen.

So, Jesus said to them, "Because of your unbelief; for assuredly, I say to you, if you have *faith* as a mustard seed, you will say to this mountain, 'Move from here to there', and it will move; and nothing will be impossible for you. **Matt. 17:20**

I was grateful God's power was far greater than any negative forces setting out to hold me back from realizing my dreams. Choosing *faith* rather than relying on the kind of facts that would never limit God seemed to be a much wiser path to pursue. One good break; one Divine connection having the potential of catapulting devoted warriors . . . those who never stopped believing and never stopped loving God was all that was needed. It's happened for so many others and we had to believe it could happen for us. To feel the touch of the silence of the soul reaching out for miracles is to fully understand those inspired words, "Let not your heart be troubled." And my response would always be . . . *God is my strength and my power, and HIS will alone shall remain and will create new for me.*

He who goes directly to the mountaintop will find all things spread out before him in the valley below. God as a living presence . . . as a guiding, animating power . . . becomes an actuality in our lives. Spiritual feeling or consciousness invariably tends to deepen and refine all modes of thought and mental action. These deeper, finer activities found in the mental world possess the power to heal and emancipate; to build up and develop our *faith*.

Faith . . .

- sees the heights, knows they are there, and believes they can be reached. Therefore, to a mind that would create a grander fate, nothing is more valuable than *faith*. It's the link in the Great Within that connects man with his Maker. It is the Divine messenger sent to guide men blinded by doubt and sin.

- is not a blind belief. It's not a belief at all. *Faith* is a live conviction, illumined knowledge that sees, knows, and understands the spirit of things . . . the spirit and promises of our Father.

- awakens everything within us that is superior and brings out the best we have to give. It unites us with the Infinite.

- becomes real when an untroubled heart relaxes, trusts, leans assured into God's ever dependable arms, and finds solitude and joy.

- is not just in our head; it's in our hearts. It speaks to our minds insisting we listen to that special voice whispering through the caverns of our souls.

- provides the stamina we need to survive in the wilderness assuring us there are no circumstances too small or too big for God.

- gives us the peace to say 'thank you' today for what we are guaranteed to receive tomorrow. Allows us to live in the NOW being really appreciative of the time we have. We cannot hesitate implementing a well thought out plan to make the best of that time.

- is sadly lost in so many people.... the ability to refuse to "give in" or "give up".

- reckons the necessity to make the whole of our lives complete, beautiful, and perfect. *Love thinketh no evil and faith is the substance of things hoped for, the evidence of things not seen.*

- is expectancy. *According to your faith, be it unto you.* Genuine faith . . . indwelling faith that has lived with us through every season of our lives . . . is the secret power of preparation. The Lord is our 'helper'.

- is taking the first step even when we can't see the whole staircase. Understanding the path of others who have climbed the same stairs will help create an easier path for our own journey.

- is universal power always at our disposal and in infinite supply. It's free!

As the world breaks down, we somehow have an opportunity now to build a better one by following the wisdom of our brave forefathers, especially if one was born of African-American descent. Deep down in their souls, they believed they would find their way even at times when they couldn't see the Light. The sustaining force holding the fine pieces together was always their abiding *faith*. 'Keeping the faith' is part of our legacy. We are a people who created astronomy, mathematics, and medicine. We created art and built empires. We have suffered dispersion and barbaric oppression. We have endured and survived. We have (I had) come too far not to go the distance. During these difficult times, the most revolutionary thing we can do is to have *faith* . . . to hold a positive vision of what we want for ourselves, for our children and their future . . . for our communities; our cities; and our country.

Realizing time was of the essence in this my "winter season", there was absolutely no excuse but to get out there and go for it. Passivity was a vicious roadblock. There are times in life when our *faith* might have to carry someone else when they don't have the degree of trust we do and we have to have an even stronger conviction for them. God will use our talents, but HE wants to receive the glory.

Understand and accept that sometimes success takes years of preparation; the right time; and yes, often the right connections and family ties. Suddenly the right door opens. Unfortunately, many people are easily discouraged just when *the darkness* creeps into a tiny crack of their life plan . . . just when those possible connections ignore being family ties. They give up. They are not primed for the unexpected. They have not built spiritual muscles nor lived by affirmative prayers such as 'I CAN because GOD CAN'! They feel hopeless and defeated. Gabriel's horn is heard from a distance. It is a melody of hope and a sign from the unseen.

Power and abiding joy belongs to those who possess one of the greatest essentials in the mastery of *faith* – definitive and high goals accomplished one step at a time. And there is nothing that causes the mind to aim as high as *faith*. *Faith* demonstrates conclusively that all things are possible, and there is no end to the path of attainment. What's more, it demonstrates that this path to greater achievements is substantial and sound all the way but may not always be smooth sailing.

My brethren, count it all joy when you fall into various trials, knowing that the testing of your *faith* produces patience. But let patience have its perfect work, that you may be perfect and complete, lacking nothing. **James 1:2-4**

Imagine a world where our *faith* is rich and formidable, and we are part of a community that nurtures hope and supports our values and beliefs. In difficult times, we stretch our *faith* so when we face life's storms, frustrations, and disappointments, we can bear up under the weight of the circumstances without wavering once more. God's purpose must take the place of our own. And I get that. But I also know some people's hearts cannot be changed and they will fight anyone's efforts to try and do so. Peace, harmony, love, prosperity (for all), forgiveness, and gratitude for the Spirit may not be their goals.

"You tell me about how I'm supposed to hold on to my so-called *faith* when people are allowed to be this mean," this lovely and quite talented young lady asked me 5 years ago in an e-mail. She had just endured the painful, ugly, and vindictive tentacles of blatant racism for yet another time. At one of the world's top media conglomerates, a black stuffed doll with a noose tied around its neck had been thrown into her cubicle in an all-white department. When the young lady decided she had taken all the disrespect she could stomach, she complained to her superiors.

Without justification or any explanation, she was immediately fired. To add insult to injury, she was escorted out of the office with the majority of the white staff singing "Celebration". I never will forget her saying to me, "Where is your God when hurtful things like this are allowed to happen and nobody does anything about it? Seems like it's happened to me all my life. How many other black people does this happen to and nobody speaks. Nobody says nothing!! I'm a good person. I'm a damn good actress. I worked hard at my craft . . . really wanted to learn from the experts in the industry. I didn't deserve to lose my job for some cruel thing 'they' did!" When asked why she would not expose them or sue, her candid reply was, "They'll lie and blackball me any way they can. Hollywood, especially for a black actress, is a strange bedfellow. Read between the lines."

I had no explanation having felt her pain in my own professional work environment and I too baffled and shaken by the depth of hatred allowed to manifest. But even in my often numbed or hurting day by day occurrences, I would not buy into the belief that the generous God of ultimate power I prayed to . . . rolled out all the praise and honor in gratitude to . . . would deny my dreams and endeavors and not provide a way for me to realize them. If I called upon HIM in *faith* and trust, HE promised to rebuke the *darkness* and help me cross through the 'valley of weeping', struggle, and malcontent. I relayed the same message to the beautiful yet temporarily broken young lady who had reached out to me. I was holding Jemma's God . . . my God . . . to HIS Promises.

It's always of value to know how the truth one finds and endeavors to give to others is embodied in their own lives; in the permanency of their own *faith*. *Seek first the kingdom of God and HIS righteousness and all these things shall be added unto you.* All will follow in a perfectly natural and normal manner and in full accordance with natural spiritual law. It is the degree in which we open our hearts to receive it and live it that we realize the genuineness of truth, and the vastness of its power to make our lives all we would have them to be. Radiate victory wherever you go. Maintain this attitude by believing in the thing you are trying to do. *Great is Thy faithfulness.*

At a parenting seminar a few years back, I recall telling the audience . . . "If you bade your child to jump into your arms, they would not hesitate even though it's so dark and they might not be able to see. The child would more than likely jump because of their *faith* in you. Confident they would be perfectly safe they would fly in the air when they hear you tell them to come. It's so imperative today that we give our children that same kind of *faith* to hold on to along with helping them to build their own. They have to know they can depend on 'Somebody'. We come here with a message for humankind that no one else but ourselves can deliver. We are co-creators of our lives with the Father.

Writer Flannery O'Connor describes *faith* as what someone knows to be true whether they believe it or not. A perfect example of the power of this declaration is an expression I once heard . . . that when God leads us to the edge of a cliff, we had to trust HIM fully and then 'let go'. A few things for certain have the possibility of happening: either HE'll catch us when we fall, or HE'll teach us how to fly. In the "winter", and even in the other seasons of my life as well, Grandma Jemma's 'good God' had done both for me. *Grace* had caught me every time I fell, foolish decisions and reckless actions included. Prayer, *faith*, my children, my husky, my students, close friends, and 'the committee' would contribute to the strengthening of my heart, washing the mud from my wings, and keeping me in flight.

The Bishop also reminds us of how this 'test of faith' would reveal the deceptive ways of the *darkness*. "Just before your seed springs forth, just before your miracle happens, just before your promise is fulfilled . . . that's when all hell will seem to break out against you. Just before you experience the fullness of God's power working in you, that's when the *devil* will try to break you." *Hear me today: You are not imprisoned; you are empowered. Take control of your circumstances in Jesus' name and arise. You are a daughter of the King, and you can arise by HIS power without hesitation. Knowing this sets you free. Pick up the pen of hope and write on the tablet of faith. Write with grace.*

Write with flourish. Write with passion. Write with freedom.
(TDJ) (Lam. 3)

This I have done. And this I know to be true. When the Lord reminds us HE is all that HE says HE is and HE will do what HE says HE will do, TRUST that HE will deliver.

The Lord spoke from the burning bush, I AM!
Exodus 3:5. I was regretting the past and fearing the future. Suddenly my Lord was speaking. "My name is I AM!" The Lord paused. I waited. The Lord continued. "When you live in the past with its mistakes and regrets, it's hard . . . I am not there . . . my name is not, **I Was**. When you live in the future, with its problems and fears, it's hard . . . I am not there . . . my name is not, **I will be**. When you live in this moment, it is not hard, I am here!!! **My name is I AM!!!**" (unknown author)

Ba'al Perazim

Chapter Five

Grandma Jemma's Prayers

***Prayer** is not an old woman's idle amusement. Properly understood and applied, it is the most potent instrument of action.* Mahatma Gandhi

Growing up, the late 85-year-old Jemma Alexander was one of the brightest stars in my life. She was always entertaining and allowing people to fall in love with her quirky, yet very wise persona. Jemma taught those she really cared about how to find God's favor through **prayer**, forgiveness of self and others, and the recognition of *grace* in everyday life. This very sagacious matriarch instructed her loved ones to call upon the 'real stuff inside them' – meaning **reserve power** – 'when they boxin' with the devil (our goliaths).

There was no one like Grandma Jemma . . . such a delightful and inspiring enigma. She talked to God like HE was sitting next to her sharing in her favorite meal of fried catfish, coleslaw, mac and cheese, and hush puppies. This very 'fine' lady of her day was so true to herself and honestly loved the Lord unconditionally no matter how rough or uncertain her road.

Mornin', Lord. I'll make this short and to the point, Jemma prays. *I love ya' and much appreciate what you done for me. I'm sure glad I woke up with the sun still shinin' on*

this ole' face of mine and that I'm still breathin' and walkin' as best I can after all these years run by me. Whew!! My purple tulips opened up yesterday, but I guess you'd know 'bout that, huh! Glad my eyes still workin' so I can see ya' magic when it comes.

Gotta ask for a whole lot of forgiveness this mornin', Lord. Me and Miss Mae been doin' awful lot of gossipin'. 'Been talkin' 'bout Miss Claudie somethin' terrible. But Lord, she's been havin' a different man comin' in and out of that house every week. Ya' know that just ain't right. And my great grandson disrespectin' his teacher like he did. Scared that po' chile to death blowin' up in that school like some kind of storm or somethin'. I grabbed him by the throat – loosely, God. Wasn't tryin' to kill my own blood, but none of my kids or their kids was raised like that. He knew betta!

Guess I gon' and don' some things right, You still lettin' me have my beer and all. I sho' 'preciate my lil' great grandbabies and the puppies Gladys just had. Lot of good memories, Lord. Lot of mean ones too, but I'm gonna thank ya' for 'em all. Want the folks I love to know ya' like I do . . . like my mama knew ya'. Don't take much. They jus' gotta see how ya' work things out and ya' do do that!

Have a good day, Lord. And by the way, I'll try and keep my big mouth shut for a while. Just watch my tulips start bloomin' some mo' and try and git rid of all these whining puppies, too! Might keep that lil' runt myself . . . nurse her back to feelin' good and all just like You do for me sometimes. I'll be back later on. Amen, Lord. Amen and 'thank you' one more time for the good measure.

Prior to finally understanding the recipe for gaining power in my faith and genuine connecting **prayers** to the Divine . . . at least to the extent where human comprehension was possible . . . there was definitely no consistency in my prayer life. Sometimes I would start the *Lord's Prayer* and would stop right in the middle of my utterance. 'Hallowed be thy Name' was continual recitation . . . going through the motions without really understanding why spiritual sincerity was imperative in carrying out my life's mission. Up until I just couldn't withstand another satanic beat down occurring frequently for decades, I didn't know what to pray for. At the time, I couldn't see where any of my previous prayers had been answered. I would have a list of people and things I wanted to pray for and then I'd forget what I wanted to ask God to do for me. It seemed more like a child's wish list to Santa Claus rather than David-like love letters to God and 'the committee'. 'The committee' now also included my 14-year-old beautiful husky who found his final resting place in heaven three years ago. I was so broken hearted that I never had the chance to say goodbye.

Often times in my attempts to get serious about my prayers and meditation, I would try to get pass the 'Our Father' or 'It's me again, Lord' sounding just like Grandma Jemma. There were times I felt guilty asking God for things I probably could have taken care of myself. In the midst of my conversations with HIM, my mind might have lingered off someplace else like having to pay a bill with an overdrawn bank account.

As a staying place, worry became self-indulgent, paralyzing, draining, and controlling while taking up a huge chunk of my time and energy year after year. Sometimes I'd go back to my childhood and adolescent beliefs that Grandma Jemma's God really didn't care about nappy headed little colored girls with crooked teeth. Otherwise, we wouldn't have it so hard. It just didn't seem right. With my own children, fairness and the *breakthroughs* have not visited them often, but so many other blessings knock at our door all the time and we knew it. We quickly and always said 'thank you'. There really was no other way.

On so many occasions, my literary and creative gifts suddenly disappeared into the dark side causing me to have to claw my way back to hope and doing what I did best. When I took worry into prayer, it didn't disappear, but it did become smaller in scope. I began to see anxiety for its true self – an imposter that masked itself as action and lassoed me into feeling sorry for myself. The victim . . . always the injured . . . constantly telling my story of woe. Brought into **prayer**, angst sat next to me and whimpered for its former place of recognition and dominance. When I focused on my **prayers** . . . on that conscious effort to engage . . . goodness stepped forward in the presence of God and concern heeled, stayed, and sometimes rolled over and fell asleep.

The Universe could not give me the answers I so desired before now due to the fact I had yet to acknowledge the 'oneness' of the Creator . . . that when I was helpless, lost, and afraid, God was not. A wise theologian and dear friend reminded me once . . . "if HE doesn't answer your prayers in a timely manner or not at all, it isn't that HE doesn't love you or that you're not HIS child. God can see what you cannot." The essence of this truth is sometimes bittersweet, yet it sustains me and gives me hope.

I had never been much of a prayer warrior able to hold hands in the company of others and fire off powerful and eloquent Osteen, Vanzant, Blake, or Jakes-like prayers. But what I did learn from these inspiring individuals was that going to God was similar to going into a court of law. I had to be prepared and lay out my case with confidence, coupled with praise and sometimes an urgent request. "Don't talk to God about how many mountains you have to climb. Talk to the mountains about how big your God is. God takes pleasure in answering prayer that comes from a faithful heart," Pastor Joel Osteen was to declare some years ago during a Sunday television broadcast. This distant 'angel without wings' to whom I would probably never meet in this lifetime would often deliver words of wisdom just at the right time resulting in my saving Grace. There would be spurts of gratitude when good things happened and then fits of angry rage when *the darkness* came after me with a huge beating stick. I had always prayed for a way to balance the two. Now as a 'winter woman' I had gained an armor of fortitude and new meaning in my conversations with my silent partner.

*Loving heavenly Father, we ask for a spirit of **prayer** to come upon us now. Increase our longing for You, and our longing for the salvation of people around the world.* It really is liberating . . . kind of cool . . . when we can come into a mindset where the Lord is so real that we can have "prayer conversations" with HIM in the context of all our activities. Most of the time my conversations with the Lord were all I had. I was convinced the enemy would not be hitting my children and me so hard if we weren't so close . . . if God wasn't preparing us to do something big for ourselves and for others. HE was listening to our hearts, hearing our *prayers*, and the devil was furious. We were positioning ourselves to eventually glorify the Lord's name in a manner greater than we had ever had the opportunity to do before. *All that the Kingdom affords is yours. Every righteous desire of the heart is promised you.*

The hour I treasure most
Is when the day is new,
Before the rush comes crowding in
With tasks that I must do.
As I humbly kneel in **prayer**,
All fears and worries cease;
There is no other time I know
That brings this inner peace.
I thank God for HIS blessings
And Seek forgiveness, too,

> For there are wrongs I've done,
> And good I failed to do.
> I ask HIS guidance for my day
> On pathways old and new,
> That I'll be kind to those I meet
> In all I say and do.
> I **pray** for each dear loved one
> And place them in HIS care;
> I **pray** all men will live as brothers
> In places everywhere.
> *Anonymous*

Grandma Jemma's spirit always floated about convincing me I still had the desire and the passion to do great things... *to Thine be the Glory!* The much-loved wise matriarch prayed morning, noon, and night for forgiveness but admittedly struggled to excuse others sometimes, especially those who chose to harm her children, grandchildren, great grands, others' children, and animals. On hot summer evenings, she seldom missed having her ice-cold Pabst Blue Ribbon beer much to the chagrin of her young doctor. After she took her last gulp, she would stand up to stretch, look up to the cloudless night sky, and say, *"Thank you, Lord. That was pretty dog gone good!"*

"I'm on my way outta' here, Baby Boy," she would tell the handsome young fellow whose diapers she had changed 35 years ago. Jake was the son of Anne Markle, a famous international artist and Jonas Markle Sr., world traveler, much admired philanthropist, and a remarkable award-winning photojournalist. Jemma had been cleaning and cooking for the Markle family for years and had pretty much raised the Markles very successful sons, Jacob and Jonas. *"Ain't no beer drinkin' up in heaven, Sonny Boy,"* she would joke to J.J. (Jonas Jr.), the other doctor in the family.

"God ain't gonna stand for that kind of carryin' on up there." Throwing her head back . . . surprisingly still full of long, salt and pepper coarse hair and laughing hardily, she takes her declaration another step forward. *"Sooooo . . . Baby Boy! Grandma Jemma's gonna' enjoy what I want, when I want, while I can."* The Markle brothers had ceased getting embarrassed by anything Jemma had to say. They also knew this remarkable sage had few inhibitions and never hesitated saying exactly what was on her mind. She would always say she didn't want anyone to misinterpret what she intended to say. After she had been blessed to live 75 years, that included God too when she **prayed**.

*Every word we speak is a **prayer** coming into reality. I can, I am, I will, I choose, I have, I love, I create, I enjoy.* Robert Tennyson Stevens

This deep prayer connection would begin to tell me who I was and might possibly lead to the big question of why I came. Amid my expressing sincere thanks and learning how to forgive, I would find solace in the freedom of being grateful and grumpy all at the same time. The scriptures said it was okay . . . that God had big shoulders and would understand. Like Mary, I would forever be reminded of how our Father's *grace* had always carried me. Like Grandma Jemma, I would talk to HIM any place and at any time. Like David, I would remain lost in a maze of utmost respect for HIS genuine greatness and would dance in praise. Like Jesus, Elijah, and Joshua, I would enter in ***prayer*** with an attitude of expectancy.

By awesome deeds in righteousness, You will answer us, O God of our salvation, You who are the confidence of all the ends of the earth, and of the far-off seas. **Psalm 65:5**

In this psalm, David is in awe at how wonderful the Lord is. This was most certainly the right focus of **prayer**.

. . to be less concerned with the outcome of our longings rather than with the relationship our prayers created with the Most High. When we treat God as if HE really is our hope on earth, praise HIM for HIS marvelous deeds, and worship HIM, extraordinary blessings can flow.

I don't think there's a wrong way to pray. You just bring who you are, and you sort of rip your rib cage open: This is where I'm at, this is who I'm thinking about, this is what I'm thankful for. The most beautiful prayers happen spontaneously. It's less about escaping the everyday flow of life than engaging with it. Ron Bell, pastor and author of "What We Talk About When We Talk About God"

True Prayer

- ❖ generates a desire to show mercy and to express forgiveness. True prayer/worship includes the full recognition of who God is.

- ❖ is communion with God. God doesn't want us to worry, get stressed out, or bothered. So HE offers a solution to those states of mind: **prayer**. Real prayer is receiving with thanksgiving. It's believing in God's promises. To think is to pray. To think rightly is to pray in *faith*.

- ❖ is waiting in silence for HIS word. Wait for HIS way to be revealed to you. To give thanks is the highest form of ***prayer***. Our hearts must be filled with adoration and gratitude . . . overflowing in joy and thanksgiving with a willingness to turn quietly and reverently to *from whence comes our hope and strength.*

It has been said that life can be as simple as love and **prayer**. Where the two mingle, there can be no jealousy, resentment, or fear. Could the miracle of becoming a person of **prayer** begin with just two words: *thank you*? We desire candid communication and conversation with God. We want to clarify what's going on in our lives and seek guidance. Whatever comes from our heart in whatever religion or ethnic culture we are born into is all that is needed.

A Prayer by William

St. Labre Indian School

Ashland, Montana

Dear Heavenly Father,
I come to you in a good way
and ask you to bless my family and me.
Keep us away from all anxiety and stress,
and help us to overcome our inner fears.
I pray that the poor be blessed, not only
the financially troubled, but also the mentally,
physically, and spiritually challenged.
I ask that you watch over their lives
and steer them away from harmful
thoughts and substances.
Thank you for letting everyone wake up
this morning healthy and able to live
another day on this earth.
Amen

In one of the many periods of some of my darkest hours, I knew God was there as did David, even though I had not sought HIM out in *prayer*. I somehow believed God understood my intimate thoughts when I couldn't find the words to say, even in silence. In desperate circumstances, we are apt to think we know what we need from God. Like a small child who cannot be consoled, we are inclined to beg HIM for what we want and when we want it. In those moments, God understands our weakness and fears. Yet, HE is also the One who uses the depth of the oceans; the magnificence of Machu Picchu; hundreds of dog breeds showcased in a famous dog show; and the wonder of the night sky filled with a perfect and mysterious white ball and blinking non-electrical lights to calm us in HIS presence.

God's perfection and HIS desire to give us an abundant life became apparent during my year of lonely nights in isolation in the woods. I was given little choice but to open my mind and heart to HIS manifestation and to the possibilities once assumed highly unlikely considering the lateness of my chronological years. I realized my worry, fear, and outrage created an aura of negativity and doubt that threatened to overpower my *faith* and weaken the potency of my ***prayers***. Once I 'let go' of how I thought the world and the people who crossed my path should have been or should be, especially in response to my ongoing plight of despair, I got the courage and strength to do what I needed to do and what HE wanted me to do with the rest of my life. I asked only to have the foresight and the strength to face the days when I had no answers and *satan* and *its* torch bearers were kicking down the gates protecting my heart and burning down the tower of the castle housing my soul.

But I say to you, love your enemies, bless those who curse you, do good to those who hate you, and *pray* for those who spitefully use you and persecute you. **Matt. 5:44**

No matter how hard it got, I would sit in my work cubicle every morning and pray silently, again and again for the enemy and for strength. The workplace mobbing was so painful. When the "giving up" button was just about to be pounced upon, I would look at the photos of some of my heroes covering the cushiony grey panels of my work space petitions . . . The Obamas, Mandela, Tubman, Malcolm, Fannie Lou, Rosa, Ruby, Biko, Malala, Dr. King, the Kennedy brothers, and Grandma Jemma. Glancing at my wrist bearing my Avon Jackie Robinson watch, I would tell myself if these great advocates and crusaders for love, brother and sisterhood, peace, and human dignity 'for all' could survive and serve others in spite of the piercing blows from their adversaries, surely the same God they served would understand, move some of the mountains aside, and protect me with HIS Divine armor while I attempted to do good work for beautiful children.

It was like I was at that same nasty roadside restroom 60 years ago asking the same questions. What did I ever do to them? What are they so afraid of?" There were days I would cry all the way to work and then sit in my car redoing my make-up before I walked into the fire. Like my children had experienced in numerous school and work environments, I never knew from where or when the next humiliating confrontation or dangerous affront or assault would come.

"Hold God to HIS promises," I heard Joel Osteen say one Sunday during another moving broadcast. "God, You said You would make my crooked road straight. You said I am more than a conqueror. God, You said You would be my vindicator. God, You said You would open the windows of heaven. You said my children would be mighty in the land. God, You said my end would be better than my beginning. God, You told me to go to the courtroom of heaven . . . that Jesus would be my lawyer and You would be the judge." I would read these words over and over until my work day began.

I would cease my Grandma Jemma-like fussing, giving God directions as to where I wanted HIM to take me. I would no longer pray my enemies would have the worse lives possible. I took great satisfaction in knowing it was not me who should be feared . . . but judgment from on High would settle the score. *Prayer* moved those negative thoughts aside and now those empty spaces would be filled with the best ways I could embrace my purpose at this stage in my life. I resolved that every word I spoke of my woes gave them power. I would no longer engage in discussions of the sort.

It's me again, Lord. Come reportin' that it was a pretty good day. Went down to the Center today to shoot the breeze with some of my ole' buddies and have my favorite catfish dinner. Loves my fish, Lord. Ya' know I do! 65 years some of us been friends. That's really somethin'. They been there for me, you betccha. Whipped Reggie in some dominoes, too. He gets so mad when he loses to this old lady. They should all know by now that I'm the Queen of the 'Bones'. Always have been – 'hee-hee'! Took some of my buttermilk fried chicken and collard greens to Fanny Louise yesterday. Know she ain't got too many days left down here . . . that she's on her way comin' to meet ya'. Wanted her to enjoy a lil' sumpen' real good fo' she made that trip.

I just think we all gotta pray harder now, Lord. This world's goin' plum crazy, and we losin' our 'babies'. Most of 'em don't even know who ya' are anymore. That's the problem! We need Your help to fix this stuff! Gonna do what I can to save my own. If I have time, I'll try to save a few more that don't even belong to me, too. I want it betta' for them than I had it. Now don't go to thinkin' I'm not happy to be here, though. I've had some real good times, 'hee-hee'. Maybe sometimes too good a times.

Eyes a closin' so I guess it's time to go. Gotta' big day tomorrow. Goin' sing in the choir caus' it's Christmas. I like those old songs, Lord. Somein' 'bout a silent night. Snowed today again. Kind of quiet and pretty and all. Saved that runt puppy, Lord. Named her Billie after Billie Holiday.

Pray for grace as you offer praise and gratitude. Often times, positive, hopeful power in the universe is without sound. Every time we ask in *prayer* and believe our request will come to pass, we are affirming GOD CAN! Visualize the chains coming undone freeing us from some form of bondage. Trust what you feel and know all will eventually be delivered . . . all will be well with our souls. The only real prayers are the ones mouthed with thankful lips. Gratitude ushers us into the heart of the Lord's blessings. **And so we pray . . .**

May the God of hope fill you with all joy and peace in believing so that you may abound in hope by the power of the Holy Spirit. **Romans 15:13**

Like Job, I was once at a place of doubting myself more than I doubted God. From a heart that was both broken and relieved, Job said, *I know that You can do everything, and that no purpose of Yours can be withheld from You.* I was now prepared to accept and be grateful for the life I had been given instead of trying to make it something that wasn't supposed to be. And when prayers continued to be answered in the most unexpected yet recognizable manner, it meant my "demonstrations" of faith had set me free from my own apprehensions and limitations. The truth would come through me as a witness for others. Just as Jesus knew He must complete God's will for Himself, He has been just as determined to do the same for us.

Now it came to pass, as He was praying in a certain place, when He ceased, that one of His disciples said to Him,

"Lord, teach us to pray, as John also taught his disciples. Luke 11:1

Our Father who art in heaven . . . hallowed be Thy name. I had to do my part and enter into a **prayer** life at new heights . . . one that would 'bless me indeed and enlarge my territory and make me whole' as the prophet Jabez requested in a simple prayer. Jabez's prayer was answered and he was even given a place of honor in the lineage of kings. (1Chronicles 4:10) It's wonderful to start the day with the Lord, praying early in the morning hours before life as we experience it is about to begin. There's a certain quality of ministry that comes only as we touch God in reality in our secret lives and then share this gift with others.

At Pentecost, the disciples devoted themselves to constant prayer until the Holy Spirit came upon them with tongues of fire, filling their lives, and giving them courage and power to witness to the world. Grandma Jemma was more than just a witness to those who would listen when it came to providing clear examples of the love and mercy of God. She would always be remembered as that 'flower of blessedness' that bloomed through the power of her words . . . *it's me again, Lord . . . Jemma here . . . comin' to ask if we could take care of a little matter that could turn out to be a pretty big problem. Ya' know me, Lord. Don't always sit 'round watching my roses bloom or playin' with puppies. I know I cross the line sometimes.*

Prayer became the foundation that kept me sane . . . kept me grounded . . . kept me writing. *Satan* pulled every dirty trick in his bag to stop the process. As the words hit the keys of my computer, I entered an unfamiliar space where what had been transpiring below the surface and in 'committee meetings' was now revealing itself. I most certainly had a partner with rebuking and healing powers. HE always reminds us: *Your life . . . your mission . . . is what you make it. Only those who are expectant of good tidings . . . demonstrate active faith . . . will bring the manifestation to pass. No matter how difficult . . . how painful . . . how dark . . . no one or nothing can stand in your way but 'you'.*

God is calling HIS people to pray more intensely than ever before. If we could only comprehend the immensity of God's plan for our lives and the importance of our **prayers**, we would stop in our tracks and re-evaluate our priorities. Let us pray . . . pray deeply and diligently with all our hearts that an army of dedicated, compassionate warriors can unite and help bring about a 'loving' change in this sadly, deeply (Divided States) of America. Let us pray more caring adults will recognize we must to do far better for our children. They certainly deserve a fighting chance.

Grant me the serenity to accept the things I cannot change – the courage to change the things I can. And the wisdom to know the difference. Niebuhr Reinold

Ba'al Perazim

Chapter Six

A LIZARD IN THE WOODS

Cultivate the highest and best and you will soon realize a life that is never lonely; never alone, for all nature will speak to you, and her great throbbing heart will keep you company and give you everything." Our Mental Children – Lily A. Allen (1917)

The rains poured, and the winds whistled and whizzed. Gushing streams began to rise in front of the guest house where I had pretty much remained isolated for months. With my common broken heart and the loss of direction and possessions again and again, how I managed to remain focused on research and writing was no question a design of *grace*. It was HIM putting me in the middle of nowhere ... in the black of night ... alone ... afraid ... just me, the wild animals of the forest that were curious of the light ... and the nemesis lizard having made its way inside a wall. The turbulent storm beat against my human house, too, but it didn't crumble. After all, my foundation had been built on a solid rock. I am reminded often that God made the rock ... that HE is the Rock. The Rock gives me strength to hold on to what is good even if it's just a handful of earth ... when I become the tree standing by itself in the valley.

Sometimes wonderful excitement would come by nature like it did for Mama when she would wake Daddy out of a deep sleep. Early one morning she had spotted a red bird balancing itself on her back-yard clothes line in the dead of winter. Decades later, the sightings of a new generation of fine feathered friends kicking wild bird seed from high above in the bird feeder reminded me so much of her and then Daddy's expression from the surprise awakening. I know now the birds' presence and hilarious fluttering about was probably a message from the Lord to get my attention . . . delivered by a member of 'the committee'. I was reminded I was much stronger than I thought, otherwise I would not have survived the recent battles I wasn't lacing up my boxing gloves by myself. It was a welcomed reprieve from the fear and constant tears. I think often of Mama and the red bird and how much joy those few moments brought her.

Several months later, blossoming morning glories brought a purple blush to a southwestern hillside. The once barren maple trees now produce fuchsia buds that open to rosy pink, fragrant blossoms. Like the magnificence of the draping weeping willows, we are reminded of the coming new season appearing during the months of expectancy. The once emptiness in my heart and soul is filled with the anticipation of a replenishment of *grace* and redemption . . . a new season. In my hollowness and silence, I had been given a clear opportunity to turn to God, the only begetter of *restoration*. There I would find a breadth of happiness and all the success and love I would need for my closing chapter. Thank you, Warrior California Congresswoman Maxine Waters. I am indeed *'reclaiming my time'*.

I know . . . most would ask . . . what could I have possibly been thinking. I knew of this Southwestern town from magazine articles my uncle brought me, and from his travel pictures and those found in my red plastic Viewmaster. As a 5-year-old growing up in a newly integrated, small segment of a Midwestern city where blacks could finally buy property (prompting 'white flight')... a city

known for its great jazz and the best barbecue in the country
... I knew I would never stay once I became an educated
adult. My career path would not be in the field of my
passion, but that reality was out of my control. I would make
the best of my limited preparation balanced with a diehard
work ethic and desires in a place where I could absorb 'pure
enchantment'. There continued to be such a spiritual and
Native lineage pull in this region that just didn't seem to
want to let go most of the days of my youth through senior
adulthood.

    With the exception of the Native and Spanish blends
of culture in a few southwestern towns, I had no other
interest in our annual summer travels west. I was alone in
the back seat of my father's precious Buicks with nothing
but my creative characters and story lines filling up Big
Chief tablets and later thick spiral notebooks. Sometimes I'd
have the pleasure of immersing myself in a new book or
magazine purchased just for the trip. It was 1957 and even
a town with such a generational diverse population did not
welcome the likes of 'Negroes'. We found ourselves eating
cold fried chicken from the bright red Coca Cola cooler and
drinking lukewarm lemonade from a jar. Mama always said
we were saving money for souvenirs when we finally got to
Disneyland and maybe shopping for school clothes once we
arrived in Pasadena where her sister lived. That explanation
as to why we couldn't stay in a hotel or eat in a restaurant
sounded pretty phony even then. I came to a reckoning of
the real truth pertaining to balancing fairness; gratitude for
life; the hypocrisy of religion; and 'colored' reality.

*... when you suddenly find your tongue twisted and your
speech stammering as you seek to explain to your six-year-
old daughter why she can't go to the public amusement park
that has just been advertised on television, and see tears
welling up in her eyes when she is told that Funtown is
closed to colored children, and see ominous clouds of*

inferiority beginning to form in her little mental sky . . . when you take a cross-country drive and find it necessary to sleep night after night in the uncomfortable corners of your automobile because no motel will accept you. Martin Luther King Jr. (from "Letter from Birmingham Jail", April 16, 1963)

As far back as I can remember the natural light and color pallets of the Southwest were so pleasantly intense and penetrating. It had to be the sun . . . the spectacular rising and setting precision displaying a powerful magnificence far beyond any writer or photographer's potential description of this geographical marvel. 'Dancing Ground of the Sun' – as the pueblo legend called the town – had the mystical characteristics of the desert expanse defined with a multitude of elements.

Changing hues and beams of golden reflections and red glow spotlighting sections of the mountainsides and valleys capture a rare and serene ambiance. Named the "Blood of Christ" by the conquistadors in the 16th & 17th centuries, the Sangre de Cristo Mountains and other ranges invited pueblo natives to *pray* to the sun helping their Father to move across the sky. Legend has it that if the people ceased their *prayers*, the sun would no longer rise, and night would descend over the world eternally. *My God, my God . . . how great Thou art.* Night skies were just as glorious as I was eventually blessed, if only for a few years, to inhabit one of the best star gazing areas in the country.

Wrote journalist, Eric Lindberg in 2005 in describing the region . . . *sun-bleached adobe churches under a turquoise sky, blue corn enchiladas drenched in green chili, and acres of art objects costing more than a new car. The city deserves its reputation as one of the West's most atmospheric 'wish I lived here' destinations. But popularity comes with a price, and during high season, the place approaches gridlock. Tourists jostle elbow-to-elbow as they eat, drink, and shop their way along brick streets used for centuries before the first automobile rolled through town. People come here for the magic of the place, and some never leave. If our appreciation of the beautiful and the idea is wonderfully developed, our enjoyment will be greater in proportion.*

Setting out in my teen years to plan a life in this place located in one of the most picturesque yet impoverished states in the country, I would eventually realize my dream ultimately resulting in unimaginable losses and injustices. The pictures I looked at every day in my Viewmaster could not capture the powerful essence . . . the matchless beauty . . . and the potent spiritual and historical vibes of this incomparable little corner of the world. Its 7,000 plus feet altitude provided some of the cleanest air and the most spectacular autumns and first snowfalls I had ever seen. There was always an array of rich tones and rainbow pastels rendering a cherry, orange-like glow off the towering mountain ranges surrounding the town in tourists bustling spring and summer months. The true essence of the majesty of God was in this place and I wanted so to soak in the power of HIS presence. It was like this famous Artist stood behind HIS cloud easel and painted The Rio Grande. The aloneness weakened my hope of finally finding a little joy, but I wouldn't stop trying. There was a distinct possibility I could leave this world lost in my sadness and pain . . . OR I could continue to fight back and heal my heart.

Native American and Spanish culinary aromas, festivals, winter skiing, holidays agleam with farolitos (sand filled paper bags illuminated with candles), and powerful spiritual, ceremonial, and cultural arts performances captured my heart. God allowed me to live my if only for a short time. One Just to think, I had gotten an opportunity to live my dream but only for a short time. As the "phenomenal" Maya Angelou once wrote . . . *we need hours of aimless wandering or spates of time sitting on park benches, observing the mysterious world of ants and the canopy of tree tops.* Each day in this captivating Forest Gump chocolate-box setting, I experienced this *aimless ambling* – a time of contentment and heartbeats of bliss etched in my memory bank for an eternity. Still, the aloneness continued to be haunting.

Solitude is for the strong, or for those who are ready to become strong. Humankind goes into solitude to seek, and that which he seeks he finds, for there is a Way to all knowledge, all wisdom, all truth, and all power. And the Way is forever opened through the unexplored silences of our being. When a man or woman is becoming great, they remain in the dark until it's time to find the light. Thoughts and pure intentions are blessed in their inception, blessed in their growth, and fortunate in their positive results.

The darkness becomes a time for healing but can be a period of fierce boxing matches with *satanic* forces, as well. Often, I would scream out in the woods in my weakest moments for *satan* just to leave me alone. Squirrels and ground hogs popping in and out of the berry bushes would look up startled. In a flash, they'd scuttle out of sight. Slowly, the tears ceased as a smile came upon me thinking of the animals' funny expressions. It reminded me of Mama and Daddy and the red bird sighting in the dead of winter. God has a sense of humor, too! Is that why HE sent the critter to scare me . . . to get my attention?

I'd hear the creepy sound late at night, especially if I turned off the lights. At first, I thought it was one of the field rats that had gnawed through the wires under my Jeep parked just outside the estate's front gate. Having been truly baffled when the car wouldn't start the very morning when I was rushing to the dentist's office in excruciating pain, I honestly had no idea these kinds of things happened to vehicles. Perhaps one of the varmints had somehow gotten inside the guest house walls where I slept during the day and researched and wrote at night. When darkness fell, I was surrounded by enigmatic wild animals roaming the dense woods along with a lot of other small, unrecognizable animals, too.

As only God could orchestrate in the evolution of HIS plan for the 'realistic' few years of my life remaining, signals that HE was ever present emerged when I would least expect. A dear friend had introduced me to a spiritual reflection written by Mrs. Charles E. Cowan in an old and powerful devotional anthology entitled "Streams in the Desert," one of the most precious and important gifts anyone had ever given me. *Here is a part in the program of God's dealings, a secret chamber of isolation in prayer and faith which every soul must enter that is very fruitful. There are times and places where God will form a mysterious wall around us and cut away from all props of human reason all the ordinary ways of doing things. HE will shut us up to something Divine which is utterly new and unexpected, something that old circumstances do not fit into, where we do not know just what will happen, where God is cutting the cloth of our lives on a new pattern, and where HE makes us look to HIMSELF. I would swing off, as it were, into the vast blue interstellar space, hanging on God alone, in touch with the fountain of miracles.* (from "Soul Food")

Talk about kindness, love, and Godliness in the back woods from wonderful, total strangers who had reached out having received heavenly instructions to rescue a 'seasoned warrior' in distress . . . someone the *devil* had banged against walls quite often . . . someone that needed a friend; a community; and an answered prayer on cold winter days and nights. I had been graciously afforded a few months of isolation, calm, and rest providing me time to figure out my next move . . . praying for a lull in order to catch my breath before the next blow landed on my being . . . and to begin the painful separation of my canine companion of 10 years. There was no way he could be with me all to get lost in the vast wooded acreage.

The everyday kindness of the back roads more than makes up for the acts of greed in the headlines. Charles Kuralt, American Journalist (former "On the Road"/ CBS News Sunday Morning)

I was too dazed and broken to entertain any other options. At one time, I thought about throwing the husky in the back seat of the Jeep where his pillow cushions and harness still remained intact and just driving until my bank account was empty. Then we would disappear someplace where no one could find us . . . maybe on one of the pueblos where I was fortunate to have worked. But my children had enough grief and these actions would be quite selfish and irresponsible . . . so ghastly to even think about carrying out such a ludicrous idea. The husky and my children deserved my pulling up my big girl panties and taking care of business no matter how badly it hurt or how lonely and lost I might have been at the time.

Total blackness. No human being within shouting distance or close enough to rescue me in case of emergency even by cell phone. The *darkness* could be formidable and all encompassing. Again, Bishop Jakes would offer truth and wisdom for this beaten down 'winter woman'. *Every now and then, satan will attempt a coup. He'll try to usurp the throne of your life. At that point, it is up to you to resist his efforts, trust in God, and exert control with your will. Satan will not stop trying, but deliverance will put you in a position to keep him from succeeding.*

Like David, I had to return to the shepherd's field (L.A. eventually), pass a few excruciating faith tests, endure emotional upheavel like I had never known before, while staying focused on literary and creative projects. It took a while, but I finally figured out why God had done what HE did by bringing me to this place at this time. At the close of my trial run of being this messenger sent by 'the committee' to do the Chairman's work, the residents could now walk the streets unafraid. I begged God to allow me to return to the fabulous sunrises and sunsets and my romps along my favorite river with a couple more beautiful animals and an appreciation of phenomenal and simple wonder.

18th century romantic poet William Wordsworth viewed nature and man as complementary elements of a whole, recognizing humans as a part of nature. Some view nature as sublime and a majestic thing. Many hold a great appreciation and respect for wildlife and the things they are surrounded by. They show nature to be a gentle, nurturing force that teaches and soothes humanity. But according to lyric poet, Percy Shelley, nature is the most chaotic, rambunctious, dis-organized system there is. Look at the fallen logs, the leaves, the "dirt", **the plants trying to grow through the rocks,** and the rains washing away the earth. It is both resplendent and deadly; a dynamic force that cannot be tamed by man. While appreciating nature's aesthetic majesty, Shelley warns man not to equate beauty with tranquility. Yet, there is a perfect order running throughout all of it. We are instinctively awed by Nature's grandeur and beauty. So many aspects of this global terrain take our breath away.

Although the world has grown smaller as transportation and communication have proliferated, the reality is that many people don't take the time or have the resources to witness all of nature's bounty in the flesh. I loved the peace of my morning walks with the Basenji in the park right in the middle of the once 'mean streets'. There was always a different 'flower of blessedness' to behold. The same ingenuity that allowed us to split the atom and crack the genetic code has barely begun to explore the foothills, let alone the heights of the diversity of life. Biological diversity is earth's greatest frontier. The love of nature balances the intense feeling of being as one with the great panoramic scenes of mountain ranges, their misty tops, and shades of purple and blue flora completing a full canvas.

In 1859, in the *Origin of the Species,* Charles Darwin wrote: "It is interesting to contemplate an entangled bank, clothed with many plants of many kinds, with birds singing on the bushes, with various insects flitting about, and with worms crawling through the damp earth, and to reflect that these elaborately constructed forms, so different from each other, yet dependent on each other in so complex a manner . . . that there is grandeur in this view of life, with its several powers, having been originally breathed into a few forms or into one.

Touch the earth, love the earth, honor the earth, her plains, her valleys, her hills, and her seas; rest your spirit in her solitary places. Henry Beston

There are moments in life when one loses bits of innocence and that's what happened when I first visited my forever favorite place in the southwest. The notion of a more beautiful place . . . a better place . . . changed my thinking about the parameters of my small life. I would go there someday, to see what my uncle meant decades ago. He said there was a locale more lovely than any other place he would have the privilege of visiting in his cut-short earthly stay.

The seasons of the region brought forth so many contributions and pleasures from so many facets of *nature*. Leaves on cottonwoods and glistening aspens seemed to change colors overnight. I saw fall today as the sun rose and the greenhouse began to fill with blooming pots of chrysanthemums and lilies. The familiar locusts' chatter reminiscent of bedtime on my Midwest childhood block echoed at dusk. Creepy insects were camouflaged in the abundance of foliage on acres and acres of old maple and oak trees.

Winter snows would soon provide the relief of moisture soaking into the parched earth revitalizing the land. Spring winds would come, and scatter wildflower seeds that often fed the sparrows, chickadees, and meadowlarks. The birds would then bury the seeds in the moistened soil for when the ground froze over and food was scarce again. In some parts of the vast blue sky, puffy white clouds build over mountain ranges slowly transforming into thunderheads and bringing forth summer monsoons and the natural drama of phenomenal lightning shows. I loved it. The blessed ones were surrounded by this powerful force and display of nature . . . the amazing omnipotence of God.

If the sight of the blue skies fills you with joy; if a blade of grass springing up in the fields or **a small green leaf breaks through the cement of a street** *has the power to move you, if simple things in nature have a message you understand, rejoice. For your soul is alive.* Eleonora Duse

In plant life, nature is constantly revealing reserve power. The possibilities of almost infinite color are present in every green plant, even in roots and stems. Proper conditions are needed to reveal them. Nature, in all her reveals, seeks to teach man about the greatness of simplicity. The aspects of things that are most important for us are hidden because of their unpretentiousness and familiarity. Nature allows nothing to become recognizable. It's an abode that teaches us about approaching life (simply and softly) from a mindset of increased wisdom, history, and a comfortable, realistic canvas of colors, passions, and destinations.

To cultivate the mental state of appreciation, I had to eliminate all tendencies of fault finding, criticism and the like, and make a special effort to see the worthy qualities in everything and everybody to whom I came in contact. The yellow rose I eye on one of my daily walks with the Basenji has 14 layers of petals. I count them one by one and am amazed. The appreciative mind has a natural tendency to look upon the better side of things, but this tendency becomes complete only when the optimistic attitude is added. To be optimistic, however, does not mean to think that black is white or that everything everywhere is all right. The true optimist can also see the flaws and imperfections in life, but they give direct attention to the good side, the strong side, and the Divine side.

The importance of appreciation of nature in spirituality can be seen in Maimonides who states that the way a person can come to reverence and love of God is through recognizing HIS enormous wisdom as contained in nature. (Foundations of Torah 2:2)

In the midst of this spectacular display of nature, *satan* came after me with all *its* brutal forces of destruction, but sometimes the dark places gave me spiritual muscle and through my writing, I began to fight back. I scribble from my Osteen sermon notes . . . *a seed cannot germinate in the light. A seed must be planted in soil . . . in the darkness . . . watered while waiting for the sun to reach it in order for it to eventually bloom. The womb – a life; a cocoon – a caterpillar – and soon a beautiful butterfly takes flight.* Interesting but not surprising that some of the loneliest and most painful nights brought out some of my most powerful writing as was the case with David. I developed a confidence in God in a way that had never happened before.

This cleansing process happened until I surrendered and decided to no longer settle for less than God's best.

There is splendor in the grass, power in the flower, and peace in the air. 'Flowers of blessedness' are in full bloom. Taking in all of nature's tapestry, I allow my feet to touch the earth and allow my fingertips to feel the layers of the birds of paradise. I experience the rejuvenation inherent in watching the birds shake off water from the bath. To master that part of fate we receive from nature, the secret is to be in harmony with wildlife and natural surroundings at all times, under all conditions, and to try constantly to employ constructively every element in nature with which we may come in contact. At the top of the lesson chart is teaching our children an appreciation of nature and about the beauty in most living things without a voice.

There is also sacredness in the commonplace, every day, ordinary life immersed in loving and caring for earthly things, miracles, and humbling moments in nature. Only a human being has the capacity to see the greatness of God in nature, and when we do so, we are being spiritual. In the woods with the isolation, wild animals, and in the cold of Southwestern winter blankets of mystery precipitation, so much natural beauty surrounded me. I would say a prayer of thanksgiving for the plants and animals . . . the great bodies of water I had seen and marveled . . . and the majestic mountains in my world. Some I could gaze upon . . . others, I might have to climb.

We may walk past trees that have thousands of leaves and give no thought to the miracle of photosynthesis and to the incomparable engineering in the structure of a branch extension. Truth is, one does not have to travel to Niagara Falls or Yellowstone National Park to have a breathtaking experience. All one needs to do is look intelligently through a microscope at a petal of a lily. The beauty and depth of nature's work is phenomenal. A prime example is of the unique environment of the island of Madagascar, isolated in the Indian Ocean off the coast of southern Africa. Eroded formations and 70% of the species found on the island exist nowhere else on the globe. We hear about the Amazon, the Pacific Ocean, and The Outback. But do we truly know those environments? Do they speak to us or bring us peace? It has been said that to see his life as he might make it, man and woman must go up alone into the mountains of spiritual thought as Christ went alone into the Garden of Gethsemane. All our greatest joys and our deepest sorrows come to us – alone. We battle against mighty weaknesses within us – alone. We live our own life – alone. We leave this world – alone. We accept full responsibility for our life – alone. And in addition, we alone can make life brighter for ourselves and others.

After losing Daddy in a cruel transition like Mama's had been, being burglarized in a second floor apartment (the culprits climbed a wall ironically using the outside security bars to balance themselves), fighting to save my canine partner's life, being fired from a state agency along with 33 others when the new political party took over, losing my most valuable work on the pueblos and my education administration position, and having to move out of my newly renovated apartment I truly loved and was so proud of, I became drained of life blood for days having experienced the same feelings of emptiness and fear so many times in the past.

    I lay quietly in the chilly, empty bed in a silent prayer conversation with God. Warmth comes over me like a blanket from the moon and starry sky. It covers me and helps lessen the nippiness making me shiver and feel so forlorn. Then the sun slowly 'breaks through' the night clouds. I think about most memorable occasions when I sat comfortably at the edge of the patio bar at the top of a famous hotel built almost a hundred years ago . . . one of the first stations of The Pony Express in the Southwest. Beside the oceans' coastal beaches, this was my favorite place to watch the sun rise and set. It was always so powerful, and when I had the chance to partake in the novelty of it all, I was given the substance I needed to temporarily overcome unexpected onslaughts of disappointments.

> I watch the snow-covered landscape
> While snowflakes gently fall
> And cover the ground in pure white lace
> With a blanket over all.
> As I gaze out of the window,
> The world is hushed and still.
> As softly falls the gentle snow
> It's destiny to fulfill.
> The time was well past midnight
> And my thoughts began to soar,
> I was wide awake, and stars were bright.
> As I looked outside the door.
> In the very stillness of the night,
> I spoke to God in prayer.
> With nothing to distract me,
> I found peace . . . my Lord was there.

Real life's true joys are revealed to us in numerous, almost imperceptible moments. Everybody needs beauty as well as bread, places to play in and places to pray in, and where nature may heal and give strength to the body and soul. Right outside the patio door, the wolf pups sneak closer and closer with each sighting. This time I catch some great shots with my Canon. They are fascinating to watch and to look at but I dare not get too close. The universe is full of magical things patiently waiting for our wits to grow sharper. But just as God perfectly understands our world, HE sees into our hurt hearts and spirits. Rest assured HE can alter a river of hate or doubt into springs of love, faith, and trust. Though heart-change may not happen overnight, with sheer will and determination and with thousands of 'thank yous', we can have the strength and intuitiveness to follow God's Biblical blueprint for experiencing amazing transformations in our lives and in the lives of others, especially our children.

Unfortunately, I would have to leave the inspiring, nurturing community of worship I so cherished before the broken pieces could be totally mended. But I had been given such a welcomed interlude while I attempted to build a new house. There were a couple adjustments I needed to make on my personal control panel. One would be how to respond to *satan's* vicious affronts that had knocked me face down over and over again, and the other was how to deal with that damn **lizard** continuing to strike fear in me each and every night. Like *satan,* and eventually the 'devil in the alley', evil popped up whenever and wherever it felt like it. Sometimes I would catch the little green menace in a box and throw it way, way out in the woods. And just like *satan* and the mean human beast in the alley, each would manage to find a way to get right back in where it didn't belong. I was convinced *it* (satan) was definitely trying to take me out.

As God's healing water seeps into my life, the trickle touches my soul and change becomes possible. For those of us willing to open ourselves to HIS will, the trickle springs up, becomes a stream, a pool, and then a river of love. I am enough for whatever God wants me to be and do in the amount of time remaining in my life. I am deserving. I am worthy. I rely on the knowledge that life offers infinite possibilities and so does God.

Those who contemplate the beauty of the earth find reserves of strength that will endure as long as life lasts. There is something infinitely healing in the repeated refrains of nature – the assurance that dawn comes after night and spring after winter.

Rachel Carson, "Silent Spring"

Chapter Seven

Seasoned Warrior

"Breath is the power behind all things. Your breath doesn't know how old you are; it doesn't know what you can't do. If I'm feeling puzzled or my mind is telling me that I'm not capable of something, I breathe in and know that good things will happen. Tao Porchon-Lynch, yoga instructor, age 96

The spirit of a warrior is a man or woman who takes action with a level of energy matching that of a trooper going to battle as did David. God's plan is for us, in some small way and step by step, to dare greatly; to embrace passion and gratitude; to take this life and love it with intensity no matter how many years we have left of the blessings of normal days filled with adventure, rewards, prosperity, health, and celebrations. As is often quoted in so many different ways and languages . . . *the main thing is not how long we are on this planet, but the quality of life we have had in our stay here. Did we freely embark upon efforts to make a difference in others' lives while doing enjoyable and productive things for ourselves, as well?*

Aging is absolutely one of the few for-certain things in life. It can be tweaked, revamped, or fashioned the way we want our lives to be, but it's still going to happen if we live long enough. I learned . . . and I do mean found out the hard way . . . that old age didn't just gradually creep up on us. It abruptly stopped me at a pretty tough intersection in my life's journey and announced, "Hey, I'm here and you'd better hurry up and make up your mind what you're going to do with the time you've got left before 'it's a wrap'.

Our culture often looks at aging as a process of deterioration; dependency and a burden upon others; reduced professional and employment potential; family dispersal; and digital incompetence. Today, it is incumbent on boomers to become role models so generations to come will be proud their parents and elders never took the gift of life for granted. Negative stereotypes of aging are so ingrained in our psyches that they are difficult to overcome, so many 'warriors' don't even try. Some are inevitably hit with the grief that comes when something wonderful and special ends, but they do cherish the memories of the laughter and the good times. A few accept a natural and unavoidable process of lying down and waiting . . . and waiting . . . with all flights cancelled.

Waiting idly "in the meantime" is an unnecessary form of self-abuse with the potential of ultimately destroying one's soul. That's not patience. That's just not too wise. "Self-neglect is sneaky," my former pastor once warned his congregation. "It's like a fire. One minute there's a whiff of smoke, and then you turn around and your whole house has burned to the ground and taken you with it." But then there are those of us connected to the Spirit who embark on finding another means of transportation . . . an alternative route to get where we want to go that involves eating healthy, moving our bodies, smelling the roses, and giving thanks for the privilege.

You don't ask to get old. You just get old. And if you're lucky, you'll get old too. Andy Rooney

Sadly, a deeply adverse shared concept of aging makes the reality something to be dreaded and fought against rather than embraced as a process affording new opportunities and challenges. Our ability to live longer, healthier, and more productive lives is one of mankind's greatest accomplishments, but we often see aging as more of a problem than a revolutionary, enriching way of viewing our individual journeys in life. We are powerfully influenced by our self-imposed limitations and lack of convictions and passion. Many people die very near the limit they set for themselves even though they are still in good health.

Regrettably, many older people feel cast aside so it's important to help them develop a sense of purpose and a positive self-image whether they are related or not. 15.8% (10.2 million older adults – 2014) faced the threat of hunger daily as a result of a lingering weak economy and a divisive, frightening political movement tearing our country apart. The title of the 2015-2017 AARP Strategic Plan – *Out of the Shadows of Poverty* - cites the following vision: "A country free of poverty where no older person feels vulnerable."

In June 2011, *USA Today* reported that Americans weren't hitting their prime until their late 60s. "A sweeping poll looking at American attitudes, health, and behaviors concluded people over 65 consistently had a higher degree of well-being than any other age group. We are both healthy, socially active, and have a family nearby. We're engaged in pursuits we enjoy. Even when aches and pains set in and health begins to decline, the older group is also less sad and depressed than any other group." Seven years later, a public crisis of boomer hunger, isolation, and the rise of alcohol dependency has dampened the celebration of once 'good news'.

There are lurking concerns that plague boomers from all walks of life. AARP recently reported . . . "Isolation is more than being alone. It's being at risk. Prolonged isolation and loneliness erodes well-being equivalent to smoking 15 cigarettes a day." A new study published in *JAMA Psychiatry* and sponsored in part by the National Institute on Alcohol Abuse and Alcoholism also reports "the soaring of alcohol abuse and dependency (a negative emotional state of being when not drinking) for those 65 pluses is a public health crisis at least double that of the general population."

The goal thus becomes how to guide our aging population in gaining confidence by steering life's transitions in ways that can benefit others. It's important for those blessed with a 'winter season' to see themselves as an integral part of society instead of being sequestered and feeling like they have come to their end. How unfortunate they should die before their time on earth is up! Not everyone's going to be starting a company or writing children's books and romance novels in their final season, but most have the desire if given the opportunity to use their individual talents and desires to enrich their lives and others too. Exploring and discovering new activities that stimulate the mind and heals the body with healthy lifestyles such as art, volunteering, book clubs, by helping others or to explore the possibilities of finding new adventures in activities such as art; volunteering; book clubs; group dinners on the town or pot lucks; crafts; travel tutoring; or opening a rib joint.

Today, as reported by AARP publications, older Americans really are 'disheveling the limits of aging' in ever more astonishing ways, e.g. Dick Richards (Bill Haley – *Rock Around the Clock Tonight* - and His Comets, touring at 91, playing his drums); the country music icon, Willie Nelson at 84 – to date - still performing 100 shows per year and writing songs (most recent album "God's Problem Child"); 84 year-old stuntman, "Judo" Gene LeBell who would like to retire and go back to racing motorcycles. And what can we say about the inspiration viewers received from the 2017 summer television hit "Little Big Shots – Forever

Young." I was floored by the 93-year-old show girl, Dorothy, from Palm Springs, CA. Popular television host and executive producer, Steve Harvey was to say, "Everything you thought you knew about people in their 'golden years' is about to change."

The way we look at growing old – a mode of thinking - will cause faith and creative forces of the mind and heart to produce the very things we don't want . . . those effects contrary to the realization of the 'ideal' life. Therefore, if those ideas incorporate weakness; hopelessness; helplessness; and the lack of exploration, discovery, and awe, then we will gradually entertain these negative attributes. On the other hand, if those ideas incorporate continuous advancement along all lines, we will continue to progress and improve no matter how long we may live. What our future is to be will depend entirely upon whether we continue to live in a limited groove doing nothing to expand our minds, or whether we train the mind to reach out. I am so much and no more, and never will become any more is such an unhealthy, non-productive mindset. Author James Allen wrote over a hundred years ago and it remains true to date . . . *As a man thinketh in his heart, so is he.*

When we actually refuse to grow old by obstinately holding on to youthful inklings and buoyant thoughts, the old age earmarks will not show themselves. The words of truth will make a change in our minds and chemical changes in our bodies. Since the Creator has so wonderfully fashioned us that it takes more than a quarter of a century for our bodies to reach maturity . . . and because we are the highest expression of HIS creative power . . . it's vital for boomers to keep ourselves as clean and as attractive as possible no matter our age. We simply have to refuse to grow old by counting our years or anticipating old age.

Are we, as aging mortals, like the walking dead? Are we living but not really alive? Are we breathing but not using our breath to create a life we really want to live? We should all be so elated that boomers are living longer and staying healthier than any generation before. Whether by choice, or by financial necessity, we are continuing to work long past traditional retirement age. And most important, many are yearning – as we have since our youth – to find new meaning and purpose in our lives and to give of our passions, experiences, and talents to those millenniums opened to receive as in Robert De Niro's character, 70-year-old Ben, in the movie, "The Intern".

Workers over 50 can be an untapped driving force for much needed economic growth and innovation. Corporations, entrepreneurial investors, and small businesses (including carefully working through the red tape of most academic institutions as volunteers) are already beginning to consider the aging population an asset in growing the market for American made goods and services and perhaps bringing a new flavor to social creativity. How many lives could change for the better if boomers would dedicate themselves to learning something new every day even if it's just taking a long walk with one's dog or trying out a new recipe? As long as we wake up to a new day, there are always infinite and extraordinary possibilities. Scholars and heroes of our past proved that very reality.

Socrates, when his hair whitened with the snow of age, learned to play on instruments of music. Cato, at fourscore, began his study of Greek, and the same age saw Plutarch beginning, with the enthusiasm of a boy, his first lessons in Latin. *The Character of Man,* Theophrastus' greatest work, was begun on his ninetieth birthday. Chaucer's *Canterbury Tales* was the work of the poet's declining years. Benjamin Franklin, at the age of fifty, had just taken his first important steps in metaphysical pursuits.

Arnauld, the theologian and sage, translated *Josephus* in his eightieth year. Hobbes, the English philosopher, published his version of the *Odyssey* in his eighty-seventh year and his *Iliad* one year later. Chevreul, the great French scientist whose untiring labors in the realm of color that have so enriched our world, was busy, keen, and active when death called him at the age of 103.

Hallelujah! Thankfully, I would declare there was indeed still hope for me. I was supposed to be planning for the end. The journey had been so arduous and tearful, yet I felt like I was just beginning a new chapter with no concern if it would be short or long standing. Instructions were coming from a well-*known* SOURCE I would trust to provide the means to do that which would be pleasing to HIM. For years, childhood friends, landlords, and church members would always say to me, "You need to write a book." And I would respond, "Everybody's got a story." And some would then say, *"Not like yours, my dear."*

What I knew for sure was that nothing in the world will make us look and feel young as long as we are convinced we are growing old. It's the idea that when we give our minds permission to rid of old age mind games and typical 'winter season' behaviors, we will not retire at sixty or at any period of our lives nor lose memory or mental capacity regardless of our years. Such a mind will be more brilliant at eighty than at 35 and both the intelligence and the working capacity of such a mind will increase steadily every year regardless of how long we may live.

Constantly affirm that you will always be young and tuned in to wellness; that you will not grow old by producing old age conditions through defeatist thoughts; that the Artist of your being intended for us all to have continual growth, perpetual advancement and betterment; that you will not be cheated out of your birthright of perennial youth; and that you are a phenomenal person with sincere intentions of using your greatness for the well-being of yourself and others. There is still a given reality of uncontrollable physical conditions associated with hereditary genes, unsavory-like living environments, and quality health care availability, but for the most part one does have choices as to how their life can and will play out.

You can't turn back the clock, but you can wind it up again.
Cars 3 (Disney/Pixar)

It all begins with a mental cleansing . . . ridding of all the negative, toxic thoughts keeping us from concentrating on God's plan rather than the past or the darkness in our lives. We embrace our personal assignment here on earth with fearless courage, gratitude, and confidence in the favor of God. No more waiting for a better day. That better day is today and all those I'd been given to be ALIVE! When we advocate for wonderful relationships, increased spiritual growth, an appreciation of the laughter and the tears, and physical blessings in the years ahead, just know God does hear and answers our prayers in 'due season'.

Our culture worships the fantasies of youth, yet we are being driven more and more by the realities of our age. The lifestyle choices we make now will go a long way in determining if we are mentally alert and physically fit and healthy in the autumn and winter of our lives. The worse thing society can do is to define people by their life seasons and decide what they can and cannot do by a certain number associated with the years they have been blessed to live.

There's no "smart pill" to ward off age-related decline but experts increasingly say lifestyle factors such as physical activity, challenging hobbies, and lots of friends or social engagements might help keep the brain more nimble and fit as it ages. We are experiencing a very exciting time

... experts estimate 30 plus years – more time than spent in childhood and adolescence. Implicit in the words "I will" is the acknowledgement and affirmation that we have the power to choose. We all want to live healthy lives, but are we choosing longevity? Do our daily habits support or diminish our chances of aging well? If we have the resolve to preserve our health and keep our mind keen, then we can develop the willpower putting us in charge. Fair warning! Don't be naïve. This aging thing is really happening!

My life had become much like driving my once owned prize Jeep Sports Wrangler and suddenly realizing I had arrived at a destination but couldn't remember the trip I had taken to get there. I was racing through my days not because I felt confident and hopeful but because I felt inadequate and feared if I didn't hurry up, life would totally pass me by. I was like a rabbit in a hole sometimes. By the time I climbed to the top, it appeared I would lose my grip after a steamroller bowled over my fuzzy feet and I'd fall or be pulled right back down.

In 2006, I had the honor and good fortune to officially publish one of my first freelance articles in a prominent Southwestern magazine entitled, Singer Rankin: Founder and Executive Director of World Women Work (Empowering women her life's mission). The subject was a then 64-year old, absolutely amazing, physically stunning, brilliant global icon woman with such a giving spirit to people and animals coming straight from the heart.

17 years ago, and since then, this phenomenal woman has traveled to some of the most remote parts of Africa and Asia in search of women artisans creating unique and beautiful products. Proceeds from sales of these items along with generous philanthropic contributions have been educating girls, helping achieve economic independence for women, and protecting the natural world where they live.

Dr. Margaret "Maggie" Hill, my beloved friend and mentor taught me more about education than any required university course two degrees later. She recognized with each student that passed her way how best to reach and have a positive influence on children having few breaks and trying desperately to overcome such huge deficits in academics and career options and preparation. Maggie also taught me so much about living a 'full life' regardless of physical hiccups, injustices, and hardships.

In 2002, Maggie's Café was dedicated in honor of this too 'phenomenal' woman. (On November 2, 2017, Maggie's Café was re-dedicated paying tribute to her illustrious career of educating and giving to children without- a voice). This small, alternative high school led by some of the finest, most respected educators in their field, had one of the first student-run restaurants in the country.

A close family friend, now 83, and before moving to northern California, so enjoyed being at a pre-school every day as a grandparent tutor in a program sponsored by a local California university. He loved the kids and they loved him. I was always convinced Rudy would never grow old. He's still contemplating performing a one-man show in the role of a late legendary black actor.

When the notable JoAnn Jenkins (CEO, AARP) introduced her powerhouse campaign and book, "Disrupt Aging" several years ago, I said to myself, *no matter what I have gone through . . . still going through . . . I have definitely been doing just that all along.* Watching Tina Turner's concert in London (in her early 70s); Betty White swinging from Miley Cyrus's "wrecking ball" at 91; and one of my long-time idols Cher after receiving the 2017 Billboard icon award and giving the world an awe-spectacular performance, the stunning super star echoed my very sentiments . . . *"Don't get it twisted. I just turned 71 a few days ago."*

Whether 'chocolate baby boomers' understood why or not, we went to church. It was part of who we were because we needed to know where we came from and why we came. No matter our choice of denomination, worship services and church activity participation gave us a moral underpinning through the company of a community and people we could trust. Before we went to the front line of the Movement, we prayed. We were in the Garden with Jesus; we went to the mountaintop with Martin; drew strength from the courage and faith of Mandela, Biko, TuTu, and the children of Soweto; and we cried with Bobby and Marion in Mississippi when a shanty town and a sewer running down the middle of the street was discovered.

As people of color, we became the best representatives of faith ever, having some of the most painful passages of lack and brutality ever recorded in history and a debilitating diaspora still continuing, but still showing up and saying 'thank you Lord' on Sundays and for all the blessings passing our way every day. Sometimes prayer and grace kept the lynch mobs, the water hoses, the vicious canines, the torch bearing KKK with a cross plastered across their white robes, and an officer's bullet abbey.

What made these times more intriguing was that 'chocolate boomers' emerged as unexpected scholars, artists, athletes, and troopers for the cause of justice. We were encouraged and taught by some of the finest educators in segregated schools; inspired by brave and committed local and national leaders, heroes, and fallen martyrs; and were molded by the love of our parents and guardians and the wisdom of our neighbors, 'real' spiritual guides, and elders. We read everything we could, especially about our ancestral history; studied and achieved; and became resolute in our demands for equality, exposure, and opportunities.

The face cannot betray the years until the mind has given its consent. The mind is the sculptor. We renew our bodies by renewing our thoughts; change our bodies and our habits by changing our thoughts. "Why Grow Old" – Orison Swett Marden

Don't think because the chronological numbers are beginning to add up that you must begin to take in the sail . . . to stop progressing. Carry yourself so that you do not suggest old age in any of its phases. A gracious and confident manner is a powerful advertisement. You can always replace old judgments with an appreciation of life. Nothing is easier than for humankind to age. All one has to do is think he or she is growing old; to expect it; to fear it; to prepare for it; and to compare themselves to others the same age. Some are left with addressing personal responses to such questions as: How will I spend my later years? Will I be vital and independent, or will I be bent over and feeble? Will I be mentally alert, engaged in living, or watching it from the sidelines of a joyous parade while throngs of boomer comrades march right on by? What life in the months and years to come may bring in my personal and professional space is not mine to decide, but it is mine to elect how I will respond . . . how I shall meet all that it brings.

Reacting to the demands of daily life instead of living in the world the person we were meant to be can be counterproductive and frustrating. Deprivation of any kind only increases the craving and makes one feel the starvation more intensely. That applies to life as well. Waiting for the right or perfect moment to live our chosen life is a miserable way to be. Make a plan in the midst of calm and not crisis and follow through. That humankind can change himself, improve himself, re-create himself, control his environment, and master his own destiny is the conclusion of every mind who is wide-awake to the power of right thought in constructive action. In fact, it is the conviction of all such minds that man can do practically anything within the possibilities of the human domain when he knows how to think, and he can secure almost any result desired when learning how to think for results. Man is as he thinks he is and what he does is the result of the sum total of his thought. If we assume an expectant, hopeful, and optimistic attitude regarding our "winter season", the time could turn out to be our finest hours.

We are the masters of thought, the molder of character, and the maker and shaper of conditions, environment, and destiny at any age. When we proceed to select the mental images, we desire to form in the mind, we must constantly be guided by the fact that every thought or mental impression should be of such a nature that whatever may be created in the likeness of that picture will be wholesome, beneficial, up-lifting, and constructive. For example, in our mind we can convince ourselves "age is but a number" – that this notion of growing old is an incorrect, defeatist way of looking at our present condition.

Our minds are the artists . . . the sculptors of our callings. Nothing in the world will make us look young as long as we are convinced we are hopelessly getting old. I learned from my beautiful mother that very lesson . . . to refuse to grow old by counting my years or anticipating old age. Although leaving this world having been brutally consumed by the (C) Monster and transitioning in her late 80s, she had long decided she would never be defined by her age or any antiquated expectations of what people living in her 'season' should do with the rest of their lives. Her mind was sharp; she dressed impeccably; loved to smell good; and praised God in thanksgiving for the daily blessings she had been afforded . . . even the meager ones that most folks took for granted.

Making a difference in the lives of others is one of the best medicines for the soul. As boomers think outside their age box, they discover that decades lived mattered far less. Intergenerational friendships have proven to be a wonderful way to enjoy inspiring group settings where new ideas and experiences are shared. I'll never forget my elation when asked to be the President of the Board of Directors for a (former) phenomenal teen art center during my residential tenure in the Southwest.

It was at this center where I met Ethaan, my 'vanilla' son, and I was his 'chocolate' Mama. When the 34-year-old gifted artist and silk screener was murdered in his own home by a burglar in broad daylight the same year I lost my literary agent to cancer (2012), I became adamant I would do whatever I could to keep both their memories alive. The well-regarded founder and executive director of the center sacrificed much to touch the lives of wonderful deserving youth. What was so beautiful about the Board's and my relationship with the talented young people who frequented this fantastic facility was the mutual respect, commitment, and admiration we had for each other. They knew we loved them and would always have each other's backs when need be. The chronological age differences were just that – numbers.

Another boomer friend became involved in an oral history project with some wonderful young people from the high school around the corner from where she had lived for many years. At their Afro-centric themed academy and Olympic training facility, these students could not graduate without fulfilling a group community service project. Gabe Phillips first led his highly engaged and enthusiastic students in a series of panel discussions regarding society's attitude toward the aging and how their grandmothers and grandfather's lives could be applauded by their positive involvement.

Hearing the "seasoned warriors" stories of decades gone by made the students think about how far our country had come . . . that was 'until' November 2016. 'Gabe's kids' (as they were often called) decided instead of using the negative descriptive words 'elderly' – 'old man' and 'old woman' – or 'senior citizen', they would change these familiar terms to 'seasoned warrior'. It gave these funny and very wise seniors with such intriguing and rich life experiences a little more class and a well-deserved honor.

The students began to journal and reflect on such topics as historical events having occurred during the time the boomers were growing up and what society was like such as music, film, wars, prices, cars, racism, education, home life, and rules (without cell phones and computers). The 'warriors' learned about the teens' lives and how so many attitudes and practices had changed. The exchange went on longer than had been planned or expected but that was a good thing. Young people were so inspired and motivated by those otherwise isolated with very few possibilities of joy walking through the front door of their nursing home.

Holiday gift exchange, pot luck dinners, dances, entertainment (like movie night and bringing in special guests), and art and music therapy most of the participants really enjoyed added so much meaning to beautiful peoples' lives . . . blessed souls of longevity and *grace.* Framed paintings from the 'warriors' projects were hung proudly throughout the newly renovated school auditorium. There had been a joint fundraiser – young and old – with the goal of raising $150,000 to diversify the school's library book collection, provide state-of-the-art technological resources the district could not afford, and to spruce up the school auditorium for off-the-chart performances. The successful interactive model led to students being more open and confident as they presented a prospectus to the mayor and the city council. They were truly committed to making sure more 'seasoned warriors' became increasingly active, cared for, and hopeful so they could enjoy an enriching and memorable 'winter season'.

The doorway to wisdom, health, and happiness is awareness. When we are present in our lives, we see clearly that God is on our side and certain situations are drawn to us to help us experience ourselves more fully, to help us grow, and to know our deepest truth. When we are fully aware of ourselves, we don't race past the moment or try to avoid it. Unfortunately, many of us love and relate from the worldview of a hungry, neglected, helpless, and fretful child. We don't see from the bird's eye view of a mature adult who knows his/her wounds and how those tender and painful places might show up from time to time. Stress and depression take a bigger chunk out of our being as we age. We have to fight twice as hard to get back on the 'happy train'.

I knew without a doubt that wherever I was, I had to be all there. I have lived the runner, panting ahead in worry, pounding back in regrets, and terrified to live in the present because I know there is no more room to hurt anymore. I had to stop sprinting and punching myself with shame and hopelessness. I would take time to notice something special; go barefoot or walk on the beach at sunset and stop off on my way home tonight for an original burger and fries and a vanilla milkshake. Tomorrow I might devour the most delicious catfish in town at Grandma Jemma's favorite 'hole in the wall' café in her honor. As we get older, it isn't the things we did that we often regret, but the things we didn't do.

Emotional, psychological, and spiritual maturity has nothing to do with chronological age. It has to do with having the courage to open our hearts, minds, and spirits to truth even though it might make us uncomfortable, anxious, and maybe scared. Age and experience can expand the possibilities in life for every member of society. Improved well-being and productivity go up while health care costs CAN come down. If younger people can change the way they address their health by educating themselves in the best proper nutritional recommendations and consistently 'move their bodies', the benefits can be huge.

When health is absent, wisdom cannot reveal itself, art cannot become manifest, strength cannot be exerted, wealth becomes useless, and reason becomes powerless. Herophilus 300 BC

The expression of age in the body is the harvest of old age ideas which have been planted in the mind. I simply refused to allow my mind to stiffen its muscles by the suggestion of age limitation. Grandma Jemma always reminded me that our bodies were God's temples and we were responsible for keeping every brick in place. "Know ye not," says Paul, "that ye are a temple of God, and that the spirit of God dwelleth in you. Shall we mar the beauty and lower the dignity of our temple of God by taking less care of it than a neat housewife does her kitchen?" The person who does not learn early in life to focus on their efforts and to centralize their power will never achieve marked success in anything at any age.

I loved author Elizabeth Gilbert's (Eat, Pray, Love) presentation for an Oprah Master Class on "The Curiosity Driven Life". She compared the flight of the hummingbird that curiously darts from tree to tree to what people should practice in search of a new passion or a different way of looking at the way we want our life to be. The message: Be curious and try something new!

There are so many ways we can all stay active, especially boomers such as working puzzles; organizing a dinner or a book or video discussion group; traveling someplace new with a friend or family member; enrolling in a course like yoga, gardening, cooking, dancing, or swimming; learning something new like a foreign language or a craft; corresponding with friends and family through mail, e-mail, or social media; considering part-time work while also sharpening technology skills; volunteering; starting a journal; tracing family histories while researching genealogical sources such as census records and ship passenger logs; writing articles and narrative stories; or getting a dog, walking him or her every day, and meeting new people along the way.

Michelle Obama and Dr. Jill Biden's powerful platform, 'Let's Move', had such a positive impact on children and their family's lives especially with physical education being removed from the middle and high school curriculum only to be replaced by standardized test scores. It's long been scientifically proven when more oxygen gets to the brain, our minds become stronger and we excel. It's also far easier to connect with new people excited about what we're doing while we surround ourselves with those who share a common interest.

A well-balanced life is a cheerful life; a happy union of fine qualities and unruffled temper; clear judgment; and well-proportioned faculties. The challenge today is to move outside of our everyday mundane existences by picking up the pace of our day-to-day living. There was no question with all the darkness plaguing every chapter of my life that I have remained mostly healthy and close to sane because first and foremost, God is a very good Father. As a "winter woman", I now exercise the ability to change my life.

The laws governing this human trek are quite simple. We are accountable for our lives especially in the age of possibilities. Decades prior, old age would have been just that - the end. Many 'seasoned warriors' are now guided by such virtues as self-respect, honor, non-judgment, alignment with the spiritual law of truth, and contentment. We become more courageous, taking more risks unlike ever before . . . not physical risks like swimming with the sharks but being more genuine, more ourselves, and more willing to try something new. It's called growing 'whole' rather than growing old. This happens by our opening more chapters of ourselves that might even amaze us too. God's truth becomes our truth as we put forth our own efforts, achieved by our own strength and fortitude, and we make God's truth our truth . . . trusting ourselves; giving love but not expecting it; giving sympathy but not craving it; and giving aid but not depending upon it.

When all the dust settles, I do believe good people . . . dedicated American citizens . . . have the capability to create a new age society with a unified, patriotic, and commonsense nationalistic spirit where aging individuals can ease into a normal life quarter knowing they can be independent but never alone. If we take care of our health and take advantage of preventive care availability while also learning to tap into organizations with a plethora of useful information and resources, we can be one of those inspiring stories of a 70 or 80 plus blessed souls having the time of their life.

As 'seasoned warriors', we have to accept the reality that certain spaces can no longer be occupied by us. It's important we begin to heal, mature, and become more comfortable with who we are right now. I believe we will see life, love, and loss in a different way . . . finding light, power, and presence as we embrace possible transformations, prospects, and wonders. We can begin by becoming active partners in our health care instead of being passive patients and waiting for life to end. Whoever said opportunity knocks only once must have died young. If we live long enough, we will discover life does give second chances – and third and fourth ones too! And we learn love comes more than once to those who are open to receive it.

The challenge is to gain confidence in navigating life's transitions and to see ourselves as an integral part of society instead of being isolated from it. Redefine your purpose, gather your assets, and keep on living, believing, and giving. No matter what our age, we haven't seen it all. Who knows, there might be someone out there who will call out, "Come in and let me love you until you can learn to love yourself." No one knows how God will end HIS book on our lives. It's quite possible HE could be saving the best for last. In the meantime, we might want to commit to letting 'the good times roll' until it's time to go.

My prayer is that I would remain as beautiful as my impending senior years would allow ... encompassing health, wholeness, proportion, satisfaction, and radiant joy. That is life as God intended it to be. I would pray to live long enough to see my children finally on their feet personally, professionally, and spiritually . . . to see them happy and whole. Included in my petitions echoed sincerely in my prayers is to be able to visit the Smithsonian Museum of African American History and Culture in Washington, D.C. while I could still walk; get a couple more huskies; a piece of land in the Southwest where my children could always go and call their own; attend a Bruno Mars and an Andrea Bocelli concert and a full season at my favorite opera house; drive a Jeep again; and possibly meet a new friend and companion. It has been an awfully lonely road.

Recently, I heard a seminar speaker once say (and quite candidly, I might add) that *life shouldn't be a journey to the grave with the intention of arriving safely in an attractive, well-preserved body, but rather to skid in sideways, chocolate in one hand and a mimosa (maybe for some hippie boomers - a cannabis cigarette) in the other, totally worn out and screaming . . . woo hooo, what a ride!*

I will pour out my Spirit on all people, your sons and daughters will prophesy, your old men will dream dreams, your young men will see visions. **Joel 2:2**

Chapter Eight
Coming Through The Valley Of Weeping

There is a brokenness out of which comes the unbroken; a shatteredness out of which blooms the unshatterable. There is a sorrow beyond all grief which leads to joy and a fragility out of whose depths emerges strength. There is a hollow space too vast for words through which we pass with each loss, out of whose darkness we are sanctioned into being. There is a cry deeper than all sound whose serrated edges cut the heart, as we break open to the place inside which is unbreakable and whole while learning to sing. Rashani Rea (The Unbroken)

In June 1992, *People Magazine* published an article entitled, "Seize the Day." The title and content were much more than a **carpe diem** interpretation. This great man was dying of a disease he at first knew little about . . . saddened by how he had contracted this monster illness while trying to save his life from another kind of physical demon and needing a blood transfusion. The writer of the piece, the late tennis legend and Citizen of the World, Arthur Ashe, left me with a truth difficult to ever shed. As grateful as I am for life itself, I shared the raw sentiments of the written words on the frayed yellowed copy I kept in a 'keepsake file'. "You're not going to believe this, he said, but living with AIDS is not the greatest burden I've had in my life. **Being black is**. No question about it. Even now, it continues to feel like an extra weight tied around me."

Being black is. Those words haunted me then and they still do today. The reality became the source of my *suffering* and that of my children. Going all the way back to my childhood, I often think I tried to fit into circumstances, relationships, and places where I just didn't belong and a few decades later neither did my children . . . where 'what was' and 'what still is' based on class, gender, and 'color barriers' continued to halt our 'rise'. No matter how hard we tried to build upon our work ethic; how good our literary and creative projects were; or how confident we were in our delivery, sometimes it was a 'struggle' to believe we were enough. There were times we could see the finish line but questioned if we could remain strong enough to ever cross it. Arthur Ashe did cross over and the reality of the price he paid has given us such great pride in his phenomenal legacy. (Arthur Ashe Stadium Center Court, Queens, NY)

My parents had moved on only one other occasion from the time I was three until I was off to college. Then the stone began to roll for me . . . 19 different times and in five states. I'm sure there had been a few other brief moves in between like a shelter and the hardwood floors of a friend's living room where my youngest child and I slept in sleeping bags. I had refused to sign off on seven 6th grade students to be promoted to junior high when they could not read and couldn't supply personal data in case of emergency. I was fired by a school district under state receivership resulting in my losing everything. With heartfelt regret that my brilliant, talented child had to pay the price, I never regretted my decision. Prayerfully, it would not be my past driving me to make amends for my missteps, but it would be whatever future remaining calling me to become the person I always thought I could be but just didn't know how to be.

Although given many special gifts of imagination and power behind words both in writing and in speaking, I was skeptical as to whether becoming a published author would ever happen. I prayed for the historic generational personal and professional *struggles* to end with my children . . . that the bus would stop where these phenomenal human beings stood waiting at their life terminals. It was time to take a trip far, far away from the frightening nightmares and sad realities of lack, loss, and betrayal. How sad that it would be their generations having to witness a segment of our once great democracy crumble. There was this horrible tolerance and acceptance of such foul ugliness and corruption . . . those carrying <u>assault</u> rifles that could destroy hundreds of innocent lives within a matter of minutes during the day and torch bearers at night having political seats in the Big House. Martin! Martin! Remind the 'good folks' again 'Why We Can't Wait'!

Mom - I was thinking about you this morning when I was driving home, and again a few hours later when I woke up. I know you worry about us the same way your mother worried about you, but there's no need. God is too good, and HE has laid in front of us everything we need to make it. Times may be hard, but there are lessons in the midst of these trials and we have to learn them all. One of my favorite scriptures now is James 1:2-4, "Consider it pure joy, my brothers, whenever you face trials of many kinds, because you know that the testing of your faith develops perseverance. Perseverance must finish its work so that you may be mature and complete, not lacking anything." This last year has not been easy for me, but at every pass, God has provided what I needed to get to the next step, and HE has provided it the way HE saw fit. I don't think it will be years for us because we've already survived a lot, but I do feel like it's coming. 2002

Sixteen years later, the struggles and heartache intensified . . . some incidents never to be forgotten but having to be forgiven in order to be free . . . some realities of our getting few breaks out of our control. As much as we suffered from *satan's* thrashings, we weren't about to give up, allowing *it* to win. We are the 'winners' because we are God's children and our God is love and HIS mercy endureth forever. That was always my declaration. What I did believe was that any Black Christian who has suffered as much individually and as a race for decades and still prays; still gives God all praise, honor, and glory; is grateful for the little blessings of *grace* and awe; freely forgives; asks no questions; and still worships as the Holy Spirit comes upon them just after the dogs and fire hoses have seriously injured their protesting brothers and sisters; while celebrating decades of phenomenal achievements against all odds and accomplished through faith, perseverance, and trudging through so many 'valleys of weeping' that now fill a museum and cultural center, I'd say that makes us a pretty powerful and impressive group of humankind. Although other minority ethnicities have suffered undeniable atrocities, especially Native Americans, the black man's 'valley of weeping' in many ways is handed down from one generation to the next. I was convinced I would never live to see it ever change and I had no explanation to my children and students as to why.

Black students have quite often paid an extra tax on their investment, vigilantly worried their future would continue to be compromised by society and the media's perception and refusal to be inclusive; an unwillingness to share in an abundant opportunity bounty; a denial of the real truth behind 89% black and brown mass incarceration, especially <u>men</u> of color; and the overall treatment of their group by the return of torch bearers filling up the pews in their all-white churches every Sunday. My children paid an even higher price because their mother drove a Ford Escort and not a Benz. We weren't naïve. We didn't hold rigidly to the falsehood that discrimination and disadvantage could always be overcome with hard work and persistence. It simply was not true. Some people's hearts would never change.

We were just months from moving into the 21st century and there I was, fighting for my children and my students who simply wanted to be free to grow into respectful, successful, visionary, happy young people with the same entitlements afforded their white peers with most wanting to make a difference in the lives of others. "There's not enough of me to deal with my own personal and professional injustices and then watch my children suffer too!" I would tell God in the midst of my tearful nights alone when it hurt too badly to fall asleep. "It's outright hypocrisy for me to sing in the choir on Sunday mornings and then on a Monday morning explain to my child what a 'nigger' is. We've had to deal with this lunacy all our lives and I am tired now, Lord. I'm really, really, tired."

When my college freshman child was confronted daily by Skinheads at a prestigious, predominantly white university, I contacted a Board member immediately. This was absurd. If my concerns were not addressed, my next move was going to be informing local news channels and newspapers. My fight was for all students of color that suddenly realized in this hostile environment that they really didn't have a voice. When Sandra Baker and the Colonel arrived on campus as representatives from C.O.R.E. (Congress of Racial Equality), they found the same frightening reality that the students of color identified immediately – in class and on campus.

Your description of events at the university warrants a careful and detailed response. My colleagues and I take seriously any situations that could be motivated by racism or lack of sensitivity to any given individual or group. I am sorry that your student has had a difficult tenure at the university to date, and I hope that the new school year will prove to be a better experience. University Board member

There was always some kind of *suffering* plaguing my trek and beginning in the critical development years of my children's young lives. I had taken my father's grandchildren out of the Midwest having no extended family support. No doubt their professional aspirations in the very difficult, inequality-based, often blatant racist, and gender biased entertainment industry along with each of their athletic pursuits would best be served on the west coast. The apple didn't fall too far from the tree. I wanted my days of frostbite on my fingers and toes to be done with and like my parents had tried to do, I wanted to give my children a chance to realize their dreams when the doors had been shut for me.

Realistically, Daddy knew there wasn't enough money in our family or through my education profession to support them, but Mama also knew I wasn't going to dissuade them from going after the life they had always envisioned . . . that I would do whatever I could whenever I could to have their backs. Few believed but that didn't stop us from striving and having faith in ourselves. We would reach a point where we would be too large to worry, too strong to fear, too noble for anger, and so happy to permit the presence of 'woe is me' to find a number in my listing of daily mantras. As inspirational author Ann Voskamp would attest, there are indeed a thousand ways to say, "thank you" Lord instead.

My thought was if God wanted me to think another way or move in another direction, that's exactly what would have happened. HE knew I wanted the mountains, the ocean, and occasionally a trip to the Southwest. My father and I remained estranged to the very end, but I would tell anyone he was a mighty good man who lived through a lot of loss, pain, and heartache often deadened by a weekend bottle; who knew about 'real love' for 60 plus years; and who knew of a kind of sacrifice few others would ever experience or be willing to bear. The kind of opportunities and life experiences he wanted for his family; saw on a black and white television screen; and read about in a magazine were a few more decades into the future. I never bought into that restricted time frame. But for what he had to work with it, he was admirably successful and found contentment in the small things in life he had worked hard to achieve.

Tainted with the racial and fatherlessness beasts, I realized I couldn't protect my offspring from every incoming bump and bruise. As children of color with a single mother trying to provide too much on one paycheck and little, if any, paternal support (thank you, EUWIN), I had to start having "the talk" far too early in their innocent childhoods. Sometimes I think I wasn't candid or serious enough . . . just too tired of not having the words to explain how hurt I was watching them hurt as I continue to do 30 years later. In a 40-year career at all levels of classroom instruction and administration, I often struggled with my young black female students with what Stanford professor Ralph Richard Banks once described as a 'segregated existence' . . . so much more likely to be single and putting most on the bottom rung of the economic and happiness ladder.

In the past, when the world was beating us up as young Black women, we could come home and share our pains and our confusions with our mothers, grandmothers, aunties, and 'real' best friends. I had Grandma Jemma, but she couldn't nor would she ever answer all my questions or respond to the prejudices that would scar my children and me for a lifetime. We also had the church, our watchful neighbors, and the best teachers and administrators in the business of educating and nurturing young minds and hearts . . . caring adults who were willing and able to recharge our faltering human batteries. With so much support behind us, we could take a breath from the harshness of a society in denial and a future we weren't certain would turn out okay. The sad reality is today the resources we once had are no longer there for this generation.

Metaphorically, I had often compared my life to that of a standard pinball machine. *Someone* or *something* else seemed to always be in a position standing at the front of the game machine pulling the spring back as far as they could or hitting a button on each side with banging force. The silver ball - that would be 'me' – was constantly whacked by the dismal and painful circumstance levers with a vicious determination to keep me from becoming whole and at peace . . . from being a winner and truly happy. But the strength in this excruciating personal suffering was that "I got it!" I clearly understood I'd never understand God's reasoning for the way HE did things . . . and couldn't always explain to my children or rationalize to myself why 'bad things happened to good people'. The puzzlement began when Robbie disappeared; white flight was in full swing; and my favorite uncle never came back to town again.

Often times my suffering was so profound and so transformative that each time I got hit, I was never the same. There were times I could blame myself and other people, and then there were other times I had to accept God's ways were definitely not my ways but that HE meant me no harm. I would just have to roll with the punches and be glad for the few *flowers of blessedness* I could still recognize. With every new city (always running); every new relationship where I could never connect all the dots; and with every professional position (most being such rewarding work and spending my days with so many phenomenal colleagues), there always seemed to be some kind of racial barrier or financial hiccup in the way keeping me from doing my very best and moving up the ranks.

    To this day, I will never forget the last conversation I had with my uncle . . . the one who had introduced me to a world that would have been foreign to me had we not had a special bond. I was 16. He was in his 50s (young sons, 3 and 5) and dying quickly of cancer ushered into his body by Parliament cigarettes in a box. "You'll always have 'rocks in your head'," he'd say trying to laugh a little through his pain. "But you're a good kid. A smart one too! You're different . . . you want to be 'out there' and that's okay. Just know it's going to be harder for you no matter how unfair that might seem. They'll let you know you don't belong. I got into their white country clubs because I sometimes had to live a lie in order to live the life I wanted. Don't listen to no-can-do voices. It might take some time, but it's going to happen for you. Remember I told you so." And then he was gone forever.

Her life has been a testament to the importance and difficulty of maintaining integrity, ethical behavior, and love while enduring the social and economic adversities imposed on persons of color in America. (1994 from a USC associate professor)

    I often think and write about the courageous and faithful wives of our once jailed and fallen leaders and heroes like Coretta Scott King; Betty Shabazz; Myrlie Evers; Winnie Mandela; and Ntsiki Mashalaba (Biko) who had to pull strength from the Well of Oneness in order to help their children and other extended family members make sense of their pain. I couldn't imagine their sorrow and uncertainty the constant fear that hate mongers might not be finished. The night is far spent, the day is at hand. Therefore, let us cast off the works of darkness, and let us put on the armor of light. **Romans 13:12**

I had begun planning for my 50th Class Reunion a year prior. The reality was I probably wouldn't see most of those who would be gathering ever again. We were the 'chocolate baby boomers' . . . many I had known since we sat on a dance hall floor not being able to attend a half-empty all white neighborhood school. I so wanted to feel good, enjoy myself, and look outstanding. But there would hardly be enough money for any of my wishes to be fulfilled . . . just enough for a one-way train ticket for a 36-hour miserable ride. If I attended, I would be leaving my children in a pretty tough financial predicament . . . one we had been living for quite some time. I had designed my event ensembles with ideas from *Project Runway* designer collections. The fabric from "Mood" was outstanding. As usual, things fell apart. I ended up wearing a $20.00 jumpsuit; had left the Aveda Salon with a color application and wet hair not being able to afford the full treatment; and attended the festivities alone as had been the case for many years.

Perhaps I should have never tried but there was a more serious reason I had to get there no matter how arduous the ordeal might be. The husband of one of my classmates (someone who had been very instrumental in being a father-figure and coach to one of my children) was sadly fighting for his life at a Texas cancer center. It was like God told me I should go to honor them. My attendance was bittersweet, but I know for sure I would have had far more regrets had I not attempted to do what my heart told me was the right thing to do. Seeing people, I had known most of my life was a wake-up call of the brevity of time and gratitude for all the great memories simultaneously. Although tears flowed off and on for the 36-hour trip back to my temporary place of residence where I didn't know what I might face when I arrived – possibly eviction – I remember vividly finally falling off to sleep thinking about my friends at Anderson

Cancer Center making my *suffering* miniscule in comparison and repeating . . . *God is my refuge and strength, a very present help in trouble.*

    Many people have come to their present spiritual path, and that would include me, because of deep unhappiness. Agony can teach us empathy for others struggling to make it through the 'valley of weeping', as well. It can humble us; encourage us to be kinder; make wiser decisions; dig deeper to find more resilience; and 'overcome' time and time again. Crisis and heartache calls upon our deepest emotional and psychological resources to face hardship and ideally conquer it.

    I knew only one person in my dream town I would head to just after my college graduate headed to L.A. and an internship in the entertainment industry. He was the co-owner of a quaint tourist oasis I had come across while browsing on-line. I would stay at the bed and breakfast until the $3,500 I had in my bank account was depleted. I had this false notion I could meet people who knew others that might be willing to help me "plant my feet on solid ground" in this strange place. But my existence was caught up in a danger zone and if I didn't start feeling and moving in a productive manner while accepting the reality that I was all alone (with the exception of my husky), I feared what could happen. I was in so much pain. The one person (my beloved mother) who fought to bring me into this world . . . who always believed in my children and me, was always so proud, and fought Daddy to support us . . . was gone and I never had an opportunity to say good-bye. It was such a cruel departure and she chose not to allow her grandchildren or her daughter to have her physical demise be the last memory we would have of her.

    At one of my lowest, most frightening and shameful suicidal-thought moments, I heard Pastor Joel Osteen's voice coming from the little t.v. sitting on the table in front of the bed. I had just augmented my awareness of a "Grace" trip having traveled 800 miles west to the southwest . . . numb and into an abyss of uncertainty. I was staying in a 100 square foot room in the charming bed and breakfast in my beautiful paradise corner of the world. Guilt ate away at me for leaving my father to the care of his relatives a year prior, but if he wouldn't come with me, I kept asking God what was I to do? I had teaching responsibilities I just couldn't ignore or up and quit; bills to pay; a dog I had to un-board and take care of; and above all else, a grief and betrayal that left me painfully speechless and paralyzed at times. This move was definitely not well thought out. It honestly made no sense, but I was somehow driven to land on my feet in this place. I had one child who needed to be emotionally pieced together after a tough and sad four-year tenure at an academic institution where many constituents reminded her daily of her blackness and aloneness while the other having horrific memories of the World Trade Center crumbling into rubble a few blocks away . . . a witness to the most shocking, brutal, unprecedented (non-declared war) event ever to come boldly and sacrificially on American soil. They were also reeling from the eventual loss of their grandparents to whom they were very close. There was little room for their mother's cries for help.

You must see yourself as God sees you . . . blessed, strong, healthy, happy, and successful, I heard the anointed theologian declare. *Unto the upright there arises light in the darkness. HE is gracious and full of compassion and righteousness. Being defeated is a temporary condition. Giving up is what makes it permanent. Your greatest battle is to remain who you are even though you might be facing a goliath.* Pastor Osteen followed his declaration with one of my favorite verses from *Habakkuk 2:2-3* . . . *"Write the vision and make it plain. For the vision is yet for an appointed time; but at the end it will speak, and it will not lie. Though it tarries, wait for it; because it will surely come, it will not tarry."* Five minutes later, the phone rang in the room. It was my dear friend, Dr. Greg Baer (Real Love Ministries) calling from Rome, Georgia. It was as if God had sent two personal messengers to save my life. The husky held such a critical role in saving my life on numerous occasions, even on this day. He knew something just wasn't right, and in that small space where we found ourselves simply being, his ocean blue eyes never stopped watching me every place I moved.

For the second go round . . . after moving back to the little piece of heaven in the Southwest (too broken to make it the first time), I was hoping to survive by finding a professional position . . . still running and running and searching and trying to find a solid place to stand. The emptiness and hurt just wouldn't go away. I had a few pretty impressive credentials and references, but they weren't strong enough to compete in the fast-moving technological evolution and the influx of highly trained and qualified millenniums contending in the marketplace.

Upon my leaving the office of one of the cabinet secretaries of a top political official, my life would change for better <u>and</u> for worse. Having had two or three meetings under our belts regarding the subjects of some of my freelance articles published in local magazines and newspapers, the secretary slipped me one of his business cards with an important name and number written on the back. It was a contact cell number for the educational liaison in charge of trying to improve the struggling school districts in a state that had long been ranked in the bottom 5 for years.

There had been on-going violent confrontations at a few high schools around the state . . . mostly between the Hispanic gangs and African American students. It had become too dangerous for black kids to stay after school for athletic practices, extracurricular interests, and academic tutorials. Brown and Black pitted against each other. After coming aboard, I never expected to be a target of workplace mobbing in the manner in which it happened from the very first day. Some days I would stand outside the building and look up to my corner office and say, "Not today . . . I can't hurt today. I have to breathe!" I would drive back home, walk the husky, and call in sick.

I was quite naïve regarding generational political cronyism being so busy trying to learn my way in a strange place. I so enjoyed reaching out to wonderful, progressive educators and nurturing parents that truly wanted to hold on to their Native and Spanish culture while also preparing their children for the global and digital marketplace. As was mostly the generational mindset, they wanted a brighter future for their offspring than they had been afforded.

I just took the time to carefully read your piece in the magazine you left on my desk. I'm just so profoundly touched by your words. While you were facing what you faced, I was watching it happen, trying to do right, but mostly shocked and devastated that this was happening in our country. And although sometimes it was not easy to keep faith, I knew – KNEW - that there were other people out there with right minds and right hearts. Thanks for all you've given me. From a beloved supervisor who taught me much. (2009)

I was a victim of a state system that persecuted me, crippled my talents and passions to help schools and families, and temporarily broke the structure of any hope I might have had for success. I had remained in "the valley of weeping' so many days of my employment and my solo personal existence. Foolishly viewing myself through a prism of false beliefs, I had convinced myself that I was quite vulnerable and unqualified . . . someone who always had to move faster than everyone else in order to maintain a professional position or simply keep up. More often than should be, I felt defeated and powerless . . . desperately searching for ways to fight back. Going back to my childhood, here I was in my 'winter season' still asking God why I had to fight for having good intentions and a pure heart. Perhaps I didn't have that 'conquering faith of David' at the time and there were far too many goliaths to slew.

You do know what your problem is, I am sure," wrote one of my late childhood friends in an e-mail that truly surprised me when it arrived out of the blue. *I surmise it as being double minded. You are astute and moral. Astuteness has allowed you to reach higher than average professional success. Morality has prevented you from being individually selfish enough to turn your back on those who still struggle. You possess a type of character that our boy Obama may not. I am waiting to see how he responds to the lady who was fired on the spot for the 24-year-old statement. A teaching moment will be missed if he does not let it be known that what she experienced was a "natural" inclination for a person from a group which had experienced racism for their entire life and how she grew passed it and began to understand it as a class struggle, poor vs. rich. The professionally successful black person will either ignore the moral issue here or seek some strategy which relieves the "boss" of embarrassment. You, my sweet, do not ignore nor cover the behinds of your superiors. I hear what you're going through and it's big. But I've known you a long time and I know your strength and resolve and that's even bigger."*

While simply wanting to make a difference in children's lives and those who were lovingly charged to serve them, and to personally survive and find some meaningful purpose in my own life, I was bold enough to think I knew what I wanted God to do in order to help me in my time of need. I was *suffering* and *weeping* from battle fatigue and fighting not to give up. Having allowed the enemy to temporarily rob me of my joy and passion . . . sorrow, guilt, and worry filled my days. I suddenly didn't know where to turn. Yet strangely enough, when 'the other' political party took over and 30 of my colleagues and I lost our positions and were escorted out of our offices with police at our side within one hour, I felt liberated. I no longer had to exist in a frightening, prison-like environment having more to do with personal agendas and political connections rather than the welfare and future of children; their schools; and their families . . . simply being kind and compassionate human beings towards one another. *Grace* was always there. I just never recognized its presence at the time. My faith was definitely being challenged so I turned away by not praying and not giving thanks for the spaces and times when I wasn't hurting, crying, empty, and disillusioned. Although we weren't on speaking terms, I realized God was still interested in listening to my silence.

It was not a matter of if but when someone would stand behind the pinball machine again and pull back the spring accelerating the metaphorical silver ball into the punishing levers. Favor was not always fair. There were some who simply slid through life normally and unscathed . . . sunning in the Riviera and marveling at antiquities in Italy and Spain. It was just one of those 'what was' realities. It reminded me of how Mama always felt sorry for the contestants on "Wheel of Fortune" who flew all the way from the northern most point of Rhode Island to L.A. to appear on the show and ended up hitting 'bankrupt' at every turn of the wheel. The woman standing beside the losing contestant amasses thousands of dollars and heads to the bonus round where she wins a sports car. She lives right down the street in Culver City. Not a thing could have changed the fate of such a disappointment.

With the exception of my parents and my uncle's passing, it took me quite some time to come through the 'valley of weeping' when I lost my canine companion . . . this stunning animal creation of God's that always caught the eye of thousands of tourists and natives alike.

How fitting that the husky, a direct descendant of the wolf, was my favorite dog breed and I had owned several. Folklore legends have historically reported that the wolf is a pathfinder; a bringer of new ideas – a harbinger of strength, loyalty, and wisdom helping to teach us about ourselves and who we are.

*It didn't matter where we lived . . . unfortunately, three cities as I recall . . . people always stopped to take a second look at this magnificent animal. In a popular southwestern tourist destination, the stunning 'wooly' Siberian husky often slowed up sidewalk traffic. Cameras were pulled out and poses were staged with the 'you-won't-believe-this-dog' sitting peacefully and taking in all the attention. He loved it. Although I walked him daily as much as I could, he **suffered** from the lack of a place he could run and roam freely . . . a necessity for good health, especially for his breed and as he grew older.*

Years later, after surviving being broadsided by a speeding big rig truck in the middle of a busy Texas highway, the husky and I bonded even more. And later, he would unknowingly manage to help me through some of the most dreadful circumstances that began to layer one on top of another. Just a hug from my furry friend slowed the flow of tears and made circumstances seem not so dire and obstacles appear not so impossible to overcome. Dogs had always done that for me, especially growing up as an only child. They protected my family and filled the lonely hours as I read to them almost every day and sometimes believed they understood.

Losing hope and believing I could no longer care for the husky, I recall vividly pulling up to the familiar dog park just before being forced to move away to another city. Opening the car door, the husky jumped out as usual and began to run freely. I naively thought of all those who had admired him over the years and trusted someone would surely pick him up and do a far better job taking care of him than I could.

As fate would dictate, just as I started to put the car in reverse, the husky came barreling through the freshly packed snow, down the hill, and towards where I had been parked. I just couldn't do it. The agony and loss was ripping my heart into shreds. The back door opened, and he jumped in the back seat of course totally oblivious to what had just been about to happen. I asked God no questions and resolved in my mind and heart that our tomorrows would somehow be handled together.

In 2010, the husky was diagnosed with a bilateral CrCl left TTA partial tear in a back leg. Grace and 'angels without wings' appeared to save the husky and me one more time. The generosity of total strangers gave me so much faith and hope in and for humanity. Their kindness was unprecedented. The headlines in the SCOOP section of the local newspaper read:

Husky's woes strike chord with many. *It's tough when your best friend is in pain. Harder still to know what would make him feel better, if only finances didn't get in the way. But add a burglary and the death of a parent. The injured Siberian husky is healing thanks to more than 30 people who donated about $2,500 to his surgery. He's back* *home so should be a welcomed sight around town in the next couple of weeks,"* wrote a former journalist.

Despite life's curveballs, I would be right by my companion's side, balancing the responsibility of making his re-hab bearable while also trying to maintain my sanity and do good work in an antagonistic work environment. I would fight with every ounce of love and strength I had left in me directed toward his survival. Within a few months, we seemed to have fallen back into step with our morning walks and Sundays and holidays in the Plaza. But then it became difficult for my friend to climb the iron steps up to our apartment and my back ached every day as I leaned over to assist and lift his 100-pound body. I didn't mind. I would endure the pain for him. We had overcome just about every crisis imaginable for a dog and its human cohort. We were warriors and we were in this fight together. Few things in life had given me the kind joy and frankly <u>sorrow</u> as my relationship with dogs, especially the husky . . . a reminder of the goodness and grace of God.

The husky transitioned in 2016 at the age of 14. I was devastated yet so grateful for the 'good' people who gave him a second chance to live a few more years and to finally enjoy mother earth . . . the smell of the lilacs in the summer and the coolness of the overnight fallen snow in the winter that he so loved and deserved. I miss the husky and cry often when I think of his magnificent presence and the irreplaceable pride, devotion, and love aiding in the natural pumping of my heart and connected it to my soul.

What was especially encouraging was the assurance I strangely felt when fortitude and truth rose right when I touched the bottom of my ocean of sorrows . . . when things were at their all-time worst. I had heard another sermon of Bishop Jakes years ago fitting to my sentiments at the time. "Instead of asking ourselves how can I find security and happiness, we could ask ourselves, can I touch the center of my pain? Can I sit with **suffering**, both yours and mine, without trying to make it go away? Can I stay present to the ache of loss or disgrace – disappointment in all its many forms – and let it open me?" This is the trick. We all want relationships and long to love and be loved, and yet we all experience the painful disappointment of rejection, abandonment, or betrayal. This kind of **suffering** had brought my children and me some of our most intense anguish.

*Tell your heart that the fear of **suffering** is worse than the **suffering** itself. And no heart has ever **suffered** when it goes in search of its dream.* Paulo Coelho

People tend to succeed who never change their temperament of hope yet never live in a cloud. **Suffering**, it was said by Aristotle, becomes beautiful when any one bears great calamities with cheerfulness, not through insensibility but through greatness of mind (that things could always be worse). Sometimes we focus too long on trying to figure out why something didn't work out the way we wanted. The secret to joy is to keep seeking God where we doubt HE might be. Passively accepting my sadness was the same as forgetting to build upon my own potential success and happiness. The most important thing was to know how to fail . . . how to lose . . . how to go through piercing heartbreak coming out in pretty good condition . . . how to hold the pain of things happening I didn't want to happen but allowing that kind of pain, with all its rawness of vulnerability, to bring forth an opportunity for something new and grand.

From the 14th of December 2012, Newtown, Connecticut would never be the same. **Suffering** from this horrific loss family loved ones, caring friends, strangers, and decent citizens were shaken to the core. Buried on a few partials of land in this quaint, beautiful eastern town are most of the 20 innocent children and 6 adults. The shock and painful incredulity made us all grieve and cry for the lost babies and caretakers; pray for the first responders and the other children who would have to return to school one day and try to perform as normal . . . especially for the parents and loved ones where ***suffering*** could never be described in words . . . only when the flow of tears had gradually slowed and just a little bit of the sorrow had subsided. What happened to those children and the dedicated educators who tried to save them was brutal. How could anyone, including President Obama, try to explain? But what we did know was these children . . . their heavenly voices . . . had given all who knew them personally and even those of us who didn't a reason to live a purposeful and joy-filled life in their memory. Children today are crying out . . . hurting . . . angry . . . wondering why there's a debate!

    Monsters with guns did exist in our children's lives. Incidents were far too commonplace now. But we had to tell them the truth . . . that sometimes they were going to **suffer** and loved ones might not be around at the time to hug and comfort them, trying our best to make things right. How could this have happened, we all asked? I can't imagine the fear of the children who left this world never understanding why. But we also couldn't forget the cries of **suffering** from black parents whose murdered children were represented by hundreds of memorial bricks still stacking upward in a 'shack' in Chicago begun by a phenomenal woman with such a great big, caring heart. She was running out of room and the 'shack' would have to be rebuilt.

We draw our strength from the very despair in which we have been forced to live. We shall endure. Ceasar Chavez

    God promises a safe landing, not a calm passage. The road to becoming like Christ often leads through the wilderness and ends in the ***valley of weeping***. Let me now express the Divine idea in my mind, body, and affairs. The more we believe in our Divinity, the greater will be our inner strength, wisdom, and clarity. The deeper our relationship with God, the stronger we feel to withstand life's many challenges. The more centered we are in God's love, the more courageously we venture forth. When God redirects a life, it often causes pain. Some people **suffer** for being foolish while others are punished for being wise. Such an irony complicated the ancient tragedy of Job and the triumphs of David.

Again, at one of my darkest hours, Pastor Joel Osteen seemed to always come through right on schedule as a crystal-clear messenger of God. On this particular Sunday morning he talked about God's night seasons. "God doesn't always show what HE's doing but we have to 'dare to trust HIM'," the masterful theologian encouraged. Like the caterpillar first crawling on the ground, then turning upside down, weaving a cocoon, uncomfortable and in a dark transformation, a *"breakthrough"* happens. The cocoon cracks open when it's the appropriate time, and a butterfly with beautiful, colorful, fluttering wings takes flight. The **struggle** has made it strong and enables it to fly.

"Your night season is temporary," Pastor Osteen declares with certainty. "HE uses it to refine our character and teach us about true integrity and faith as HE did with Paul and Silas in prison before the earthquake that happened at midnight freed them. You wouldn't be alive if God didn't have a spectacular future ahead. Know that 'all is indeed well'. The heavens are about to open. Just like the butterfly needs adversity to become what God intends it to be, so do we."

When I hear your children speak – and speak so wonderfully (like mother like offspring) - I want to say to *you, don't think of what they've been through as something you should (or could) have saved them from. Celebrate it as what has helped make them what and who they are; made them strong; given them what they need to know about what love, compassion, and life's meaning and purpose truly are. You can't save someone from being human or from **suffering** in ways that all human beings suffer in this world (yes, even rich white people), nor should you. All you can do is love them and that's more than enough though it does pain us to see our children feel pain . . . always has, and always will. You've been in charge all along, my dear, making it happen, whether you knew it or not.* BM (2003)

I seek the power of the words "I can" and "I will". These words speak to me of victory over trials and defeat; of a commitment to my children, other children, and myself and pray for the strength to execute it; to pursue lofty and daring enterprises and of imaginative aspirations that might be out of our reach, but I can still try; and recognize the thousand and one solid impulses by which I will master hurdles in the way of my climb to the top. There is a depth of determination, resilience, decision-making, conviction, vivacity, and individuality in round, ringing tones that characterizes my faith.

Seasons do change. It's the first day of spring. 'Flowers of Blessedness' are *breaking through.* On a day of HIS choosing, a Divine revelation will surface. What has been won't always be. That has always been God's promise. The cold and barrenness of winter has passed. An elderly Abraham laughed at the absurdity of God's promise to make him the father of many nations. Jacob wrestled with his Lord over the uncertainty of what lay ahead as his soldiers reached Jericho. David openly expressed his despair and helplessness in circumstances beyond his control when he had to face a giant. Job accused God of being unjust. Now we know the truth without question. HE lay us down to sleep. Trust and HIS *love* tucks us in.

According to Dr. Henry Emmons *(The Chemistry of Joy; The Chemistry of Calm)* resilience is the power to keep going when life events bring us down. The ability to get back up again and keep going so long as we need to is the key. I've had to do this very thing most of my life often times exhausting all of my 'reserve power". "It's not that we won't **struggle** or feel sad, but rather if we are able to experience the discomfort, accept a changed reality, and go on living life with meaning and purpose." For now, I believed I could do it with HIS help. I just kept on writing, sketching, and sometimes speaking at local churches. My prayer was simple every morning: *"Thank you* for opening my eyes and letting me hear my heart beat and the melodies of my fine feathered friends; for feeling healthy; and for being assured YOU are near . . . my strength and my refuge in these times of troubles but in the midst of a multitude of blessings and wonder."

Suffering has a great deal to teach us. If we use the opportunity when it arises, suffering will motivate us to look for answers; to be better; to look better; to feel better; to pray more; and to never take joy and success for granted. Jesus encouraged us not to worry about tomorrow since today presents its own share of problems. In the weakness of stormy and unsteady emotions, we may need to settle for short steps, the wisdom of the moment, and the present reassurance of the One who says, "I will never leave you nor forsake you." Trust HIS word to be true today more than ever before. Bless us, Lord, bless us indeed for these our gifts.

German philosopher Friedrich Nichetche once wrote *. . . a person who has a why to live for can bear almost any* *how. In the **valley of weeping** and darkness, I had found a light.*

Ba'al Perazim

Chapter Nine

Letting It "Be"

Forgiveness is giving up the hope that the past could have been any different. Oprah Winfrey

Forgiveness is a process requiring honesty and courage as portrayed by a black father who stands up in a courtroom with tears streaming down his face and *forgives* the white police officer who murdered his unarmed 12-year-old son. The officer is later acquitted on the pretense he feared for his life. On June 17th, 2015, 9 beautiful, spiritual warriors, including the senior pastor of Emanuel A.M.E. Church in Charleston, S.C. left this world in one of the most gruesome hate-crime massacres ever recorded in modern day history. It wasn't the number of innocent individuals who left this world during a Bible study, but how and why they perished. *Love is always stronger than hate, so if we just love the way my mom would, then the hate won't be anywhere close to where* **love** *is.* **WE FORGIVE YOU**. Chris Singleton (mother Sharonda was one of 9 victims in the Charleston Massacre)

As broken hearts cried out and disbelief obscured any rational thinking, faithful members who had lost loved one's shocked believers around the world when they declared their *forgiveness* for the young white man who opened fire on virtuous people with personal intentions of starting a race war. But we recall the words from one of the legendary Beatles plethora of consistent Number One hits back in the 60s . . . *And when the broken-hearted people, living in the world agree, there will be an answer,* **let it be**. God asks us to be obedient and to trust . . . trust that some questions just wouldn't have an immediate answer or none at all and that's okay. Whatever the matter being addressed, it's important we forgive ourselves and forgive others. If that is the action required in order to be free, then we should want to proceed accordingly and then move on.

As I advanced rapidly into my 'winter season', I learned forgiveness would prove to be liberating . . . it happened, it's over, and now it's done. *Lord, please help me to simply* **let it go** *. . . to let it 'be'.* I had heard these words, sometimes adhered to the challenge, but I wasn't sure if 'moving on' or understanding the world as this now evil and mean place could happen as quickly as need be. I tried desperately to find my way out of the same kind of darkness on that fateful day in December in Newtown, Connecticut in 2012. It would take me some time to begin the process although I knew my task, and gladly so, was to be obedient to the law of the Divine. *Forgiveness* would always be necessary. HE never said it would be easy.

Over the past several decades, I had found myself locked in an emotionally claustrophobic space . . . like being squashed in an elevator or subway when far too many passengers were packed like sardines. The electricity suddenly goes out. I am numb but cannot give way to blackness of night. I had either overlooked or was just too obstinate to accept the fact that I personally held the key to unlocking the way to a more logical passageway toward the light . . . a pathway out of the black hole of despair and lack. It would begin by my forgiving myself and then forgiving those who had "trespassed against me". Bishop Jakes calls the opposite attitude and action - the act of an unforgiving heart - a 'defense mechanism' . . . *like drinking poison and waiting for someone else to die.* I learned through hard-knock experiences that sincere undertakings of **forgiving** were forever on-going. It was an act of contrition lodged against resistance and often requiring a lot of hard work, but it had to happen.

Even when hurt seems too great to repair, God tells us . . . "I will remove from them their heart of stone and give them a heart of flesh." **(Ezekiel 11:19)** We experience a heart of stone when we are too angry, too selfish, or too frozen by the pain others have caused us. A heart of flesh, while it may be vulnerable, is compassionate. This heart sees that while we are feeling severe distress, the other person may also be hurting for the pain they have caused us. On the contrary, I always believed those who 'trespassed against us' knew exactly what they were doing and the degree of hurt they were inflicting. Perhaps that was not always the case.

It is true people need to be held accountable for their actions. But these people also need patience from us and I needed patience from God. Practicing patience with another and holding on to the hope and vision for a relationship with them is a demanding task. It is indeed a true act of kindheartedness and unselfish regard. Wisdom dictates I invite the Lord into the journey and ask for the courage it will take to be good-natured with others and embrace the understanding needed to see they too are working through the pain that needs forgiveness.

In journalist Nicole Weisensee Egan's (February 2016) *People Magazine* article "Napalm Girl: Finding Forgiveness" (with Associated Press photographer Nick Ut's Pulitzer Prize winning photograph), the brave survivor, Kim Phuc, proudly chronicled . . . "I've learned how to move on, how to cope, and I'm thankful," she says. On June 8, 1972, 9-year-old Kim Phuc couldn't help but stare. Napalm bombs were accidently being dropped on a South Viet Nam temple where she and her family were seeking refuge from the North Vietnamese during the Viet Nam war.

In that moment, a bomb landed on Kim's left shoulder and neck and over the back of her body, igniting as they touched her skin. She was burned over 65% of her body. Doctors gave up giving Kim a 100% chance of dying. She was angry, bitter, and full of hatred while suffering debilitating agony from her injuries. Converting to Christianity when she was 19 brought her a peace and joy she now shares with others around the world as an inspirational speaker. Her message is one of "love, hope, and *forgivenes's*". She teaches everyone if that little girl in the award-winning photo could learn how to *forgive*, we most certainly had no excuse. I have been inspired by her message.

Forgiveness is defined as 'giving to that which is prior before our present moment and the gifts of your future'. But the idea of *forgiveness* meaning sins are washed away is one of the reasons why some might shy away from any manner of amnesty. We surmise forgiveness means forgetting and that feels wrong and unfair. Sometimes we feel we need our resentments to educate us about the people in our circle and in the world; that we require a list of animosities to guide us in ways we should respond to particular individuals and circumstances. We feel like we need our memory of past hurts, so we can maintain boundaries with people. But the Lord is all-knowing and mercy itself—therefore, there must be a way for knowing and forgiveness to exist together . . . a clear-headed clemency that forgets nothing but forgives all.

Here's one way of thinking about it: how might it feel to look at someone who has hurt us and not feel anger? Is this even possible? That's how angels are described . . . "those who have charity hardly notice the evil in another person, and instead notice all the goods and truths that are his; and on his evils and falsities they place a good interpretation. Of such a nature are all angels, it being something they have from the Lord who bends everything evil into good." (*Secrets of Heaven* 1079)

    I am aware people can be drawn back into an attitude of indignation or feelings of betrayal believed conquered a long time ago. We might run into a former love interest or friend who has not changed and knows exactly what button to push in order to change our mood from happy to sad. Once again, we're disappointed because our having a productive, enjoyable relationship moving forward appears not a priority nor feasible. **Let it go.** Remind yourself you are worthy of good thoughts and deeds; wise enough to use your time and energy wisely; and protective of your heart from those who wish hurt feelings or harm upon you. Often the way we keep multiplying mercy is through the actions we take to demonstrate our inner freedom and David-like faith. We give ourselves this gift of redemption when we understand the perpetrator is not exonerated but the victim is set free.

    When one finds themselves starting to go back to those familiar thoughts and feelings of malice and vengeance do think on God's words. "Whom the Son sets free, is free indeed". Think of something pleasant and peaceful. Just don't let your mind go back to that dark place. Continually ask the Lord to heal you and to help you *"let it be."* To just say we're not going to think those thoughts anymore won't do. The more we do this (like exercising a muscle), the less time it will take to make the menacing thoughts go away. Eventually these obstacles will rarely enter our minds.

    Forgiveness does not mean we are excusing or condoning bad behavior. It is like cleaning out a wound. If it isn't cleansed early, it festers, hurts, and it doesn't heal properly. Once the bad stuff is removed, it can mend itself. When the soreness has subsided, there might be a scar but it won't hurt as badly. So that means *forgiveness* is for us. It's not for the person that wronged us. It's to set us free. It's so we are not held prisoner paying the price for someone else's wrong doing. Often the person who has hurt us feels nothing . . . no shame, guilt, or remorse. The wrong doer may even have forgotten the event, but we can stay trapped in resentment and rage, refusing to forgive for years. It can affect our emotional, mental, spiritual, and physical well-being while the other person is absolutely oblivious to our pain. I was a victim to many unnecessary self-inflicting wounds.

To forgive doesn't mean we're ready to reconcile; to become great friends either. It might be hard to trust after one has been hurt or betrayed. And if the perpetrator is unrepentant and we're convinced they will probably repeat their bad behavior taking into consideration past incidents, then we have to set boundaries, steer clear of abuse of any kind, clear our hearts of thoughts of revenge, pray for the person to be forgiven, and then 'let it go.' We also ask a favor of the Lord. *God, I hope it's okay, but I'm handing this person over to you. I'm praying I can forgive them and they can forgive me if I've done something wrong. I want to be free, so I'll let it be between You and them.*

The business of *forgiveness* is about re-budgeting our energy supply and attention span toward something other than what happened to us in the past. There's no one size fits all formula for **forgiveness**. For each of us, the struggle will be individual. But I've found forgiveness to be the key to genuine freedom. It releases us from the bitterness and resentment that might otherwise destroy us. The crying eased up the day I forgave myself and became confident God had done the same . . . that I had truly opened my heart to HIS love and *grace* and the *forgiveness* of others.

For some reason, we believe others are affected by our experience of remaining upset, hurt, or angry. Once we accept no one else is going to get us out of the messes we find ourselves in, we stop kissing frogs looking for a magic prince to come rescue us. Instead, jump right in to working out solutions for the problems. As Dr. Phil McGraw always says . . . *name it and claim it!* List the hurts; the resentments; and past debts and transgressions. Ask God to forgive you for not wanting to forgive others and to forgive yourself. Be confident in Divine promises that these arcs in your journey are behind you and you are at liberty to enjoy a different kind of life now. Our prayers for redemption and restoration must be sincere and consistent and could be answered in ways we could never imagine.

In the case of continued racism, *forgiveness* for the audacity others have to hate and want to return to the way "America used to be" (the white oppressor and the black oppressed) is a difficult one. What do we tell our children who have no control of gender or ethnicity but who might have to study or listen to conservative media that insist blacks make an issue of race because they just won't 'let it be'; that the race should forget but respect the past and then stop using race as an excuse? Tell that to the family of Stephon Clark, young Black man shot in his grandmother's backyard with 8 bullets in his back. What do we tell our 'charcoal children' when they face what Bishop Jakes refers to as "atrocious miscarriages of justice" (e.g. miseducation; poverty; hunger; low self-esteem; jail cells; and a lack of exposure, opportunity, belonging, and hope) in violation of all reasonable consciousness"? "Somebody needs to talk to us about *forgiveness* before we destroy everything that's important in the process of proving a point," he declared.

Every twenty-four hours, God has a fresh new supply of grace, favor, wisdom, and *forgiveness*. We learn to take the good with the bad; be pleasant, appear happy, and smile even when our heart is breaking, and we are sad, feeling down and hopeless; and have no regrets once we have become wiser by lessons learned from our misdeeds. Things will go wrong, and people will change. We will too. But as we issue out our "I'm sorry(s) and turn away from dead ends, we seek open roads towards forgiveness. We find that life does go on and there are always tickets for the second show left at the will call window in our names.

Sometimes, it's really difficult to forgive our own shortcomings. We feel really awful when we've let ourselves and other people down. But one day, we have to develop a little amnesia and allow the sun to shine again in the darkest valleys of our hearts. There's a huge difference between blame and responsibility. To deserve blame, we must have intended our actions or recklessly disregarded their consequences. By contrast, responsibility simply means we were in control. Accountability or responsibility does not imply intent or thoughtlessness. It only says we did or allowed to be done whatever led to the outcome. I have an excellent memory and sometimes I drive myself crazy reliving past mistakes and piercing hurts. Bah humbug! I just want to get a mental bottle of white out to delete the old story of "woe is me" and replace it with . . . *let me tell you 'bout how my God is able and willing.*

By itself, energy is only a commodity until we expend it on something like moving on after the darkness has been penetrated by light. No, it won't be that easy, but it will be infinitely more productive, satisfying, and effective than clinging to the blockage siphoning off our vigor and preoccupying our thoughts for so long. Acrimony, fury, and hatred are poor tenants and never pay their rent. It's time before we run out of numbered days to evict them from our hearts and move into a clean, inviting, creative space within where we can occupy and enjoy our own life. God wants us to do that because HE knows guilt and condemnation will keep us from becoming who HE has created us to be. Salvation and Christ's love are special gifts. We don't earn it. It's freely given. There is also liberation in forgetting, too!

We move pass what the apostle Paul called the process of "forgetting those things that are left behind." Over our lifetime, the accumulated offenses of numerous perpetrators and the unintentional pain we may have caused others will eventually begin to mar our soul like graffiti sprayed painted across a wall of an abandoned building. It may be a matter of having that hard conversation we've been putting off and simply telling someone the truth about how we feel and what *forgiveness* looks like.

Know that forgiveness does not depend upon someone else saying "I'm sorry". Pray that God's love liberates those forgiving and being forgiven . . . and then we're able to forgive ourselves. Writer Bryant H. McGill pens . . . *There is no love without **forgiveness**, and there is no **forgiveness** without love.* Eventually we learn that forgiveness is a powerful act of self-love and self-discovery. The action does not erase the memory of an experience but can and will neutralize its impact. Re-examine your approach to the painful infringement and consider alternative possibilities in rectifying the issue. Then pray, *Lord, please help me to simply "let it be".*

Taking BIG Steps towards *Forgiveness*

- ➤ We must first acknowledge we made a mistake and that it is an incident requiring attention quickly.

➢ It's not a crime to make mistakes. The penalty is when we continue to think our actions were okay and assume no one was hurt in the process.

➢ It's important to examine the impact our actions had on the victim or us. Be honest and willing to accept the consequences. It is sometimes easier to overlook the dormant impact when the immediate one is so big and dominating.

➢ Remember, no one is perfect. Be kind to yourself and others. We're going to do some things right and with good intentions and then we're going to do some things wrong maybe for the right reasons. It doesn't make what happened excusable, but it does leave room for us to accept our imperfections and shortcomings and try to improve.

➢ Devise a response to your troubling heart rather than simply reacting to an incident or words that are piercing. We can't go stuffing our feelings in some hole someplace because feelings buried alive don't die.

In a flash of a moment, I realize there is no separation. Life is truly circular. Karma! What goes around really does come around. Forgiveness opens our mind and heart, so we can recognize the healing opportunity when it shows up. That means we can't live outside of ourselves. We must look within and identify the garbage. Whether it is fear or hostility or shame or guilt or whatever it is, we've got to clean up the stuff muddling our vision and our true heart's desires.

If we fail to accept this law and continue to perceive the world and react to it as a victim . . . adamant in the belief that we are "right" so the problem can't possibly be our fault

... we won't be able to move up from where we are and get to where we need and want to be. If we don't disarm our precious egos, sometimes compromise on our viewpoints, and maybe adjust our attitude when definitely called for, then we can't possibly create meaningful and lasting changes in our lives.

We are a mass of energy; that's why we get tired ... that's why we have to go to sleep so that we can refuel and re-energize. And I would think if we spend all our time energizing what has happened in our past, it begs to question. If we energize our history, what will we have left for our future? If we continue to expend all our fuel on the sometimes-rough road we've traveled, we'll have an empty gas tank and have little hope of circumstances changing and a few dreams being realized. It's imperative we relinquish the heavy bags and the mental children of resentment, deep-seeded grudges, and pure disdain. Look at the positive side of it all. Those that wrestle with us strengthen our nerves and sharpen our skills. Our antagonists become our assistants helping to reinforce our stamina.

Forgive "you" for all of the unkind, unloving, unsupportive things you have thought about yourself. Ask yourself what you "could have" done with the time and energy you poured like oil flooding into a gulf by comparing yourself to someone else ... grumbling over actions which you had no control? What chances were poisoned by that wasted energy? Now is the time to decide where we're going to direct this attention that was being poorly utilized by keeping our ire and frustration alive. Now is the time to be happy and strong as we praise and give thanks to the Giver of Light.

Guilty as charged. I am even more addicted to *Law & Order*, *CSI*, and *NCIS repeats*. These crime-and-punishment dramas support our beliefs that everyone and everything must be judged. For every crime, there must be a punishment. On any given day, we are all judge and jury in the cases we build or hold on to in our minds. In the realm of consciousness, a judgment is a classification. It is a thought that classifies people and things as right or wrong, good or bad, or fair or unfair when measured against what we believe.

At the core of all judgments there is the belief that things are not as they should be, as we want them to be, or need for them to be, but they are what they are. Sometimes the things we detest and judge in others mirror the very things we cannot accept about ourselves. It is the power of love and restored faith that opens our hearts to *forgiving* those who tried to rob us of that freedom. It doesn't mean we like what they said or did, but it does say forgiving them will assure we're okay to move forward with our lives and that God's love is ever present even in the midst of chaos and hardships.

Bearing with one another, and *forgiving* one another, if anyone has a complaint against another; even as Christ forgave you, so you also must do. **Col 3:13**

We each have unique purposes in life designed by our Creator. That purpose carries with it the responsibility of obedience and letting go. Forgiveness caps the leak in our own energy enabling us to stop the damage it can cause; minimizes the peripheral damage that's a given; and ultimately restores us to the infusion of momentum denied to our dreams by the emotional and physical drain on our heart and soul. Forgiveness is truly between God and HIS warriors. Unfinished business . . . issues passed down from generation to the next that linger in our lives . . . impedes progress and the goodness of heaven sent *grace*. There is no need to forgive what's behind us if we aren't going to embrace what is before us.

Let us birth something more worthy of our attention, all the minutes and hours. Let's prepare for the future by making ourselves available for the next opportunity waiting just around the corner. Isn't it time to unwrap the present we've always carried around? Each generation has the ability to choose: stay the same and continue the pattern or be so contradictory to what has been passed down that others won't know who you are. There are these intricate pathways in our lives that intersect and bridge young and seasoned. Our children pray we get it right, so they can be released, and we can be healed.

It's a fact we can't change the past, we can't change others to be who we want them to be, and we can't work on changing ourselves by ourselves. Prayer and asking God to help us forgive provides the space for HIM to come into our hearts and move aside the indignation we feel towards those who have hurt us. Each time we forgive, it paves the way for the next time we need to forgive.

Be available for what's next. Step out of the box and embrace the life of blessings God has always had in store for us all. It's about immersing ourselves in the flood of fulfillment that has been blocked by the dam of past disappointments. It's about turning our head around from looking behind us, to realizing where we are right now, and then looking forward to the future.

What the world needs now is . . . *love*

The sheer truth that you are a soul who has a body makes you worthy and deserving of love. Hill Harper (actor/author)

I love the ingenious writing of some of the high-tech, modern day television commercials, especially the one where the father at a school bus stop is so apprehensive about letting his precious daughter go. The depth of love is so powerful and real shown in the worried lines across his brow. Everyone needs someone to love them that intensely . . . like the characters Fitz and Olivia on the popular (recently ended) television series *Scandal* or Yuri and Lara in one of my all-time favorite movies, *Dr. Zhivago*. I know I certainly do, but perhaps it might be a tad bit too late for me. I am a realist. Love's what's been missing for most of my journey and probably for a lot of others, as well.

I fondly recall the powerful impact the story of former Bernstein High School (Hollywood, CA) Coach Masaki Matsumoto had on me when I first saw the ESPN interview six years ago. I often wonder where some of these fine young men ended up on the success and happiness ladder. Another football story about how 'love' changed the lives of sons and parents all of whom faced the harsh reality of urban poverty every day. I just sat there watching and thinking more parents should hear about this free power of 'love' no matter their personal or career status.

As a long time, educator, single parent, and forever sports enthusiast, I applauded Coach Matt's simple formula for re-directing his players' raw talents and passion for the sport while inspiring them to reach for the heights with confidence and faith: LOVE – that's what it's all about! The gridiron leader sadly admitted that many of his young players didn't feel they mattered and some didn't have a family to go home to. "They have no motivation to stay in school or make good grades."

After sending a letter to the parents/guardians of each of his players encouraging them to in turn write a letter to their son(s) expressing their *love* and pride in what their offspring had achieved in the face of so many odds, life changed drastically for all involved. Success knocked at their locker room door and champions emerged. Year after year, young men whom society had counted out became their own heroes. "Confidence comes from knowing you've put in the work . . . that you gave it all you had even when things didn't go your way," the coach would tell his hopeful players. For the first time, these deserving students (some participating in the 'Second Chance' program offered by the school) began to excel in 'life' . . . in the classroom, on the playing field, and as a role model for others all motivated by the letters and later actions of their parents. (E:60 Pictures 2012)

Things were different now that there was someone else besides Coach Matt that truly cared about them. But this passionate 'leader among young men' was the one who taught those who had the good fortune to pass his way how to love themselves. In many of my keynote addresses, I never fail to use a quote I read once that summed up this impressive coach's philosophy . . . *Having a mother (a parent) who knows your heart, supports your dreams, and shares your journey is the greatest gift in the world.* Let there be LOVE and light to heal our children's broken hearts and our country's divide.

No one is born hating another person because of the color of his skin or his background or his religion. People must learn to hate and if they can learn to hate, they can be taught to love. It is only through education that we find the wisdom to trade hate for compassion. Nelson Mandela

Real Love . . .

- sometimes means allowing others the painful lessons of their own life experiences, just as we experience and grow from our own.

- changes our viewpoint when we seek the help of others who can love us, see us clearly, and help us see ourselves for who we are.

- can move us from a place of fear, anger, and loneliness to a condition of peace and happiness. Add courage and a heart willing to open one more time.

- is becoming wise because we feel love and we have decided to share that love with others.

- requires us to come forward when there is a need.

- is about someone's happiness without any concern for what we'll get for ourselves and without any standard that must be met by the person we love.

- doesn't mean loving someone because they are intelligent or looks good, or because they can do something for us. I am and receive 'real love' because everyone needs to be loved.

- knows that in order for a relationship to work, partners should share similar values, interests, and goals, and who each have a capacity for intimacy. Each knows they are indeed worthy of the best life has to offer.

- is experienced when we have seen the worst in a person and have not forsaken them. This is the love our heavenly Father has for us. One cannot run from the only answer there is to the questions of life. This is not the kind of love one would seek from humankind.

- comes from that man like Jesus, the Lover of our souls. This love is the love that God gives to compensate the thirsting heart that has drunk from the waters of humankind's hollow promises. It is the brook we come to when no other has quenched the thirstiness of our lives. It is the cool, refreshing knowledge of a love that calms our desperate cravings and clinging.

- calls for humankind never to become bitter as we rummage through relationships, looking for Divine love from human hearts. Trust God wait on HIS blessings and HIS timing, and we will have the kind of blessings that add no sorrow.

- is not when I do what you want, and you like me. It's 'real love' only when I'm flawed and foolish – when I get in your way and don't do as you wish – but you don't feel disappointed or irritated with me. If we are empty and afraid, not only can we not see the needs of others, but we can't recognize the truth about our own behavior.

- does not need someone else to make us happy. It is 'real love' when you care about others happiness without any expectation of return for yourself. Say something kind and supportive. Touch them gently on the hand. Look them in the eye as you speak. As we pour out 'real love', it somehow multiplies miraculously, and it leaves us with more than we had originally.

And now abide faith, hope, love, these three; but the greatest of these is love. **I Cor. 13:13**

The best relationship is one in which people's love for each other exceeds their need for each other . . . to accept one another without trying to change them to meet our own needs and to realize that we don't have to be needed in order to feel worthy. Sometimes we won't' share who we really are because we're afraid people won't like us, and then we'll feel unloved and alone. But as soon as we hide who we are, we can guarantee we'll feel unloved and alone again.

Some people will resist our love no matter how hard we try but we have no right to expect everyone to accept that which we offer. When one demands the kind of love someone cannot give at the time, they will gradually shut down and maybe go away. Letting go of a destructive relationship is hard but is necessary and can happen without experiencing disabling depression. Supportive friends, family, and healthy interest can be the antidote to the personal pain of hurt and betrayal.

Know that God's grace is sufficient for your needs and your scars. HE provides the Divine glue. We learn valuable lessons through the process . . . that it's okay to be open and trusting with good people as long as we don't expose ourselves to the exploitation of those who are not interested in our well-being. But then often times it's easier to believe we have the good qualities we don't because then we don't have to make the effort to change. In order to genuinely care about the happiness of other people, we must remember they cannot feel loved and happy without telling the truth about themselves. No one ever told us about the importance of belonging to ourselves. Aloneness is the condition most painful to us. Those without love attack only because they are empty and afraid.

Extraordinary challenges have been overcome by ordinary people who love God and appreciate themselves.

Be grounded in the presence of the Lord and identify proudly as a child of the Most High. Be a model for the heart knowledge you know to be true. Know always God is good and God is **love**. Believe as an unalterable, incontrovertible truth that all that is not good and all that is not of the nature of *love* is not of God's creation. Love thinketh no evil. Out of these two great fundamentals will grow all that is necessary to make the whole of one's life complete, beautiful, and perfect. And ever has it been that love knows not its own depth until the hour of separation.

*I'm not perfect but through it all I have learned how to hold firm in a storm not by holding on to whatever I can find for as long as I can, but by trusting the one thing that matters in this world that will never let go of me. That's what 'perfect love' is. Perfect love casts out all that pain . . . all that fear . . . and replaces it with **hope**.* Signed, Sealed, and Delivered for Christmas (Hallmark)

Trust what your heart tells you. Sometimes you might have to stand while others are sitting – have a voice while others are silent but then you can look back upon your life and know that the moments when you were truly alive were the moments when you did things in the spirit of **love**. If we desire to do well in the world, let us begin to love humanity . . . to realize more truly the great dominant note that sounds in every mortal despite all the discords of life, the great natural bond of unity that makes all men brothers and sisters.

Love is the wondrous angel of life that rolls away all the stones of sorrow and suffering from the pathway of duty. If there are holes in our hearts needing to be covered, we should safeguard them with *love*. Love is far more than just being sentimental. It is indeed a way of life. Simply pray for more courage and kindness and a little bit of magic. But remember, people don't have to be nice. There are unfortunately many mean and cruel people in this world.

Some live in big houses. Those residents have never accepted that love is a choice.

I couldn't allow the fear that God wasn't close, wasn't passionately caring, was intentionally trying to keep me from seeing the sunrise spilling ***love*** all over the world, and purposely taking my blessings away. I believe our lives are intended to be infinitely richer and more abundant than they are at present. For now, I would dream and believe the day would come when I would live on this earth like it was heaven; that I would dance like David danced, at times as if no one was watching; that I would sing songs of praise like Mary as if only God was listening; and that I would love for the first time like I could never be hurt again.

I like living. I have sometimes been wildly, despairingly, acutely miserable, racked with sorrow, but through it all I still know quite certainly that just to be alive is a grand thing.
Agatha Christie

Chapter Ten

Ya' Know, Father, I'm Good!

God, I have prayed for years. I have done everything I know to do in order to see my dreams come true. I have had seasons of working hard and seasons of "letting go and letting God" and, still, the things I have believed You for seem like they will never happen. I have had one disappointment after another. And it's almost too late. I feel like Sarah – like it is impossible for me to ever hold the one thing I long for most. God, do not let me miss my destiny! But do not let me hope for things that are not a part of Your plan for my life. Bishop T.D. Jakes

      A favorite, gorgeous young commercial actor always made me smile when he fantasized about driving a big car like his Dad. With his buddies watching in amazement from the sidelines, he imagines many of the joys and frustrations associated with the privilege of being behind a steering wheel he can barely see over. He decides driving on the busy city streets and coming within minutes of getting a parking ticket after his grocery bag filled with oranges burst from the bottom and spills all over the ground wasn't much fun, at least for the time being. He was putting himself in places he wasn't prepared to be or shouldn't be at all. **"Ya know, I'm good,"** he tells his Dad as he drives away in a play car just his size. I utter the same words to the Lord whenever I feel alone and dejected, and when there are moments I get scared and fight to steer my mind on something more positive, happier, and productive. "I'm good, Father. I really am . . . and by the way, thank you!"

Most people who really knew me felt I had a lot of nerve moving into this strange town where I knew one person I had befriended on-line. I had visited this mesmerizing place every summer beginning as a soon-to-be kindergartner fascinated by the brick streets and the natives selling their wares on the street corners. Each year, I became more and more intrigued by the hundred(s) year old architecture and the powerful mystical ambiance that emboldened the people present at the time. This place was even more exciting than Disneyland or the 1962 World's Fair for me. The only thing missing was the ocean. It was this fascinating place where I didn't have to feel that piercing hurt when a white kid would wait for the next time the Ferris wheel came around to keep from sitting next to me.

It wasn't until I was an adult that I would be able to spend more than just a few days with each visit. After the blows I took from an estranged extended family after my mother's passing, it was a place I could hide, have time to try and grieve, and to gain strength to survive the next day and the next as I did when I first came into the world. I had an urgent need for a plan of action but mainly a *miracle*. Empty and alone, it was the husky . . . his magnificence and unconditional love . . . that gave me so much pride, hope, and solace. This was the kind of place where one could become absorbed in a stroke of good luck, or get chewed up, spit out, and shown the out-of-town route. Sadly, the latter would happen to me with two failed attempts.

For years, I had read every magazine article and book I could find (especially old *National Geographic*) on this Southwestern region and its native and Spanish history and culture. I dreamed of one day living in this place I would describe as another world . . . a powerfully enchanting little corner of the country. To eventually live there and work on the pueblos and in rural school districts was such an honor and for many years a blessing constantly prayed for. It was exciting, rewarding work with so many beautiful children, passionate educators, and loving parents. Neighborly and community unity in support of their children's education complemented high expectancy, the integration of generational history and culture, and rendered exemplary achievements for students and for schools. These were some of the rare academic laboratories where I witnessed, without a doubt, 'real learning' taking place. But I was alone; the focus of daily workplace mobbing; and totally and painfully out of balance. I couldn't enjoy the rewards of my hard work because my heart was always broken, and I never knew when the next insult or assault would occur.

This number (71) seems so strange to me now and I often become quite sad. The summer and autumn seasons had disappeared in the ravages of so much loss and voids clouding my vision; temporarily dousing my hopes and spirit; and hampering any possibilities of laughter and success. "The Committee" speaks to my heart and even my beautiful husky companion barks. I miss my canine friend. These beautiful human beings and the husky connect me to my past . . . memories from letters and photos in an old wooden trunk found in the attic of my childhood home. The words and images on the yellowing, dingy pages tell me who I am and the lineage from whence I had come. Sadly, at critical times in my life when I truly needed to connect with family, they were never there nor did they care to be but my 'true' friends were.

Like Job, instead of listening to the accusing voices, I cried unto the Lord in my trouble and HE answered me. When I lost all hope, HE snatched me from the depths of death . . . numerous times. Hives closing my throat and cutting off the oxygen flow I so took for granted; pepper spray and the pitbulls; a speeding big rig truck crushing the husky and me in the middle of a busy Texas highway; and a burglar and a gun happening three times. It had taken my getting to the "winter season" of my life before I clearly understood I had surely been saved by *Grace* for a reason.

Many times, I felt my own 'charcoal children' and those I had the privilege of teaching over the years should perhaps have gotten "the talk" long before we shared a truth few wanted to discuss. I certainly didn't want them to suffer as I had for the lack of street/color/class/relationship common knowledge. We all would have benefitted from being provided psychological counseling on how to navigate and survive being black and living in a white world of entitlements. I also wanted my children to understand I was human and to be human was to sometimes err. I was fending off *satan's* blows alone while trying to give them more than I should. Still, despite the treacherous personal and professional trek for some of us, many 'chocolate baby boomers' and their offspring have had a surprising measure of success and some of us did quite well without integration.

Like their grandparents had hoped, I wanted my children to have the best education possible in a state-of-the-art facility with knowledgeable and passionate instructors, especially at the university level. Unfortunately, my desires for their brighter future came at a hefty price. Their mother had witnessed 'white flight' from its beginnings in the 50s and then watched as a white college fraternity rode on horseback through the streets of a well-known college town brandishing confederate uniforms and waving confederate flags in the late 60s. This shocking event would result in the spark setting off a firestorm of serious activism . . . fighting on the front lines right after the King murder.

A painful guilt ate away at my heart attempting to rationalize why I would place a martyr role in my children's life paths 30 years later . . . that they would experience the same frightening images of that same racist flag and suffer the same cruel and bigoted intentions of the flag and now torch bearers. Daddy would say I had caused them unnecessary 'suffering' by enrolling them in predominantly white schools, living in predominantly white neighborhoods, and starting tennis lessons for my youngest child at 5. He would tell me I should learn to stay in my place. I would add to our father/daughter estrangement by asking, 'what place is that'?

God had heard and answered my mother's prayers. The plane traveling 1,500 miles had landed safely and there was enough money to pull all the celebratory festivities together. People had come from around the country . . . those who had known my child for years; those that admired the courage and determination it took to survive and come out victorious despite suffering through incidents of the unthinkable at times. This college experience would not be as joyful and meaningful as most students having the opportunity of building on their knowledge base and planning an exciting career. It was a war of black/white and class ideologies; dangerous and brazen bigotry; and a test of 'wills' sealed in a mother's undying love, support, and prayers.

One might wonder whether the accomplishment of earning a degree was worth the painful price my youngest child had to pay in the four years she would have to walk pass the Confederate flag displays on her way to class every day; the fear she endured walking home from the library at night with her finger on a can of pepper spray and the other on aa switchblade knife she would have to carry on her person for fear of a Skinhead attack; and the lack of coaching and team support that broke her heart and should have caused her to quit. Sheer guts, tenacity, and a willful determination to overcome and fulfill the promise she had made her grandmother propelled her to achieve her goals. We all prayed Mama would live long enough to see the degree in her grandchild's hand, so she would be able to transition in peace.

On that June day, 2003, we would make merry and not worry about what sad events we might have to face the next day or the next. We all knew the end was near. I try to catch my breath. I look into my mother's eyes and know she is dying. I cannot reach her soul or let her know how much I love her and how sorry I am. The heartache and tears block my saying 'thank you'. The cancer is razing her body and there is nothing I can do to stop it. She has held on just long enough to realize her dream of this day.

I watch my father and know his mind is slowly slipping away into the grips of one of the meanest diseases ever. Still there is no doubt in my still clear mind he realizes his soulmate is leaving and he wants to go with her. If only there had been a brother or a sister to lighten the grief and responsibility . . . who could have truly understood what I was going through and could have helped in making important decisions. I was weary and lost but adamant in playing out my role as mother and daughter and doing what I had to do for the days ahead of sole obligations. I hadn't quite recovered from the last *satanic* rampage.

Somewhere out there, a tall palm tree is swaying in the midst of a fierce storm. The tree might bend all the way down to the ground for quite some time, but it will soon stand straight and tall once the winds and rains have subsided. At this very moment in our current existence, a misty waterfall is cresting a cliff and the sands of beaches shift under many feet. We struggle to stand tall like the amazing palm tree. Our hearts are so broken, and our souls torn asunder. September 11th, 2001.

My first born was alone and devastated some 3,000 miles away and walking across the Brooklyn Bridge with thousands of others. The World Trade Center towers had crumbled behind them. The air was full of heavy grey soot, cement and metal chips, and shirt sleeves were covered with grime and sticky wet tears. When the second plane hits, there was no communication. I was numb with fear and disbelief. Life now seemed so surreal and uncertain. I kept imagining the fear my child must be enduring with all the rest of stunned citizens of a once free world. This could not be happening, I thought – not on American soil.

Terrified, innocent people are in the middle of it all – death; sirens; flashing red and yellow lights; fire trucks and police cars at every intersection; mounds of rubble strewn about; and painful cries of loss and devastating shockwaves. A budding acting career is cut short. The lights on Broadway would not shine bright for quite some time. All lights out – NYC 2002 – the very next year! I tell my child how sorry I am but how blessed they are. In all the upset, pain, and sorrow (along with the anger that my students had no clue as to where Afghanistan was on a world map or anything about Muslims or radical terrorists of all nationalities), I foolishly failed to thank the Lord for sparing my child.

I thought of my beloved late mother today more than usual. Somehow, I felt I had come to the exact place where she probably was though my path had not been nearly as unforgiving and unkind. Seldom, if ever acknowledged, was internalized emotional and 'lack' demons haunting her most of her life. Often frustrated because she felt few of her **prayers** had been answered after the loss of four babies and sadly watching the man she had loved most of her life writhe in his brokenness, she internalized her agonies and said very little.

My father was a black man coming of age in the 30s and 40s and wanting so much more for his family and his mother. Even in his weekend and holiday inebriated dispositions or my mother's broken heart that radiated through her eyes and silence, they both still kneeled every night on their respective side of their small bed and prayed. They always worshiped. For their only offspring, it took some mind and heart readjustments to get to a point of being that forgiving and to understand the process of surviving as a 'charcoal child' in a selfish and vicious white world. Now that I have been blessed to be living in my 'winter season' and have indeed experienced a roller coaster ride on most of my days, I look forward to spending quality time smelling the roses and appreciating all of the ***flowers of blessedness***.

Become the master of yourself. Operate your days flowing gracefully and with as much poise and depth of being as possible. Prepare for opportunity never denying the King of Glory a seat right beside you. HIS presence and mercy will keep doubt, fear, and apprehension from locking the gates of your heart and preventing all the good that is possible. There might be times you will struggle in silence and could be uncomfortable for a season or two, but in the meantime, remain constructive in the maintenance of your mind, body, and soul. While in waiting, be happy anyway. I learned long ago that as long as humankind has a dream in their heart, they can keep saying to the Lord, *Ya know Father, I'm good. I really am.*

Believing I still had a meaningful purpose, I prayed God would give me time to fulfill it. I long to give others hope and bring a smile to their hearts. On those late August and early September middle of the night early morning hours, I flip on CNN news watching the horrid happenings after Hurricane Harvey, Irma, and Maria while also remembering the blatant ugliness of humankind during Hurricane Katrina and my heart breaks as I watch the children hoisted on the shoulders of Coast Guard seamen and volunteers and grown folks clinging to plastic bags containing the few irreplaceable valuables, documents, and pets they could grab quickly. They report they are happy to be alive . . . to have survived the floods having been rescued when others were not . . . but now, where will they go? What will they do? How will they start all over again?

As I walk down the street, I hear people arguing. Their voices get louder and then someone screams. It's the same day they find two more bodies in the mudslides having happened in an instant and in many cases without warning. Shut up! I say silently to the people I hear at a distance. How dare you complain and be so ugly to one another when there is so much sadness and sorrow all over the country and the world. Count your blessings and just say 'thank you' God for my day and the pancakes and milk I just had for breakfast.

It would be so unappreciative of me to choose to shut the open door through which "all blessings flowed". No remaining idle or doubtful, living a life unworthy of a child of God. If we fall into that pit, we have no one to blame but ourselves. I would seek the good in the Now making my present task so pure with faithful and whole-hearted endeavors. All things bend to those who conquer self. Author, television personality, and spiritual guru Iyanla Vanzant challenged me, and I'm sure many others, when she wrote . . . *There is no greater battle in life than the battle between the parts of you that want to be healed and the parts of you that are comfortable and content remaining broken.* I would fight to heal by gluing the broken pieces together and making my life stand for something more.

There was a great poster I saw on-line one day that read . . . Philippians 4:13 – **I can do all things through Christ who strengthens me.** *The road to success is not straight. There is a curve called failure; a loop called confusion; speed bumps called friends; red lights called enemies; and caution lights called family. You will have* *flats called jobs.* But if you have a spare called determination; an engine called perseverance; insurance called faith; and a driver called Jesus, you will make it to a place called success. I look forward to the day.

Chasing Rainbows

Pursuing happiness is like chasing a rainbow. The faster we go, the harder we try, the farther off it becomes. I have learned that happiness is not a pursuit – it's a choice. Happiness is a state of mind, obtainable at any time, in any moment of your choosing. Darren Hardy – SUCCESS publisher and editorial director

Happy is the man who dwells not long as the purely natural man, but is early transformed into the spiritual, and so in whom the Divine Word becomes incarnate. Accepting the truth that there are things we simply don't understand (but God does) is the ticket to our freedom. Cultivating wonder grows gratitude and being in thanksgiving yields much joy.

We are in charge of our own **happiness** but most often our options are quite limited. Children are a true blessing with the exception sometimes when you're a black mother and your offspring are most likely to be raised in poverty and fatherless; to be unsuccessful in school because many children in underserved neighborhood schools are being mis-educated; or are likely to be victims of violence, conspicuous discrimination, or a number in the criminal pipeline (victim or perpetrator). And the ones not in any of these categories trying to earn degrees or succeed in industries long having their doors shut to people of color, especially women and wondering what they could possibly be doing wrong when they have given their assignments their very best.

Happiness is like those palaces in fairy tales whose gates are guarded by dragons: we must fight in order to conquer it.
Alexandre Dumas "The Count of Monte Cristo"

It is by making active choices in our lives that might include friendships, careers, education, hobbies, family relationships, and other interests and passions that could make or break our happiness zone. The more options we have, the more ability we have to change the direction of our journey to being unreasonably overjoyed. All unhappiness comes from a lack of power . . . the void of a necessary connection to the Infinite Source bringing forth contentment, financial freedom, marketable skills, and increased academic prowess; a higher level of spiritual connection; a confident and suitable presence; a grateful demeanor; and a healthy lifestyle. Sometimes it's the energy we exert in chasing after happiness that makes us the unhappiest.

What then creates a fulfilling life? According to Holocaust survivor Viktor Frankl ("Man's Search for Meaning") there must be a fundamental change in our attitude toward life. "We had to learn ourselves and, furthermore, we had to teach the despairing men that *it did not really matter what we expected from life, but rather what life expected from us.*

- What is required is for us to stop asking about the meaning of life, and instead to think of ourselves as those who are being questioned by life – daily and hourly.

- Our answer must consist not in talk and meditation, but in right action and in right conduct never taking no for an answer when going after what we want in life.

- Life ultimately means taking the responsibility to find the right answer to its problems and to fulfill the tasks which it constantly sets for each individual; never to be identified by one's brokenness.

- Life – like music, passion, and love – requires courage and commitment. In all human affairs there are efforts and there are results and the strength of the effort is the measure of the result.

I am happiest when I first wake up. *Thank you, Lord. Another day with infinite possibilities. I'll take it!* I am happy when I approach life from a place of positive energy, desire, and enthusiasm. It took me far too long to conclude that life may be difficult; it may not be fair; but God needed me to know and accept that life is still a precious gift. I once heard a motivational speaker jokingly point out a simple reality about feeling joy. "Licking my favorite lemon sherbet ice cream cone makes me *happy*. But if someone accidently knocks the cone out of my hand, I'm no longer happy. In other words, **happiness** can be fleeting and unstable like my ice cream cone. It's really just a temporary sensation of pleasure like entertainment, a great meal, or shopping."

The love in our hearts is the divine alchemy of life, transforming all duties into privileges and all responsibilities into joys. We continue in the attitude of perfect peace, retaining this harmony of mind under every circumstance. As we do so, we retain power and a capacity and talent so we will always be equal to every occasion. It's important to remain open, honest, and honorable in all our endeavors, establishing high standards, principles, and values for ourselves and inspiring children in our charge to do the same.

In everything, we must strive to keep our word . . . completing the task at hand and honored to have the privilege. Create credibility doing what you said you would do but without the necessity to impress others or seek their approval. Stand in your personal space. It serves no purpose to dream we would be happier in some other place, in some other circumstance, or being someone else. But for many women of color, trying to reach that higher ground is sometimes a monumental task requiring God's armor and holding HIM to HIS promises without the expectation of an explanation as to why.

The problem black women (young, middle age, and seasoned) have to face in analyzing why they are or are not happy is pretty much dependent upon the adults in their lives at a young age. Children have to be advised in understanding relationships but women who haven't resolved the role of male-female relationships in their own lives may be unable to help their children with the same issues. I am quite guilty and assume responsibility for my failure to inform with candor and compassion. At the core of the problem is that nearly twice as many black women as black men graduate from college. So what are educated black women going to do when there are only half as many black men in their college classrooms or professional work environment and the other half is behind prison gates?

In his often described 'controversial' book, "Is Marriage for White People?" (How the African American Marriage Decline Affects Everyone - 2012), Stanford University law professor Ralph Richard Banks addresses one of those "I'd-never-really-thought-about-it-that-way" sad realities analyzing why black women are the most unpartnered group in our society. "The title comes from a young African American boy in Washington, D.C.," informed the author. "When a journalist visited his 6th grade class, one of the other boys said he wanted to learn about being a good father. The journalist volunteered to bring some married couples to talk about child rearing, but the boy said he wasn't interested in learning about marriage. Then his friend interjected, 'Marriage is for white people.' The boy's statement jarred me. It captured an accepted reality more poignantly than anything I had ever read, not simply the fact of the black marriage decline, but also its emotional valence. The boy's observation stirred in me a whole range of feelings, anger, sadness, and confusion."

According to Banks, Black women have the thinnest pool of partners within their race. They are the least likely to marry, the most likely to divorce and become impoverished, and have the least chance of remarriage. 1 in every 10 black men in his 30s is in prison or jail on any given day. The percentage of black children born to unwed parents exceeds 70% not because single women are getting pregnant more often, but because black women are so much more likely to be single. Any number of factors contribute to this conversation such as a high incarceration rate for black males (profiling and targeting, forcing a large majority into the system); the building of more prisons than academic institutions; the increase in gay and bi-sexual (sometimes down-low) population; and interracial dating (more black males and white females).

Recently, a beautiful bi-racial actress, humanitarian, and women's activist . . . with her stunning black mother seated proudly to one side of the gold and jeweled altar of St. George's Chapel in Windsor Castle . . . walked down the aisle on the arm of her future father-in-law and the future King of England in anticipation exchanging marriage vows with her British prince with red hair and in the presence of his beloved and esteemed grandmother, the Queen of England. Hope floated over the lives of so many young girls of color that day . . . providing the possibilities, they too could one day become a princess who falls deeply in love with a handsome prince and living happily thereafter. Fairy tales did indeed come true.

Some years ago, Jill Nelson, then *USA Today Weekend* journalist wrote about the dismal status of black women in a way few wanted to admit, let alone discuss. I wonder if this reality has changed much in 2018. "The happiest Americans are in order . . . white men, white women, Black men and, at the bottom of the happiness barrel, Black women. Most disturbing than the statistics is the fact that black women have few collective voices with funding and action behind them (more positive prospects recently) . . . organizations or leadership to address issues that make us unhappy."

We have long been demonized by politicians in the name of welfare reform and ignored by media gurus and ad agencies that once singled out blonde hair, colored eyes, and a size 4 as the only model of true beauty; to more of our share of domestic and professional violence and abuse; to the once excessive expense and inconvenience of maintaining black hair; to just being lonely. In most cases, Black women have some of the lowest salaries often for routine, unrewarding work without benefits. And yes, in 2018 they can still get fired because they refuse to straighten their natural hairstyle and they can be emotionally and psychologically damaged due to workplace mobbing precipitated by the color of their skin and having been denied exposure and fair academic and professional opportunities. Is it any wonder we're so unhappy?

Untreated mental health issues had been passed down from one generation to the next. Not only were my parents and I victims, but I was a perpetrator, as well, passing the same trauma down to my own children though intertwined with many achievements and successes. To my knowledge, therapy carried such a stigma in the black community until recently that few would ever discuss the need. I just kept on moving in spite of the numbness and the pain and my willingness to be accountable for those decisions and mistakes that were definitely in my control.

"The tragedy is that most of the time no one cares about black women, including us. Until attitudes change, nothing else can. We need to figure out how to connect our experiences as black women at home and in the larger culture and translate them into a voice and action that speaks for all of us. We need a national organization for sisters." (There has been a great beginning: October 2017 – *The National African American Women's Movement – Conversations – Atlanta, GA*)

Like one of my true heroes, Nelson Mandela, when it came to **love** and **happiness,** I too was a romantic and a realist. Wrote author Richard Stengel in his book "Mandela's Way" . . . *for much of his life, love was something distant, existing more in his imagination and memory than in reality. And when it was a reality, it was often a source of pain rather than solace. Yet he never gave up on the idea that love would be in his life.*

Happiness is a birthright but it's also ours to choose. Unless we learn the lesson of self-appreciation and practice it, we could spend our lives imitating other people and depreciating ourselves. We tie ourselves up in stuff we simply cannot control. This notion that happiness and fulfillment hinged upon radical transformation was true for where I found myself in this 'winter season'. It had been a life with hardly anyone in it . . . like a frame without a picture of a normal and blessed 'happy' family. Still, it's so good to still be here, rising every time I fall and praising the Father simultaneously for the many blessings and 'good times' in my journey I would never take for granted.

He has shown you, O man, what is good; and what does the Lord require of you but to do justly, to love mercy, and to walk humbly with your God? **Mic 6:8**

What qualities do I need to embody in order to be happy? It's not the pursuit of happiness I should concern myself with, but rather the pursuit of fulfillment and significance. If I have created a life of meaning in which I have a deep sense of purpose and value, that won't change because someone knocks my ice cream cone over. Fulfillment is a state of existence, not a fleeting passion.

I had reached a place where 'soul holes'; pains of the heart; and betrayals and losses I had consistently endured throughout my life had brought me much needed wisdom but honest emotionless. When I really needed the strength, I always drew from memories of the close relationships I once had with a few loved ones and close friends who suddenly departed from this world far too soon or disappeared from my friend and colleague circle. These great individuals . . . *the committee* . . . had taught me so many life lessons and had given me so much laughter and a feeling like I belonged at the top of their love and caring list. But they could never fill all the holes, and no one could occupy the vacuum after *the committee* members had transitioned north. My (live) and stuffed animals and white dolls looking nothing like me couldn't talk back but their unconditional love filled some of the empty spaces of my silent, rainy days.

For now, I could feel very little, but I certainly wanted to live the rest of my life doing good and pinching off a little joy. I also recognized my faith and survival had to be an example for my children . . . and other people's children . . . and someone else needing to know what I knew about *grace, forgiveness, prayer,* and *gratitude.*

- ❖ Get rid of the life you planned so you can have the life that has been waiting for you all along.

- ❖ Make aging a choice; not a challenge.

- ❖ Accept that every bridge crossed brings you closer to a higher level of fulfillment.

- ❖ Be proud of your attempts and failures; getting back up and starting all over again; refusing to give in and give up even when you can't see your progress.

- ❖ Know God relies on us to be the tangible evidence of HIS love for the world.

- ❖ Continue to be thankful for all you have while still remaining creative, innovative, thinking differently, and more positive. When life gives you 500 reasons to cry, feel sorry for yourself, and simply fade away like you never existed, show life you have 5,000 reasons to smile, know you're blessed, and be confident this too shall pass.

- ❖ Believe you can face your past without any regrets; conduct your present with certainty and a willful determination; and be fearless in approaching and preparing for your future for however many years remaining. The most beautiful thing is to see a person smiling . . . free . . . void of the luggage they have obviously been pulling behind them. Even more beautiful is the possibility you could be the reason behind the smile and the happy demeanor.

Cherish your visions; cherish your ideas; cherish the music that stirs in your heart, the beauty that forms in your mind, and the loveliness that drapes your purest thoughts for out of them will grow all delightful conditions and a heavenly environment. If you remain true to these things, your mansion will at last be built. It is the broad life; the deep life; the lofty life; and an ever-expanding life that we should seek to develop continually. If man does, day by day, the best he can by the light he has, he has no need to fear, no need to regret, and no need to worry. We can see the smile of God in everything if we look close enough. All things become mirrors reflecting the joyousness and the sweetness of warmth from on High. Darkness changes into light; pain changes into pleasure; tribulation changes into peace; adversity changes into love; and life becomes a dance like David danced in praise and honor to the Lord.

If we hold on to optimistic ideas, we can drive out pessimism . . . the great breeder of disease, failure, and misery. If we stand guard at the door of our minds, we can possibly keep out all the enemies of our happiness and potential for future achievements. "Let the mind be in you which was also in Christ" - that is the mind that gives health, peace, and *happiness* along with harmony, justice, truth, and beauty a shot at being real. Unless we live, move, and have our very being in HIM . . . unless we abide under the shadow of the Most High . . . no combination of those 'good virtues' can ever exist.

During my early morning coffee conversations with God, I would pray . . . *if it is up to me to understand my place and standing, give me the strength and foresight to push forward without fear and doubt in the precious gift of my days ahead. If I have to wait on Your time, give me patience, reinforce my faith, and protect me with your* **grace.**

Ba'al Perazim

Chapter Eleven

Flowers of Blessedness

Dear God,

*YOUR love continually inspires, renews, and prospers me. I am filled with gratitude for the **'bouquet of blessings'** in my life. Blessings keep my awareness of life's holy potential ever present. They awaken me to my true being.*
I WILL do this!

One night while watching one of my favorite television programs, *Madam Secretary*, I heard a speech line that appropriately summed up the completion of this book. *"Sometimes the stories we want to hear the least are the ones we need to hear the most."* Perhaps this was one such story with Divine-directed, powerful messages threaded throughout the text . . . veracities that could turn out to be someone else's saving grace. It was quite simple. With God, we have the power to overcome, clarify and balance our thoughts, and then strategize next step possibilities. My prayer would be that the words on these pages might give a few good souls food for thought or prevent a few dismayed and hurting folks from giving up before they deny this life just one more try. So many dear to our hearts were never given the blessing of a second chance.

I struggled desperately to find my way through this life maze as a 'charcoal child' wanting so much more than what society was willing to give. The "Green Book"; women's liberation; and later stationed on the front line protesting for civil liberties next to Black Panther Party comrades. We really weren't that keen on the expensive food at the "Top Hat Culinary Hub". We just wanted the privilege of sitting at a table far from the back of the elegant dining room or the busy kitchen swinging doors if we chose to do so. Hundreds of troopers of all hues boycotted every weekend until we got the owners and the city's attention.

Days later I would be wearing my academic honor roll and perfect attendance pins on the lapel of a suit jacket I had designed, and my talented seamstress mother or tailor uncle had created just like my sketch. My designs would hang in my closets for many years with no possibilities of ever making their way to the fashion marketplace. Weeks later, I would be donning my fabulous debutante gown created by another amazing black designer who would have rivaled the Versaces and Posens of the 21st century. The prestigious ball was one of the most urbane affairs for deserving, up-and-coming African American high school girls, escorted by some pretty impressive young men, their parents, and guests of a historically black sorority. Even then I was asking why everything had to be so separated by black and white.

I tried to rationalize how Black nationalism ended up entrenched in the Black church whose all-black congregations prayed to common depictions of a white Jesus whose hair was supposed to be like wool and his skin like bronze or brass but instead looked like the people who had lynched some of our great-great grandfathers and raped or sold many of our great-great grandmothers on the slave auction blocks after they had birthed numerous babies in the cotton fields while the father/master oppressor looked on. Talk about a deeply rooted quest for discernment I eventually accepted would never come.

Enjoying a little success throughout this journey, I would surmise my victories were due to an eventual and unshakable David-like faith; a mother who prayed for her only surviving child constantly; a father who insisted I get a quality education and who started saving for it when I was six months old . . . a little in a college savings on his 49 cents an hour job . . . an education neither parent could nor would ever be afforded; that I know right from wrong at all times and 'do the right thing' for the right reason even when no one was looking; that I would always keep my word and take care of business; that I presented myself well both in dress and preparation; that I would stand for justice and fair entitlements for my children, myself, and others (especially youth) and fight what I perceived as injustice at every turn; and above all else, that I would grow to love God with all my heart and obey HIS will. No dress rehearsals or encores in life. This is indeed the show and no matter how desperate the circumstances, we are obliged to perform and be glad.

The Basenji yanks at the leash suddenly. There's a squirrel balancing itself on an electrical cable right above our heads. He, in all his canine, nonsensical wisdom is determined to capture the elusive, fuzzy-tailed creature. The contractors working across the street from where we walked had begun their day quite early before the rains came as had been forecast again. They laugh at this crazy dog standing on his hind legs trying to climb a huge tree in a futile attempt to catch the swift, medium-size rodent. I look pass where the nutty animal and I continue our hike heading back home. There they are . . . those beautiful flowers in an array of brilliant colors popping up more and more each morning. The unexpected rains over the past two weeks had been such a nature boost giving the wilting blooms what they needed to come back to life. The Lord does that for us from time to time. Welcomed, sudden showers of blessings come our way out of the blue just when we're about to concede that all is lost.

My current personal conditions bore semblance to the subject of journalist Jennifer Gould Keil's (NY Post) inspiring story I read several years ago . . . *A New York tycoon found a friend – and her dog – living outside his office building.* "Billionaire Steve Witkoff always saw this homeless woman and her dog when he came to work each day. He eventually learned 43-year-old Lasharn Francis Harvey's story . . . a college graduate; had gone into business; failed attempts at making anything she tried work; finding herself with nothing; but always keeping a positive outlook telling people passing by her sleeping bag and cup for donations to "have a blessed day."

I came very close to finding myself in a similar position as Ms. Harvey . . . the husky and me . . . had it not been for that rescue potion I freely consumed often referred to as *Grace*. Having personally lived this one woman show most of my life – through childhood without siblings and later void of an extended family; into adulthood without a 'significant other' almost forever; and in motherhood doing the best I could with one paycheck on a teacher's meager salary or having to work two and three jobs; and giving what little I had been taught and knew to be true about surviving as a woman and mother of color. There was no turning around, going back, and starting all over again. The option door was closed and would soon display a deadbolt lock.

It was tough and confusing especially when we were compelled to go to church and hear "we will understand it better by and by." I was on the last leg of this human race, coming around third base and heading for home plate. 'By and by' had just about passed me by. I remember being on punishment for weeks when I asked Daddy why the white kids that looked like pictures of Jesus had to understand something far different. I understood 'white privilege' at a very early age while perched on the front line during the changing of the racial guard and being bitter because I had never been allowed to participate wearing my personally designed ensembles in the Plaza Easter parade. My children and my grim college experiences in predominantly white university settings showcased 'entitlement' even more and made the reality of our blackness and class status crystal clear.

When we think others are getting the breaks we feel we deserve, sometimes it's hard to stay on God's plan. No question. I would stray so many times, searching for that which I thought I needed or deserved but seemed to never be intended to be mine. I had this dream world based on what I had stared at every day in my red Viewmaster as a child; read about in books and magazines as I grew into my teens; and then eventually never missing an episode of the t.v. program *Julia* starring the beautiful Diahann Carroll . . . that was once we were finally able to afford a black and white television.

This was one of the first middle class 'colored' shows whose producers took what they would describe as a 'big risk'. The show's plot stepped away from the typical and accepted buffoonery depicting Black life to a solid plot where a strong and determined widow; single mother (having lost her husband in the Viet Nam War); and career nurse blended in quite well with the gradually evolving media industry. Carroll once wrote . . . *Pursue your passion. Don't speak until you know what you're talking about. Life has given you the right to say what needs to be said at this moment.* This was an incentive the character of "Julia" gave me the first time I saw the program. From that day forward, I was never afraid to speak the truth no matter the consequences.

"Julia" had my kind of attitude . . . always believing there wasn't anything she couldn't do or couldn't have if she was willing to sacrifice and work hard. While having the privilege of waking up to the world in a big city, she learned to relate to people of different ethnic backgrounds . . . a melting pot of cultural offerings where all could participate. (It was the kind of ambiance I eventually received from the native residents in the Southwestern town I so loved). The inspiring female character raised her young son to never feel he was 'less' than any other child as I did my own children and always instilled in my students. I never will forget how this gifted actress, the same color as me, had been such a powerful influence and role model during my early adolescent years and then how First Lady Michelle Obama's praiseworthy confidence, integrity, fashion savvy, class, commitment to so many important causes, and obvious appreciation for her favors and special gifts had propelled me and so many others in modern times to strive to reach new heights and realize our dreams.

Later down the road, I longed to have that Tyler Perry "will achieve" spirit as I once heard him proudly admit in an Oprah Winfrey interview . . . *I took my own route to success because the easiest paths were blocked by a turbulent childhood. But the pain gave me the tools I needed to hack through trees and underbrush and blaze my own trail.*

Flower Power

No matter what our line of life . . . what our need . . . we should feel we have within us infinite, untried strength and possibility, and if we believe and do our best, the angel of reserve power will walk by our side and even divide the waters of the Red Sea of our sorrows and trials so we may walk through in safety. (Sun Books, Santa Fe)

It is said reserve (alternative) power is always plugged into the universe. This power is in every living, breathing thing in existence. It's always at our disposal and in infinite supply. It's free. We don't need a laptop computer, a house on the top of a hill overlooking the ocean, a professional sport or entertainment contract, or anything other than who we really are . . . the way God made us to be. The wisdom of our ancestors and the Word of God encourages a true connection to this power that can aide us in securing a life of meaning with dependable and loving relationships; a link to our values and beliefs fostered in a faith-action spiritual community; a sense of well-being and healthy lifestyle habits; a natural tendency of kindness and empathy towards others in need; a fearlessness against on-going challenges especially in sickness and growing older; exposure and opportunities for relevant and rigorous learning where progress and rewards are the norm; and when an increase of heart-to-heart prayer conversations with the Lord can give us the strength we need to find a way out of the dark valleys in our lives.

I thank and praise you, God of my ancestors: You have given me wisdom and power. **Daniel 2:23**

Life follows visions so if we can re-program our minds with new beliefs and more positive and constructive thoughts, we have within each of us the potential of creating wonderful, uplifting, joyous events in our lives. We must teach our children the same. It's about choices and priorities and the appreciation we should have for the blessings bestowed. Being brave requires tapping into our reserve power. It is like the manna given to the children of Israel in the wilderness. Only enough was given to them for one day. Each successive day had its new supply of strength.

Our top priority as human beings gifted with life is pleasing God . . . seeking the Blessor and not just the blessing. Stepping forward with conviction and trust, even in the darkest pits of despair, does take chutzpah sometimes. But how will we ever know what's ours to have if we never make an effort to realize what is in our reach? Be grateful that God has put a measure of faith inside each and every one of us. With the recognition of *grace*, the necessity of *gratitude*, and the power of *forgiveness*, we are given just a few of the beautiful jewels of wisdom . . . another way to describe the multitude of the "flowers of blessedness". They are the result of long and patient effort in self-control and consistent prayer.

It has long been said that life is not measured by the amount of breaths we take, but by the moments that take our breath away. When 'old age' finally got my attention, I realized so many new gifts of wonder had been right in front of me all along. I no longer took their beauty and majesty for granted. My hope was that most deep thinking, cognizant, and grateful individuals would also stand in amazement at the magnificence of the mountains; the meadows of sunflowers and daffodils; the total eclipse; and other marvelous works in nature and come to a more meaningful reverence for and with God. The realization of what God has provided for us in nature will lead us to love HIM even more.

Wisdom dictates we train at this very basic level because of the widespread suffering in the world. A divided, hateful, avaricious, fearful, and controlling small segment of society is said to be the greatest nemesis blighting happiness, breeding discontent, and causing some to wallow in a sovereign panacea for malice, revenge, and all the brutal propensities weakening what was once the most powerful country in the world. My desire is to use my gift of writing and speaking to reach more youth and their parents with an honest truth; a model of faith and hope; an example of the moral strength required to navigate unparalleled political chaos and senselessness; and a way to find a renewed purpose and passion for building a better world for us all to live and prosper.

The child having been taught nothing about the power of learning and accruing knowledge; contributing to a caring and happy kind of humanity and community; and of the Lord's free-flowing mercy . . . of *love* being the greatest disciplinarian, the supreme harmonizer, and the true peacemaker . . . will never witness cruelty melting away at the altar of kindness or evil intentions dissipating after running into an antidote of sweet charity and tender sympathy.

The child having never been brought to realize the claims animals have upon humankind for protection and compassion will grow to be thoughtless and cruel toward them. And if cruel to them, that same heart . . . unchanged and untouched by adoration . . . will grow to be cruel to himself, his family, and to his fellow man. On the contrary, if our children can begin to envision more cheerful, happy, hopeful, and abounding prospects for their lives and their future, there is the potential to revolutionize our splintered civilization and advance our standards immeasurably.

When asked of Dabo Swinney, the highly admired and successful football coach at Clemson University, after his young players defeated the number one Alabama Crimson Tide for the 2016 NCAA Football Championship, how he believed his team pulled off what many have called one of the greatest upsets in college football history, he spoke more of what made his players champions of the heart as well as champions on the field. "Loving God, chasing greatness, working hard, believing in themselves, respecting their coaches and teammates as brothers, being committed to doing their best, and giving life their all . . . that's what we teach," the mellow, yet motivating, expectant, and deeply spiritual coach swanked with great pride.

Former Clemson star quarterback DeShaun Watson, now an NFL quarterback for the Houston Texans, spoke of how their coaches, year after year, nurtures each member of their team with valuable life and game wisdom while also openly displaying sincere compassion; how team members are taught to have confidence and have no fear; and of the necessity of slowing down the moment before it is totally lost. Watson knew that very thing could have been the case in the last play of the title game. "We're encouraged to be humble, hungry for success, and above all else, to always give God the glory . . . to let the light that shines in us be brighter than the light that shines on us."

"Give courage and strength to those willing to go beyond their daily loving service for individual children to advocacy, mobilization, and organizing for all children, to ensure that our rich and powerful nation truly 'leaves no child behind'," wrote Marian Wright Edelman, legendary founder and Executive Director of the Children's Defense Fund (leading our nation since 1973 to ensure a level playing field for <u>all</u> children).

In her unending commitment to giving children a healthy, safe, and moral start in life, the renowned educator, humanitarian, and writer has also given us beautiful prayers for our children in one of my favorite books, *I'm Your Child, God.* One of her petitions is for children to find "a stronger inner anchor and spiritual grounding in our too materialistic, too violent, too busy, too secular, too individualistic, fragile, and ever-changing world where ties to family, community, and the sacred are becoming increasingly frayed."

When parents fully understand their teens have intrinsic worth simply because God loves and values them, then they too can do the same. This acknowledgement takes adults beyond a sense of duty and closer to a depth of wise, devoted, and loving guardianship. It causes God's love to be the motivating force as we usher our adolescents through difficult issues of their precious lives and for some, the frightening reality of a gun and a bullet. How do we walk the fine line of the real truth without causing the innocent unnecessary concern and angst? Children can no longer remain naïve about events affecting their future and their caretakers can no longer remain silent. Prayer is requested. As author Beth Moore, in a powerful daily devotional, "Believing God, Day by Day" (2008) once wrote . . . *I want my children to love God. I want them to love His Word and discover life healing, and power within it. I want them to love people and treat them with compassion and kindness. But more than anything on earth, I want glory to come to God through their lives and ours.*

It's often been said one can tell much about a person from just how gracefully they handle change, wrestle with guilt, try to forgive, sum up their losses, and then 'let go' . . . 'letting it be'. I had gone from the pueblos to the 'hood' where dangerous bomb-like explosives and gunshots could not be distinguished from one another until shell casings were found on the sidewalks the very next day . . . from streets filled with tourists from all over the world enjoying festivals, amazing art venues and performances, centuries old fascinating history, and fine native and Spanish cuisine to where blue was crossed out by red graffiti spray painted on a nearby multi-million dollar building overnight; from driving a brand new State authorized car and a personal Jeep to going 6 years without touching a steering wheel; and from being totally immersed and strengthened by powerful worship services to having no church home at all. In spite of the estrangement from friends and extended family members suffered by my children as well, the unexplainable would become inexcusable if we would suddenly give up and stop pursuing our dreams.

"Jesus went outside the box to choose His disciples and those warriors who would stick with Him no matter what. They were ordinary men like Moses, Joshua, (Mary's) Joseph, and David chosen to do great things. They had an innocent willingness and wisdom directing them to give God the Glory in all things," master theologian, Bishop Charles E. Blake (L.A. West Angeles Church of God in Christ) concluded in one of his powerful Christmas messages delivered before an overflowing audience years ago. "Even if you are laughed out of the conference room because of what you believe, your *faith* will reconcile what you lose and more than make up the difference in what you will gain." I was an ordinary woman still believing I had been chosen to do extraordinary things . . . indiscriminate acts of kindness for my children and others I cared for deeply. I prayed there would still be time. What I did know was no matter where I found myself, there would always be God, spirit, infinite good, infinite wisdom, infinite harmony, and Divine love. It could not be otherwise.

This would be the foundation upon which I would rebuild my life. I had to believe my faith would activate God's power in a new way and I might live to see this truth come into existence. Had David focused on the reality of facing a giant, he would have gone down in defeat. Instead, HE focused on what God promised HE would do. Life is too big of a task to handle without God. Alone and without his nest, the eagle cannot fly across the sun guided by the Master's map. Our lives will thus be spent with the Dweller in the Innermost . . . in that region where God speaks directly to the soul, and where growth and evolution is a silent, metamorphosing force within the heart, mind, and body.

"There are holes . . . big ones and lots of them," a dear friend and pastor conceded in a summation e-mail after one of our frequent counseling sessions. "I get it! But there's also a strange kind of 'extraordinariness' about you I can't explain . . . so many things you do quite well. Your children exhibit the same productive traits. That should count for something. Maybe you shouldn't be in this ugly predicament, but you are and you've got to figure out how to come from under all this grief. I don't know how much longer you will be able to deal with all of it alone." I remember that very moment when I lowered my head and breathed a momentary sigh of relief. Finally, there was one person who understood my heart was hurting but prayed with me for the jubilee to come just over the horizon.

"It never surprises me how you seem to always find a way to get through the muddle and flood waters right before you spill over or drown. You've managed to take the limits off God because you're convinced HE wants you to reign supreme in your life while also giving Glory to HIS." My pastoral friend smiles as he stands to bid me adieu for the time being. "My wife tells me a lot of women in the church look forward to seeing what you'll wear every Sunday . . . *that you always look stunning,* she says. I think that's the word she used. That's so funny! Those are pretty wealthy and influential ladies so that's really saying something especially since you told me you always shop at Ross." I too smiled at the irony.

Wisdom Nuggets

- Don't wait for extraordinary opportunities. Seize common occasions and make them great. When in doubt, just take the next small step. The best decision anyone can make when a problem arises is to decide not to decide.

- Often times we bring on unnecessary pain when we blame ourselves for the wrong thing happening when we tried to do the right thing. Sometimes we just have to accept 'what is' out of our control.

- A strong, successful man or woman is not the victim of his environment. His own inherent force and energy compel things to turn out as he desires.

- Remember to remember to be prepared for opportunity. As long as humankind has a dream in his heart, he cannot lose the significance of living.

- Don't allow changing times and aging to change who you are. Our state of affairs might transform and we could feel empty and unfulfilled. The possibility of rebounding even better than before can be real. Ask the spirit of Job.

- God knows there are many things only a person who is full of years and experience can contribute.

- The worse thing is to assume everyone will see life from your side of the fence. They didn't come to life with others' life experiences. Maybe it's as simple as accepting there are things we don't and won't ever understand but HE does.

- ❖ Humankind does not attract that which they want but that which they are. When we vibrate to success, happiness, and abundance, the things symbolizing these states of consciousness will attach themselves to us. Thou will keep him in perfect peace whose mind is stayed on Thee. Our wishes and prayers are only gratified and answered when they harmonize with our thoughts and actions.

- ❖ Life isn't tied with a bow, but it is still the ultimate gift along with the health of our bodies. It is worth living if live in a noble manner. We don't own our lives to do with at will. We have a life-interest. Before we know it, it will be time to surrender with an accounting.

- ❖ It will not be how we have started this race; how we made it around the sharp curves and tight lane straightaways; but how we have strategized the possibility of winning. Once we start out on this pursuit, we will realize that crossing the finish line is not what's most rewarding. The journey itself and the anticipation of achieving our goals is what's so exhilarating and wonderful.

The reason most people give up is because they tend to look at how far they still have to go, instead of how far they have come. (NBA icon and Hall of Famer Shaquille O'Neal)

When Oscar-winning actress Anne Hathaway dances with her childhood friend towards the end of the movie, "Princess Diaries" (after she finds out she has inherited royal status), he asks 'why me' now that you've become a 'real' princess?" I would surmise her response might have been in essence, "Because you saw me when I was invisible . . . not so important; just a school girl named Mia Thermopolis who had a cherished cat companion named Fat Louie." Quite possibly, God feels the same way about our *faith*. We receive blessings from "The Invisible One" we have trusted all along because we finally became confident HE'd always been there and would be by our side accepting us just as HE wanted us to be.

A dear friend once reminded me about blessings being distributed in my direction. "When the depression really hits,

And you can't forgive yourself or those who have broken your heart and when you have little hope in just about every aspect of your life, get a map and a census report of the world. Think about all those many millions who would gladly exchange places with you." I concluded there was no time for pity parties. When God sees what we can do, HE promises HE will do the necessary things we cannot. It was incumbent upon me to trust HIM to perform HIS miracles as only HE could do . . . those promised in the Word.

Successful, happy, and contented people find it in their hearts to understand more compassionately. They love God and themselves and feel and exude confidence, optimism, and worth. They reside in their personal spaces reinforcing and realizing they are quite fallible yet always possessing *reserve power* coming from the main Source. Jesus taught that the Father within each and every one of us could be absolutely trusted to guide, protect, and provide when humankind believed it possible. I believe. I believe one can be changed by the agonizing events that might happen in their lives yet can refuse to be reduced by them. I whisper *Aloha* in my prayers . . . *consciously manifesting life joyously in the present.* This would indeed be my goal.

Seizing the power of understanding in the journey of others, I psychologically and spiritually created a new path for myself. Wherever I have lived, my walls were filled with large framed posters of those who have inspired me by the sacrificial stands they assumed for a cause and for the people . . . those I have studied, long admired, and have given me much needed faith in humankind. My next framed poster would be a blow up of the front cover of the GQ Magazine bearing a wonderful picture of Colin K. I knew what it meant to take a stand knowing there might be irreversible consequences.

In 1965, just after high school graduation and three months into my collegiate studies at a then Big 10 university, I was invited to write and publish a column in the award-winning university newspaper I entitled "The Other Sheep". The associate editor had been impressed with my editorials in the Black Panther newspaper although I wrote under a pen name. I never knew how the respected journalism student found out who I was. Surprisingly, he had written a scathing editorial himself accusing the university of 'unfair and blatantly discriminatory practices' when it was reported students of color and women had been denied enrollment in the journalism school although having strong writing sample portfolios and impressive references.

The gossip and isolation precipitated by the subject matter of some of my editorials forced me to have to transfer to another university. Without a normal college experience and not being able to follow my dream of becoming a photojournalist, there would be no reason to stay. Mama understood my dilemma; my shock; my hurt . . . especially having no Greek or social life while trying to keep up with courses of no interest, some quite difficult. This wonderful lady always hung in there with me no matter what. I believe I wrote and spoke about the facts and sentiments needing to be said and saying what others were probably thinking but too afraid to say.

What I didn't do in taking so many different risks or stands against injustice was to measure whether it was worth the level of bravery and raw stamina it took to overcome and succeed in spite of the naysayers or the odds and the negative effect my radical actions would eventually have on my children. Sometimes things worked out and I would believe I had done the right thing. Other times, I was on the edge of a cliff and my children would sadly have to pay the price of martyrdom. I often wonder what my life might have been like had I chosen to remain silent. My only regret was losing an academic scholarship and not being allowed to enroll in yet another journalism school once I had transferred. It appeared to be common practice across the university boards not to accept African American female candidates, with exception of the progressive institutions of higher learning on the east and west coasts that my parents could not afford.

As Malala Yousafzai, the young Pakistani activist and advocate for education for girls and the youngest-ever Nobel Prize laureate, always encouraged, "There's a time to be silent or stand up," Malala continued to challenge even after a critical personal injury inflicted by the Taliban. "Speak what's inside your soul. Life is sacred – a consciousness beyond all borders - not because it is unique but because it is not. Sometimes it doesn't work, but you can't give up. You have to keep trying." Malala has been and should be an inspiration . . . an ambassador of hope . . . bringing forth the love and decency within us all.

For so long, I had not been tuned in to God's frequencies . . . the signs HE presented in such subtle and often obvious ways. Happiness parked at the front door of my life refusing to come in. Ignoring the clear blessings, I woke up with every day injured my soul and prevented me from moving on until the 'winter season' was upon me and in full swing. I believe my eventual awareness had a lot to do with talking to and about the mountain simultaneously.

Upon deciding to make a better version of myself, I would embrace capabilities and let go of some of the painful past transgressions holding me hostage. God's mercy is bigger than our mistakes. HE steps in to clean up the pandemonium we've created. HE helps us see that regret and envy will never get us what we lack, but it does make us miserable and blinds us to the blessings already in front of us. I believe just as Rahab from Jericho did that most people saw my shortcomings and dismissed any possibility for my future success, but God never did. HE still saw a diamond in the rough, even in my 'winter' years.

I will instruct you and teach you in the way you should go; I will guide you with my eye. **Psalm 32:8**

When the world tempts me to feel life has passed me by, my soul calls out to my heart informing me I am not finished yet. I believe God would give me wonderful relationships, increased spiritual growth, and physical blessings in the years ahead. I know for sure the enemy does not anger and lash out because of where we are. It's where we're going that makes *it* raise *its* ugly head. Think of Moses and the fact that God had this all figured out from the beginning. It was a destiny moment. God positioned Pharaoh's daughter to be at the right place at the right time. The Lord is indeed exact and precise and if tuned in to the right frequency, HE's quite obvious. HIS message blares in sight and sound. Why would Pharaoh's daughter find Moses' mother to help her care for the baby that came to her in a straw basket floating down a river?

Ruth came to Bethlehem at the time of harvest. She couldn't have gotten there any sooner. It was a set time when things were to begin to happen. Although I would never comprehend the necessity of the pain in my journey or why God chose to act or not act upon my prayers, I became aware that the Lord knew and so did I. If HE would have given me my harvest any sooner, more than likely I would have messed it up and would have never come into the fullness of what HE had in store for me all along . . . HIS messages brought forward in the pages of this book. In Boaz's field, Ruth didn't sow; she followed the reapers becoming, like David, more experienced, wiser, and far more mature. Heartbreak and an inkling of fear and dismay were part her journey as is the case for so many. Like Ruth, God would escort me to a place I had never been before. My life would count for even more.

The results we produce for the Lord are even greater because we've gained a greater ability to influence the people and culture surrounding us. Our survival out of the battering storms of life demonstrates the power of our faith and the intentions of God's mercy and grace. Regardless of our position or past, God raises people up equally. No matter how many mistakes we have made, it is our *faith* HE honors. Opportunities we think have been long forgotten in our past become tools to help cut together the blessings that will save us in our future. God gave Abraham a vision . . . a picture depicting the petitions of his prayers. When it looked like the Promise would never be realized, he looked at the stars that gave rise to his *faith* despite the miles he had traveled in his journey and the anguish he had experienced.

The essential unity of human life with the Divine life is the profoundest knowledge we can attain. Nothing real can be threatened – nothing unreal can exist. Therein lays the peace of God. Can you remember the times when you were at the bottom and how quickly and miraculously you were lifted up? Know for sure that the real winners in life are the people who look at every situation with the expectation they can find good, make it better, and cause almost everything else to work out okay in the end. Humankind can find every truth connected with our being if we will take the time to explore the substance of our soul.

We cannot make the mistake of becoming too anxious to improve our circumstances but be unwilling to examine and take action in improving ourselves. The shackles will not fall off and we will remain bound.

Long ago, author Lily A. Allen (Our Mental Children) reminded readers of a way to walk around the darkness and find joy in this life . . . *not to fight old traits but to let them go; to think strongly and look for the beautiful in all things; to replace the 'dark, sad-eyed children' called hatred, fear, pride, insincerity and suspicion - with love, truth, honesty, purity, and Divine Universal Law. If we have not found the 'beautiful' within our own hearts, we shall not find it in others, and scarcely shall we find it in the world.*

It became apparent that finding the beautiful required focusing my attention on the present . . . the power in the moments where I lived and breathed in the NOW. We all have a voice in our heads that hardly ever shuts up. This voice can take us anywhere, anytime, and especially when we are studying but our brain is at the beach enjoying the sun and surf or having daydreams of true love and success coming into our lives when we least expect. It took three lifetime seasons for me to realize that when the voice was silent, I could create and expand my awareness. Time would cease to exist, and I could forget worries, aches, pains, reasons, excuses, and justifications. Life could be magic and a foreign excitement for what the future might hold.

My prayer is that God will allow me to continue to be a champion of my faith, not just when it's easy, but when chaos and conflict test my constitution. Sadly, that state of affairs happened quite often. Faith is tough, especially in the darkness. But when prayer and faith mingle, there can be no fear, no jealousy, and no resentment. There is also the realization (in most cases) that in life there might be devastation, sickness, aging, disappointments, heartaches, and betrayals. That's pretty much a given. What's not an absolute is how we choose to get through it all. If we look back far enough, we've done it and we can do it over and over again if need be. I hear God whisper from the warmth and glow of my soul . . . *I am all that I am, and life is grace, goodness, and love by MY presence.* Instead of being distracted and hurt by those who left or betrayed me, I would celebrate those who believed in me and stood by my side . . . those who have climbed over such huge emotional and spiritual hurdles with me. I would rejoice in thanksgiving for their love and true friendship and live my life not out of my circumstances but out of a vision.

Embrace the truth that God meets us at the level of our expectancy, so we should anticipate unprecedented favor with a future superseding the heartbreak and letdowns of our past. Whatever we focus on is what we are moving toward. By directing our minds, we direct our lives. And it is in the valley when true character is revealed; not the peak. We cannot control fate or our genes; making things right instead of left; going up rather than coming down. What we know for certain is that real success can be achieved in knowing we've done our very best. It's never enough to set out to make things work. We must set out to make things happen. As one of the "America's Got Talent" contestants once announced to the judges . . . *I didn't come here to "try out" . . . I came here to win!*

It is our duty as men and women to proceed as though the limits of our abilities do not exist. Perhaps in the final season of my life, I will be in a place where God has always wanted me to be. This confidence begins with a consciousness of promise and personal triumph . . . the assurance that God loves us because of who God is, not because of anything we did or didn't do. If we keep searching, we will find there is far more in us than the tears we have shed as a result of the struggles we have endured.

*He who will step aside from the passionate press, and deign to enter the byways here presented, his happy feet shall press the incomparable **flowers of blessedness**, his eyes be gladdened with their beauty, and his mind refreshed with their sweet perfume.* (Sun Books)

All too often the difference between happiness and depression; progress and regression; failure and success; and balance and imbalance is simply a matter of priorities and perspective. We see more of what we don't have instead of celebrating all the blessings we do have. In the end, what matters are not materialistic goods or the accolades we gather, but the 'pay-it-forwards' we manage to scatter along the way. These deeds, freely given, document what kind of life we have lived. The things we desire most have no price tag dangling . . . a life with a much music and laughter; an overflow of gladness, good health, and well-being that manages to wash away every disappointment; initiating into play enough joy to dissolve every sorrow; and receiving an abundance of love to ease every pain.

There are several visions in my head. The first picture is one of a weathered, winter woman and only child struggling with grief after her father's estrangement and passing and never having the chance to say goodbye. There was also little time to grieve for the horrible transitioning of her mother. She looks lost, fragile, and diminished. The second most recent picture shows a mature woman successful and thriving. How did she get from there to here? She remembers the journey well. She arrived in the place that is here by faltering. She made some really great decisions and some really stupid ones too! Each time she fell down, she eventually got up, brushed off the dirt, and moved on. Her fortitude and tenacity continue to be a marvel to those that know her well.

I pass the vase displaying the closed, faded white and green elongated main flowers of the star gazers. It's always so fascinating to watch the flowers complete their transformation right before my very eyes. They would soon open up into beautiful blooms of stark white petals on the outside and maroon dots and streaks of dark pink painted on the inside. Green and gold core stems and buds bring forth fuzzy, burnt orange tips dripping in a calming fragrance. ***Flowers of blessedness.*** In one plant of magnificent blooms, so many wonderful gifts of *grace* are freely presented and offered to those opened to receive.

So, we come to the table exactly as we are, some days on top of the world, other days barely getting by. Sometimes we might feel like a number; like the shiny silver ball in the metamorphic pinball machine being hit from all sides - like a mere cog . . . beaten, severed, and separated from the depth of good life things. On this day we probably feel like so many others. When and while walking constantly through the fire, I often think about Harriet Tubman when she received Divine instructions to become a conductor for the Underground Railroad. *"The Lord told me to do this. I said . . . oh, Lord, I can't – don't ask me – take somebody else. And HE said, "It's you I want, Harriet Tubman."* She remembers God as a prayer. She hears HIM, and HE gives her strength. *"HE set the North Star in the heavens. HE meant I should be free."*

There are also times we wake up to life feeling tuned into a song, fully being, and hyperaware of the God who IS still all. The point of the experience isn't to create a special space where God is over and against the rest of life where God isn't. The power is in the striking ability of this experience to open our eyes all over again (and again and again) to the holiness and sacred nature of life. That's God all in all, bringing together our bodies, our minds, our souls, our spirits, and all the parts and pieces that make us *us*. Our eyes are opened to the good, the bad, the ugly, the beautiful, the breathtaking, and the gut-wrenching to the presence in all of life of the God who is with us, for us, and ahead of us. Although swimming upstream is always challenging and requires extra strength, it is still possible as are so-called impossible dreams.

One of the most agonizing problems within our human experience is that few, if any of us, live to see our fondest hopes fulfilled. The hopes of our childhood and the promises of our mature years are unfinished symphonies. Dr. Martin Luther King Jr.

I often wondered what gave good people like Dr. King and so many other warriors for the cause the strength to do what had to be done when they often had to respond to the unthinkable . . . the unspeakable. I concluded they suddenly realized anxiety, worry, and fear of the unknown made men slaves and were destroyers of health, prosperity, and joy. They refused to be weakened to the point of asking why and then giving up. I refused as well, and I continued to instill that same fighting spirit in my children and those I continued to extend a helping hand.

The scriptures remind us 'all is well' even when it seems unwell and we must wait for God's timing, not rushing ahead of HIM. We find some contentment when we respond in faith like Moses who kept right on going because his heart remained connected to the Invisible One. At times, the esteem of others can claim such importance that it becomes our way to measure our worth as a person. After his conversion, Paul understood that God's evaluation of his actions was what mattered, not his own opinion of himself. The pleasure our lives give to God should be our motivation to live righteously; trust what is received as *grace*; and utilize our freedoms of thought, passion, and purpose that can provide a perfect guide for a happy and prosperous life.

When we take with us the deep, persistent, constructive power of right thought, we take with us a power that is positively invincible. With such a power in our possession, we need never feel disturbed for a moment. Our life is our own; our future is our own; and whatever we may wish to become, it is our privilege to make our dreams come true and make real our highest idea. We must convince our children of the same and pray they understand the importance not just to try but to make what our God tells us is possible really happen.

Today I share my excitement for life with other people through the pages I write . . . through the words I will eventually speak. I'll make someone smile. I'll go out of my way to perform an unexpected act of kindness for a stranger or someone dear. I'll tell a child just how special he or she is, and for those even closer how much I truly care. Famous actor, Leonardo DiCaprio recalls his father, George DiCaprio once telling him, "I don't care if you're successful or not. Just have an interesting life." I always wanted that blessing for my children, my students, and in the time that was left for me as well. It is true. Hope is the aspiration of the soul, the persistence of the mind, and the affirmation of the heart. Hope blooms like Mamacita's beautiful roses amidst the thorns of life.

"'Feliz navidad', Mamacita," the card read. It was a rainy and windy Christmas Eve. I was hoping the little poinsettia plant I had sat in front of her door wouldn't blow away. I simply wanted to say, "muchas gracias". My dear friend on the corner would never know how she had moved my sadness and fears momentarily and on so many occasions given me an unplanned interim of pleasantness. I constantly prayed for a breakthrough . . . a much-needed miracle. Miracle performances is the kind of business my co-author gets a standing ovation for. Most often, there were many requests for an encore.

In the end, there were obvious signs I had been in the right place for the time being and would eventually complete one of my Divine assignments with the writing of *Baal Perazim.* A television commercial aired throughout the holidays for Merci Chocolates and the words of thanksgiving for kindness shown by ordinary people had long been the title for the chapter on *gratitude. Ya' didn't have to do what you did but you did, and "I thank you".* All throughout the college football playoffs, I kept hearing about the decisions of 'the committee' and I thought about our 'heavenly committee' of ancestors, close friends, and the husky being chaired by the Lord and keeping close tabs on my children and me . . . always providing the *grace* we needed just in the nick of time. I look at the cover of this book and think in amazement at an auto commercial that ran for only a couple of weeks. A precious daisy had grown from a crack in the asphalt street. Like me, the flower was wilted. The car suddenly stops and backs up. A finger hits the H20 button on the dashboard. Sprinkles of water fall on the petals, and instantly 'poof' . . . as I hoped I would be soon . . . the daisy is revived and continues to bloom and multiply. I knew then, without question, Thy Will would be done.

I loved the tribute t.v. personality Kathie Lee and her family paid to their late, great husband, father, and sports icon, Frank Gifford, on his passing several years ago. *He lived fully, loved deeply, and he leaves an amazing legacy of lives touched and changed.* The power yet simplicity of those words would be a proper adios for me as well.

***

Three Components to Creating a Breakthrough: *strategy, story, and state of mind. The way you approach a goal, your beliefs about life, and your mental game form the foundation for any success or failure. But by learning how to take control of these forces, you can take massive action and can* *create the quality of life that you've always wanted.* (Tony Robbins, Podcast – 1/23/2017 – Oprah.com – Inspiration)

Aftermath

Where Is The RAGE?

Give me the man who believes in the ultimate triumph of truth over error, of harmony over discord, of love over hate, of purity over vice, of light over darkness, of life over death. Such are the true nation builders.

Former President Barack Obama

There was an eerie quietness on these once mean California streets on November 8th, 2016. It was late but the hour meant nothing to our then 12-year-old Basenji. When nature called, we gladly scurried to answer. To still have this 20-pound, very smart, cute, and loveable canine companion was truly a blessing and a joy. He always made us laugh just when we needed to the most. The unconditional, infinite love flowed as if he instinctively knew when we were hurting or not feeling well. The husky was like that too. We always carried pepper spray when walking, and in the wee hours of the morning my children carried their late grandfather's switch blade knife in case of an unexpected personal concern or affront. The Basenji was famous for going after strays and even dogs on a leash 10 times his size. We had become quite fearless walking him now having no question we were forever protected by **Grace**.

It was indeed a strange night . . . a numbing kind of fear and disbelief not directly tied to any immediate foreign threat (or at least we thought at the time). Frightening and potentially ruinous political ramifications loomed in a haze of total shock, despair, and chaos. What could we do about what had just happened in our "once upon a time" democratic country now deeply divided and fragile with fear, anger, ignorance, greed, deep-seated hatred, and corruption.

The <u>United</u> States of America was now jarred by splintered national and world politics and clothed in classism, selfish egos, personal agendas, and a refusal to be accepting of cultural, ideological, and religious differences. One of my former students described the state of affairs as 'national terrorism' perpetrated against true American patriots so proud of how far we had come as citizens . . . notably African Americans, Muslims, Hispanics, and the LGBTQ community. We were under attack by a pseudo official governing body and bigoted, misinformed voter base threatening the very fabric of American freedoms and enduring peace. We owed it to our children to tell them the truth and to fight back.

"'They' disrespected the Obamas for 8 years . . . as we say at the Academy (a classy act to follow)," this same student wrote in an e-mail just after that fateful November day. "He sure did some good stuff while he was in the White House even though 'they' always tried to hold him back. Never could figure out why if he and his 'peeps' were making good decisions for the benefit of <u>all</u> the people. Liked Obama's strut. 'Broths' called it a *swagger*. Showed a lot of class and confidence in who he really was. He's like you - fearless when it comes to causes for the good of the people. Especially for the kids. He's cool and like me he's a fan of basketball and good jazz.

"Loved your class!" he continued. "Just think about it! International Baccalaureate diplomas in the 80s in the inner city along with sold out performances of *The Mikado* and an all-black cast! That was really big! But then none of us could go around bragging about how smart we were because we lived in the 'hood. We would have been bullied every day if we tried to do what was right like the Obamas and the Bidens tried to do. I hated that, he admitted. They were sharp dudes and they were bullied too just like me. Now those same folks that went after "the man" are making stupid decisions that have a chance of ruining futures of young folks like me and my friends. That's really messed up."

In an interview several years ago with journalist Michel Martin (*Time Magazine*), Bishop T.D. Jakes, called one of "America's Best Preachers", summed up many of our fears today. *I am very troubled by the times in which we live. The death of civility in our generation is very disturbing. I know there have always been conflicts in Washington but now they have reached a level whereby we have lost all sensibility and reason. There is so much hostility and deterioration of families, marriages, and community.* The inspirational theologian goes on to describe the *unforgiveness* and *hatred* as a cancer because it never stays where it is first found. *It spreads and left unattended will attach itself throughout our bodies. It's a systemic, pandemic problem in our personal lives, in our public lives, and in our professional lives. We have lost all reason.*

Words could not describe the quaking jolt and anger as to how life in America had suddenly changed so drastically and sadly in just a blink of an eye. I had no explanation . . . not for my own grown children or any of my former students who had stayed in close contact over the years. A somewhat feasible clarification required our digging deep in our rationale response bucket and convincing them there was still a chance America could get things right.

I couldn't imagine how painful and difficult it must have been for our then Presidential <u>leader</u> standing at a podium in Poland in front of world leaders attempting to come up with a reason why our semi-egalitarian way of life seemed to have unexpectedly disappeared in an instant. "This isn't what America is all about," Barack Obama would find himself saying again and again. Some called the results of that November day "one of the most tragic days in American democracy."

Eight years . . . four years prior . . . people from all walks of life were elated by the outcome . . . by the possibilities . . . by grasping the triumph of this beautiful family soon to occupy the White House and to steal a little piece of our hearts along the way. How vividly I recall running down my cul-de-sac street that 2008 historic night while living in the town of my childhood dreams. Clad in my Tasmanian devil onesy p.j.s, and with my bright blue plastic curlers falling from my hair, I cried uncontrollably. It was a frigid winter night and my tears were freezing cold rolling down my cheeks but I didn't care. There were no words to describe it all. Funny how I never knew my next door neighbor was a staunch Republican and was furious at my one-woman celebration.

Exhilarating, overwhelming joy occupied my usual weakened spirits that night as I witnessed this amazing milestone unfold. When the Obamas, all fashioned in black and red, walked out on the stage at Grant Park in Chicago hand and hand and with smiles beaming, I thought of Martin and Mandela; Biko and Malcolm; Bobby and John; Medgar and Emmett; and Rosa and Maya . . . all sitting up in heaven conversing with the Lord and thanking HIM for the 'change having finally come.' It took me back 58 years when I sat between my parents, ironically among a predominantly 'white' audience, seeing and listening to Dr. King for the first and last time.

I was young, yet so awestruck and captured by our soon-to-be martyr's presence . . . his strong voice, the "big" words he used, his undeniable confidence, and obviously a Divine assigned mission to right a long-time crime against people of color and the least of our brothers and sisters. This wonderful human being fearlessly declared that the historic discriminatory and blatant and dangerous conditions could and would no longer be ignored or tolerated. *Freedom is never voluntarily given by the oppressor; it must be demanded by the oppressed. This is why we cannot wait.* Everyone knew the danger and what the ultimate sacrifice could entail, but with so much conviction he told the audience that night, "Now is the time!" Can we not say the same today? NOW IS THE TIME!

With the exception of the loss of his life partner of 65 years, I had only seen my father cry one other time. When newscasters Brinkley and Cronkite announced on that ill-fated April 4th, 1968 day that Dr. King had been murdered, he pulled out his white handkerchief from the back pocket of his familiar corduroy jeans, wiped his face, and walked outside to his garage where he would spend a few hours to his own thoughts and prayers. I remember that double pain even to this day . . . the loss of our hero and seeing the anguish in Daddy's face like it was yesterday.

Within hours there was a another painful level of incredulity and fury with the sounds of broken glass, sirens, fires popping and lighting up the night skies, uncanny cries of anger and anguish, and federal army tanks rolling down the neighborhood streets of my childhood heading towards the Plaza to protect the million dollar mansions of the rich and famous. 50 years later the same scenario would play out in the streets of Ferguson, Missouri after a young man's lifeless body lies for hours without covering; a devastated mother and father cry out; and the white police shooter acquitted. Again, we would ask why all the hatred and resistance was ever necessary in the first place and now why a new generation would have to still explain why "Black Lives Matter". Statistics never lied if calculated honestly.

When a bee hovers over a garden of varied flowers, what it beholds is not the difference between the flowers, but the honey within them. Amma

I often wonder what racists' prayers were like. What could they possibly be saying to God regarding their abhorrence and bigotries? "Now, Lord, I'm going to church Sunday and all, but Tuesday night we got an order from the Grand Wizard to go and drag this colored boy to the square 'cause he done disrespect us. Went and drank from a 'white only' drinking fountain'." Would Grandma Jemma's God think their stone hearts and ignorant thinking and actions were as absurd as we believed they were and still are?

With Barack Obama, there was so much hope coming from this wonderful love story for country and each other while exuding such dignity; class; beauty; and brilliance leading the country from the heights of Washington D.C. It was a new kind of family and they looked happy, healthy, and confident. They were different and an eventual divided country would either celebrate or sulk. We didn't always have to agree with their opinions or administration's policies, but most would conclude the Obamas and Bidens were class acts.

It didn't matter how many blows *satan* was landing on my person, I would be committed to the "Yes We Can" new movement and was quite proud of my role in the first campaign. It had been such an honor working at one of the campaign headquarters side by side with some pretty funny, quite knowledgeable, and commonsense-wise-beyond-their-years young people so enthusiastic and optimistic about their future.

The brilliant red-head Nick and several others on the campaign trail stayed in contact after they landed well-earned positions in the White House after President Obama took office in 2009. They would sadly fill me in on the depth of willful and vicious factions purposely orchestrating destructive dysfunction, displaying bold and blatant contempt, bullying mannerisms, and out-in-the-open threats . . . unprecedented disrespect for the leader of the free world. 'Their' adamant refusal to acknowledge or cooperate with a new changing of the guard made it so difficult to sustain a motivated and cooperative governing force charged to get the country back on its feet and its citizens progressing and enjoying better days.

I had followed the future 44th President from the time he became the first African American trailblazer of the Harvard Law Review in 1990. It was the same year I had appealed to the city's most reputed civil rights activist for SCLC, and for a representative of Department of Justice to immediately come to my oldest child's high school. Skinheads had actively been soliciting membership for the slowly integrating community across the river and students of color were being threatened in the halls and classrooms and outside of the school campus. Again, I continued to remain vigilant at my station on the front line of protest and yes, at the time I prayed even though I didn't quite understand why I had to since this curious racist dynamic was being allowed to fester anyway.

Many who heard the young man with the unusual name speak at the 2004 Democratic Convention predicted he would one day become President of these <u>United</u> States. I read as many articles and books written about and by the new leader as I could outside of my writing every day and was empowered by Stephen Mansfield's "The Faith of Barack Obama." Dr. King's message would resonate in law abiding, morally decent people's hearts that day and sadly 50 years later . . . *the nation is sick, trouble is in the land, confusion all around. But I want you to know tonight, yes, that we, as a people, will get to the Promised Land.* The subtle challenge kept us grounded with common hopes, great expectations, and lofty aspirations for the blessed todays and tomorrows in our lives and those of future generations.

Journal Entry: January 23, 2009 - *I had never traveled to Washington D.C. Flying and crowds were not in my 'favorite things to do bag'. Yet, I tried to imagine what it would have been like to just be there – to personally participate, experience, and witness "The Moment" and "The Miracle." In front of my little 9-inch TV, I stood and saluted the flag, cried hysterically, clapped my hands, and tapped my feet in a rhythmic jig. As I watched the inaugural celebration taking place at the Lincoln Memorial, my body shook all over as Challenger and Mr. Lincoln, America's symbolic bald eagles, spread their wings in the caverns of that majestic monument and then took flight.*

I had been invited to watch the inauguration of the new President with an absolutely stunning, creatively talented, and academically/historically astute group of Native American children. The school is indeed one of my favorite places to be – an amazing staff and strong pueblo support led by a young Harvard-grad principal who, like Obama, "gets it" – understands what works for his staff and student body . . . for the Native community . . . <u>for the people</u>. Like the Obamas, he was willing to sway from "doing business as usual" if there was new and innovative academic methodology that could truly make a difference and render more positive results for children. What a powerful morning! God and 'we' the people had become the wind beneath Barack Obama's wings.

For those of us who understood the historical evolution miraculously happening at the time, we took great pride and were so grateful to still be alive to see the day of Obama's inauguration, especially the "chocolate baby boomers". And what could we say about "the Lady" . . . still my First Lady . . . the remarkable woman, mother, wife, daughter, sister, aunt, scholar, and role model especially for children of color. "My desire for this country is that we remain hopeful and that we find a place in our hearts to love each other," Michelle Obama would challenge. Sadly, quite the contrary has occurred.

Writes Dedrick Asante Muhammad in recent report findings for "Prosperity Now" . . . *African American households are making middle income money but have the wealth of a white high school dropout. By 2020, median black and Latino households stand to lose nearly 18% and 12% of the wealth they held in 2013 respectively, while median white households are projected to own 86 times more wealth than black households – 68 times more wealth than Latino households.* The authors cited the legacy of discriminatory housing policies, an upside down tax system that helps the wealthiest households get wealthier, and the economic and political effects of mass incarceration. African Americans make up 13% of the country's population but occupy 2/3s – 86% of the prison population. And so I must ask, *where is the rage?*

What a beautiful sighting of excited D.C. children and visitors with containers filled with vegetables and fruits and having the time of their lives sitting at a long table with the our former First Lady and enjoying a delicious, nutritious lunch. Some are experiencing new tastes and learning so much about proper nutrition and keeping their bodies healthy by exercising. Their parents have been encouraged to practice the same habits at home whenever possible. Programs such as "Let Girls Learn", "Let's Move", "The School Lunch" and "My Plate" (began in hopes of helping curve the epidemic of childhood obesity within a generation); the "Reach Higher Initiative"; and "Joining Forces" . . . while also opening doors for so many other talented and deserving young people (e.g. fashion designer, Jason Wu) were just a smidgeon of accomplishments of this two degree Ivy Leaguer who took on controversial issues she believed could no longer go unnoticed and not acted upon. "When they go low, we go high!" she would proclaim after each personal affront and obvious lack of support. A distinguished Second Lady, Dr. Jill Biden, advocated gallantly right by Mrs. Obama's side.

Ours is a story of people that felt the lash of bondage . . . the shame of servitude . . . the sting of segregation but kept on striving and hoping and doing what needed to be done so that today I wake up every morning in a house that was built by slaves. Michelle Obama, former First Lady

When darkness fell upon an Orlando nightclub; a San Bernardino community center; a Roseburg (Oregon) community college; a Chattanooga recruiting center; a Charleston church; a Kansas Jewish community center; an elementary school in Newtown, Connecticut; a Sikh temple in Wisconsin; an army base and a naval yard; a Congressional event in Tucson; a movie theater in Aurora, CO . . . all mass shootings, I kept wondering just how much more heartache our then compassionate leader and once progressive, humanitarian-based country could take.

Shattered parents and loved ones; shaken first responders; and citizens around the country and world were stunned by these horrific crimes of barbarism. News reporters struggled to be professionally informative while simultaneously harnessing their own raw emotions. One of the many somber speeches of our former distinguished leader, halted by overwhelming sentiments as a proud father himself, brought him to a point of momentarily no words but not without a song in his spirit of God's *amazing grace*.

Broken hearts ripped apart in excruciating pain and disbelief cry so many tears and whisper *'thank you'* Mr. President. This admirably moral and intellectually astute young warrior sorrowfully offers his family and administration's condolences and then asks, as did Dr. King, *where do we go from here?*

Many of us held our breath for fear the furious backlash of a black family residing in the White House would eventually and dangerously boil over. Apparent *grace* wrapped ITS arms around this family. Oh, if only Mama had lived to see this day and Daddy could have released his once sharp mind and loving, funny antics from the shackles of Alzheimer's, I know they would have been so surprised and quietly quite proud. They would have watched history make a new and 'just as grand' entrance as Dr. King and others did in the 60s. Both men started out successfully persuading their followers "Yes, We Can!" but I would contend there were far more roadblocks than there were failures. Both giants in the struggle for justice remained in the political arena for the good of 'all' humankind.

It is not the critic who counts; not the man who points out how the strong man stumbles, or where the doer of deeds could have done them better. The credit belongs to the man who is actually in the arena, whose face is marred by dust and sweat and blood; who strives valiantly; who errs, who comes short again and again, because there is no effort without error and shortcoming; but who does actually strive to do the deeds; who knows great enthusiasms, the great devotions; who spends himself in a worthy cause; who at the best knows in the end the triumph of high achievement, and who at the worst, if he fails, at least fails while daring greatly, so that his place shall never be with those cold and timid souls who neither know victory nor defeat. "The Man in the Arena" (an excerpt from the speech "Citizenship in a

Republic", delivered at the Sorbonne in Paris, France on 23 April 1910 by Teddy Roosevelt)

As I stood up after knotting one of the bright blue poop bags we tied to the leather handle at the end of the Basenji's worn out leash . . . something I wished other dog owners would have the decency to use . . . I looked straight into the eyes of a young African American man coming non-threateningly in my direction. He was really good looking, tall, well-built, and neatly dressed. It was late, and the November night air had suddenly gotten chilly. Tears were streaming down his face but for a far different reason than my elated Obama waterworks 9 years ago. What a stark and so very sad contrast!

I surmised he was around the age of my youngest child who was just as dumbfounded, heartbroken, and troubled. "I'm sorry," Ma'am," he spoke apologetically while wiping his face with a couple fingers. "I mean no disrespect, he continued, but can you tell me what just happened? What are people thinking?" Momentarily, we were both silent as he looked up to the starry night sky searching for an answer from my silent partner. "This shit really hurts," he muttered. "What's going to happen to us . . . black people and those folks too as he nodded towards a Hispanic family walking on the other side of the street pushing a baby carriage?"

There just wasn't enough time for me to tell the young man . . . to tell somebody . . . just how ashamed and frightened I was and am for our country. I had gotten caught up in not thinking clearly after so many mind-boggling events of the day . . . so upset that I foolishly fell for a very sophisticated Microsoft computer scam that even AARP warned seniors to be on high alert. I hope Jeff from PC Techmart (a fraudulent white elephant company) enjoyed the $150 he had no problem taking from my bank account with the information I had freely given him.

With no-apology vindictive thoughts, I was hoping one day someone would pull a similar kind of con on his mother or grandmother and he would know just how devastating it could be, especially for a senior on a set income, living alone, and struggling just to survive. I was able to catch myself the first time they tried before the transaction took place. This time, the fear was they would clean out the bank account where my social security check had been deposited for quite a few years. I had lost my cherished sterling silver kokopelli earrings that day, too. When I learned of the election results, I threw them as far as I could in total frustration. Afterwards, I couldn't believe what I had done and then I couldn't remember in which direction I had shifted my throwing arm.

How tragic, I thought, that we had come so far and yet now we were suddenly swathed with the disdain, hatred, venomousness, inhumane, and dangerous climate now plaguing our country. How many cities practically went up in battle sounds and flames before, on, and after the 4th of July? How does one describe this kind of anger and hopelessness? Where is the rage . . . a call for a 60s kind of revolution? From Rhode Island to L.A. – small towns and big cities – internet-instructed-man-made bombs give children fright (those not participating) and some senior residents near strokes and heart attacks after having an explosive blow up right in front of them. They fear fire and the loss of their animals.

Riots. White flight. Skinheads. Neighborhood criminal onslaught of black-on-black mostly teen murders. In the Movement . . . demonstrations . . . positioned on the front line! I had been a part of it all. Right after the (1992) Rodney King riots I would travel to Andover, Massachusetts for an interview for a teaching position at the prestigious Phillips Academy. Ironically, during that week I would have the pleasure of running into Bobby Seale, the co-founder (along with Huey Newton) and the national chairman of the original Black Panther Party upon my arrival.

After attending a two-week Classical Greek curriculum symposium two year prior, I had decided I might want to consider the possibilities of my youngest child (a tennis player *the hard way*) to have this top quality academic and state-of-the-art 'court' opportunity I would never be able to provide. My oldest child had found their own niche having such extraordinary talents, physical and spiritual handsomeness, creativity in every aspect of the gift, and an iron will that could provide a passage to the heights. It had been such a difficult and undeserved road to travel at such a young age for both of them.

While sipping on a little Hennessy and eating out of boxes of a variety of some of the best Chinese cuisine I had ever tasted, we talked about the Panther audacity and brazenness 'back in the day'. "White entitlement just wasn't going to fly with us and we set out to address the finality of it *by any means necessary*," he professed pensively. "We wanted our piece of the rock. We still do."

We talked about how my love for writing became more serious when I started writing articles for the Black Panther newspaper. We sadly recalled where we were in 1969 when Fred Hampton (Chairman of the Illinois Chapter of the Party and Deputy Chairman of the National BPP) and Mark Clark (a Peoria party leader) were assassinated while sleeping in their apartment. "Still slaughtering brothers like that," he said. "They just make it happen now behind bars . . . what we call 'modern day slavery'. They could do whatever they wanted to us and there wasn't a whole lot we could do but try and stay together and protect ourselves.

That's what scared 'them' then and that's what scares 'them' now, he continued . . . when people of color stick together and grow strong as communities outside the prison gates." When he said that, I thought about that powerful 60s civil rights activist Fanny Lou Hamer again when she said . . . *actually, the world and America is upset and the only way to bring about a change is to upset it more. It's time for America to get it right.*

"We just got tired of it all and decided no one should have to live that way, especially our kids," said the still defiant revolutionary. "But the party also taught us there were 'good' Jewish and white folks who deplored the injustices without accountability and were willing to help us even in the face of potential danger and often the sacrifice of their own lives. Sometimes their fighting by our side gave us a little hope that our legitimate uprisings would not be in vain. We knew who was 'real' and who wasn't. As Malcolm X found out too, they weren't all devils."

What was truly beneficial was when our leaders made us read everything they read . . . the first book being John Hope Franklin's, *From Slavery to Freedom*. "That was a pretty big book," I remarked. We learned early on from our loving parents; extraordinary educators (black and white); courageous community leaders; and our national and global heroes that high interest and the right kind of literacy would enrich our minds with an accumulation of useful knowledge giving us permanent power for the rest of our lives.

It had been an honor meeting Bobby Seale that May evening and remembering his fiery speech that made a lot of elitist students quite uncomfortable. Those sheltered from the real facts and truths and never having to entertain what it was like to live in a foreign world inside their own country would rather avoid what they believed at the time really didn't concern them. Some respectfully stood up and walked out. The teaching position was not offered but that was okay. There were no hard feelings. I clearly understood the certainties and surmised the majority of white privileged students and instructors were so far ahead of us in exposure to life opportunities most of them took for granted. That included my child's tennis prowess, as well. There were serious doubts if we would have been welcomed with opened arms. Class status and academic deficiencies would have held us both back and success and happiness might not have been the end results.

The recent emerging regression did have the potential of wiping out all the good will we had achieved and progress we had made. "Like my own children, I really wish I could offer you a rational justification behind it all. I have none. In all sincerity, I'm sorry for your generation and for our country," I said to the young man as we headed out in opposite directions. "Things will work out in the end," I tried assuring him, not totally convinced I believed that hope myself. "There are still 'decent' and 'caring' people in this world. The 'good' will eventually prevail." I always remembered that sentiment from my reading and the teaching of "The Diary of Anne Frank."

On November 9th 2016, I received a moving, thought-provoking e-mail from the founders and owners of one of my favorite children's clothing companies. The communique provided honest insight and echoed much of my personal emotions for the moment and continuing to this day. I would believe there were probably others who felt the same.

Sometimes it feels like the world changes overnight. It certainly has felt like that today. This morning, we didn't know what to tell our kids about the meaning of this election, after a campaign that did not reflect the ideas we at our company hold dear – kindness, empathy, and inclusiveness.

From the very first day, my partner and I founded this company to make the foreign familiar. We want to open the world for all children – to celebrate the common humanity that we share with all people no matter the color of our skin or the nationality of our birth – or even the color of the state we live in!

We truly believe that all of us have more in common than we think. Everyone – every single one of us – has beauty that deserves to be respected, heard, and celebrated.

Today, we realized that our work is more important than ever before. We can be a force for good in this incredibly complex world. As a company, as female leaders, as parents and people who love this country, we are committed to this goal – that every day when we wake up, we will strive to make the world a better place . . . a kinder, more open, more curious, more inclusive place.

And we know we are not alone. We know that all of you in our community want to give your little citizens a better world, too.

So let's do it together. We come from so many backgrounds, worldviews, opinions, and experiences and complexities – all of us deserve to be heard and treated with deep respect.

We are going to stay curious. We are going to stay hopeful. We are going to keep traveling and learning and seeking inspiration. We are going to keep celebrating the things that make us all different and the things that make us the same. But we're also going to dial up the importance of citizenship, of understanding, of connection, and of common humanity – whether around the world or across our own street.

Let's go there. Let's do it together.

We had started out 8 years ago *going there* and doing this thing called citizenship and brotherhood/sisterhood 'together'. Three weeks into President Obama's (he would always be my President) first term, the new leader would keep his promise making the good people in Elkhart, Indiana, the first place he would visit after his inauguration. The town had been hit harder by the recession than almost anywhere else in America. Unemployment was on its way to nearly 20%. Companies having sustained the community for years were shedding jobs at an alarming speed. And hard-working families were losing their homes and health care along with their livelihoods.

When Obama spoke to the people of Elkhart in February 2009, his administration promised if we all worked together, the community and the country could rise out of the depths of hopelessness and become strong and progressive once more. It wouldn't take forever for them to come out more determined and more successful than ever before . . . like Job. In 2016, unemployment in Elkhart had dropped to 4.1% and the President returned to celebrate "with the people" as he had promised. Those were the days, my friends!

After the numbness that grabbed all of us when we were shocked and saddened by the tragedy at Sandy Hook Elementary School (December 2012) in Newtown, Connecticut, and 200 plus school shootings since (recently Parkland, Florida, and Santa Fe, Texas) it should have been a catalyst for Congress to make necessary changes in gun control expeditiously, if nothing else but background checks and magazine bullet sales to start. Was there a feasible explanation we could give our youth as to how we got to where we are today – how 'monsters' with guns had started to invade their privacy and necessity for sound sleep instead of nightmares; how the human rights of common decency, commonsense, and security had all but disappeared; and how grown men and women could behave worse than them? So many of us want to be the co-authors of a collective revolution and evolution for positive change . . . a compelling new story of our potential as a whole human species where there would be collaboration of all classes, ethnicities, religions, and political parties of choice. As one of the blessed survivors of the Parkland, Florida, mass shooting challenged . . . *listen to the cries of the children.*

I would have to leave a little time in between viewing my tapings of *Michelle's Mission; Michelle Obama says Farewell; Christmas at the White House; Obama: 60 Minutes – Barack Obama: Eight Years in the White House; Dateline: Barack Obama: Hope; The Legacy of Michelle Obama; Taking the Stage – The Smithsonian's National Museum of African American History and Culture in Washington, D.C.; The Tonight Show with Jimmy Fallon – First Lady Michelle Obama; Obama's Farewell Address.* Watching would only add to my already depressed demeanor as it pertains to leadership, priorities, and our country's future. A black child recently wrote . . . "I hope one day I will have as many rights as a 'gun'." That is the reality . . . the 'real' honest to goodness truth.

I wanted to savor the memories of the First Daughters along with Bo and Sunny (the handsome White House canines) growing up in this magnificent place and time. It was so wonderful to watch as the entire family conducted themselves in a multiplicity of national and global people circles with such poise and self-assurance. Over the years, one of my favorite photos was that of the former President going over a stack of documents seated at the back of a rehearsal studio while his youngest daughter, Sasha, was hard at work in a dance lesson. Millions who saw that photo felt the magic and felt so much pride.

After that November day (2016) I have watched many "Law and Order" repeats in place of news. It still hurts too badly. Being the historian, I have always been ... having taught some aspect of the discipline and the literature associated with the particular eras in the U.S. and the world for 40 years, I would forego staying informed. No information any political analyst could comment on would serve any purpose. The entire scenario was too bizarre ... absolutely unprecedented. I don't think anything else could have blindsided me more.

This wasn't about blue or red states. It was about the obvious realities of corruption; financial waste when so many other needs, especially for our children and the least of our brothers and sisters, were being ignored; the total loss of morality; and the barefaced and unexplainable injustices, lies, and deceit. I would thus fill my remaining days still counting my blessings, building a house of personal restoration and joy, and giving back whenever and however possible. "People said they were voting for the current occupant of the Oval office because they didn't want a politician anymore. When you go to have surgery, do you go to someone who's not a doctor?" asks one of my favorite Hollywood (Atlanta) screen icons, Tyler Perry.

Greg Popovich (San Antonio Spurs) had always been at the top of my list for exceptionally skilled, wise, cool coaches, and a 'real honest man'. Bravo! What a testament to a life well lived! He had no problems expressing his personal political sentiments that I and many others agreed. This much admired teacher and mentor to so many deserving and talented young men deplored the current, frightening leader of the so-called free world's use of "fear-mongering, race-baiting, and any other scare tactics" to get elected. He also noted the newly elected top official's lack of sensitivity and morality, his bullying style, disgusting language, tone, and comments that had been 'xenophobic, homophobic, racist, and misogynistic'.

"Half of the population ignored all of that to elect someone. It had nothing to do with Obama or a political party. We live in a country that ignored all of those values that we would hold our kids accountable for. They'd be grounded for years if they acted and said the things that have been said by this individual." Any shame running through the streets of American cities will have no place to go. The sewers where all the muck and trash had once flowed and disappeared are now clogged!

In 476 C.E. Romulus, the last of the **Roman** *emperors in the west, was overthrown by the Germanic leader Odoacer, who became the first Barbarian to rule in* **Rome**. *The order that the* **Roman** *Empire had brought to Western Europe for 1000 years was no more.* (Google Research)

A large portion of Americans believe it's still an 'us' and 'them' world now more than ever in recent history. When the word 'nigger' was spray painted across a security gate of the multi-million-dollar Brentwood, CA. mansion of one of the greatest athletes in the world, the basketball legend was not surprised. "On the eve of the NBA Finals (2017)," Lebron James expressed with ire and sadness, "I have to sit down and talk to my kids, especially my oldest son, about what it means to grow up being Black in America. This kind of hatred is why Mamie Till wanted an open casket for her son Emmett Till so the world could see what *hate* did to him. At the end of the day, it doesn't matter how much money you have, how famous you are, or how many people admire you. You are still Black in America and around the world. As much as it hurts, this incident will shed a light on what we all know. There's a lot of work still to be done." My children; our children will continue to ask . . . but why?

I am no longer accepting the things I cannot change. I am changing the things I cannot accept. Angela Davis

The truth of the matter is that our children should not have to endure such personal pain; lack expectations and promise; or ever go hungry. We have enough food in this country to feed them, our homeless (especially veterans), and many suffering the worse in Third World countries.. (Thank you, Tom and Sylvia) We can choose to form barriers to keep *satan* out, strengthened by the Light, courage, kindness, and much love. There's enough beauty and loveliness in the universe to keep us in awe, in thanksgiving, unafraid, and with 'hope in the unseen'. But there is also a reality that remains unaddressed, buried in the messy chaos of some of our days, and painted with signs of have and have nots; black and white.

The energy in the world flows from God at the center and then back to God. The sages see life as a wheel with each individual going round and round through birth and death. I would believe nothing that happens is beyond the Lord's domain. Nothing can touch us that the heavenly Father can't deal with, and no event can ruin HIS plan for 'good' in our lives. But admittedly sometimes I did want to ask, "Did You picture this horrible, repulsive bedlam we see closing in on us today?

I still believe in greatness and possibilities . . . continuing to feel love and success would come even in this 'winter season' of mine and in the midst of all the madness and sad actualities of present times. There are those of us who have experienced strength in numbers . . . power in the combined voices of people from all ethnicities, religions, and academic/career backgrounds. We know it works especially through our freedom to vote. We're convinced there are ways to weaken this lunacy keeping us from being who we really are, who we can be, and keeping us from being proud of the country in which we live. We pray for signs of hope and love from and for a nation reeling . . . for more and more *grace* to help fortify our desires to always bring God the glory, give Him praise, and enjoy the fruits of HIS abundant blessings.

Time moves by so quickly. No matter how I shift in and out of my days – in laughter or in sorrow, I will do so having proof of my David-like *faith* and the Lord's everlasting *love*. I would wrap myself in **gratitude** for the roses in an array of beautiful colors and species, designed and painted by the most famous Artist in the world. I believe I will . . . my children will . . . our communities will . . . our country will . . . eventually find the sunlight to make the **flowers of blessedness** bloom 'all in due season'. And as Martin continues to speak to us 50 years later, I echo our fallen hero's heartfelt sentiments in my todays and tomorrows too!

I believe that unarmed truth and unconditional love will have the final word in reality . . . I have the audacity to believe that people everywhere can have three meals a day for their bodies, education and culture for their minds, and dignity, equality, and freedom for their spirits. I believe that what self-centered men have torn down, men other-centered can build up . . . I still believe that we shall overcome. Dr. Martin Luther King Jr.

Ba'al Perazim

Made in the USA
Middletown, DE
16 September 2018